ESSENTIAL SKILLS IN MATHS

BOOK 4

Nelson

Graham Newman and Ron Bull

D0183550

First published in 1996 by:
Thomas Nelson and Sons Ltd

Reprinted in 2001 by:
Nelson Thornes Ltd
Delta Place
27 Bath Road
CHELTENHAM
GL53 7TH
United Kingdom

03 04 05 / 15 14 13 12

A catalogue record for this book is available from the British Library

ISBN 0-17-431443-4

Printed and bound in China

Contents

NUMBER

ALGEBRA

SHAPE, SPACE AND MEASURES

HANDLING DATA

Number

1/ STATING THE VALUE OF A DIGIT WITHIN A DECIMAL

The value of a digit within a decimal depends upon its position within that decimal.

	10s	1s	$\frac{1}{10}$s	$\frac{1}{100}$s	$\frac{1}{1000}$s	$\frac{1}{10\,000}$s
5.0456		5	0	4	5	6
14.302	1	4	3	0	2	

EXAMPLE

▶ State the value of the underlined digits in (a) decimal form (b) fraction form:
5.04<u>5 6</u>, 14.<u>3</u>02, 34.7<u>6 9</u>

5.04<u>5 6</u>   4 means (a) 0.04   (b) $\frac{4}{100}$

           6 means (a) 0.0006   (b) $\frac{6}{10\,000}$

14.<u>3</u>02   3 means (a) 0.3   (b) $\frac{3}{10}$

           2 means (a) 0.002   (b) $\frac{2}{1000}$

34.7<u>6 9</u>   6 means (a) 0.06   (b) $\frac{6}{100}$

           9 means (a) 0.009   (b) $\frac{9}{1000}$

Exercise 1A

State the value of the underlined digits (a) in decimal form (b) in fraction form.

1	0.8<u>7</u>25	**2**	0.9<u>5</u>54	**3**	0.008 <u>7</u>5	**4**	0.18<u>8</u>9	**5**	0.02<u>4</u>7
6	0.007<u>6</u>6	**7**	0.09<u>7</u>2	**8**	0.051 <u>4</u>6	**9**	0.83<u>7</u>5	**10**	0.047<u>6</u>1
11	0.3<u>4</u>89	**12**	0.041 <u>2</u>5	**13**	0.000 <u>5</u>69	**14**	0.95<u>3</u>3	**15**	0.018 <u>7</u>4
16	8.8<u>4</u>72	**17**	72.1<u>5</u>76	**18**	2.2<u>7</u>61	**19**	17.4<u>7</u>48	**20**	11.2<u>8</u>67
21	2.34<u>6 1</u>	**22**	24.9<u>1</u>82	**23**	11.9<u>8</u>72	**24**	110.8<u>5</u>01	**25**	29.094 <u>2 7</u>
26	18.<u>5</u>176	**27**	6.015 <u>8 6</u>	**28**	724.06<u>8 7</u>	**29**	81.00<u>6 3</u>	**30**	23.095 <u>3 1</u>

Exercise 1B

State the value of the underlined digits (a) in decimal form (b) in fraction form.

1	0.8<u>7 5 4</u>	**2**	0.8<u>4 9 2</u>	**3**	0.07<u>5 4</u>	**4**	0.09<u>3</u> 85	**5**	0.<u>7</u>436
6	0.091 <u>2 3</u>	**7**	0.031 <u>4 2</u>	**8**	0.078 <u>2 1</u>	**9**	0.<u>6</u>153	**10**	0.051 <u>6 8</u>
11	0.8<u>3</u>61	**12**	0.009 <u>1 4</u>	**13**	0.3<u>6</u>42	**14**	0.006 <u>3</u>15	**15**	0.000 <u>1 6 3</u>
16	19.3<u>1 4 2</u>	**17**	1.<u>1</u>937	**18**	17.1<u>7</u>28	**19**	2.6<u>5</u>94	**20**	42.3<u>1</u>42
21	49.4<u>9</u>82	**22**	53.3<u>1 2 4</u>	**23**	1.<u>7</u>471	**24**	18.052 <u>8 6</u>	**25**	1.002 <u>1 4 3</u>
26	85.2<u>9 8 7</u>	**27**	9.0<u>2 8</u> 96	**28**	29.003 <u>5 9 4</u>	**29**	172.3<u>8</u>1	**30**	41.03<u>2 7</u>4

2/ MENTAL MULTIPLICATION AND DIVISION

When multiplying or dividing a decimal number by a power of ten you need to move the decimal point.

EXAMPLE

▶ Write down the answer to (a) 345 × 1000 (b) 674 ÷ 100.

(a) Multiplying by 1000 means multiplying by 10 three times; each multiplication by 10 moves the decimal point to the right one place.

345 × 1000 = 345 000 (You have to add three noughts.)

(b) Dividing by 100 means dividing by 10 twice; each division by ten moves the decimal point to the left one place.

$674 \div 100 = \frac{674}{100} = 6.74$

When multiplying or dividing one number by a multiple of 10 the problem can be broken down to enable the calculation to be done mentally.

EXAMPLE

▶ Write down the answer to (a) 567 × 3000 (b) 648 ÷ 4000.

(a) 567 × 3000 = 567 × 3 × 1000 = 1701 × 1000 = 1 701 000

(b) 648 ÷ 4000 = 648 ÷ 4 ÷ 1000 = 162 ÷ 1000 = 0.162

Exercise 2A

Write down the answer to each of the following problems. Do not use a calculator.

1	13 × 40	**2**	29 × 900	**3**	41 × 20	**4**	369 ÷ 300
5	561 ÷ 30	**6**	238 ÷ 200	**7**	86 × 400	**8**	750 ÷ 3000
9	87 × 4000	**10**	1024 ÷ 40	**11**	1505 ÷ 5000	**12**	38 × 500
13	1418 ÷ 20	**14**	5733 ÷ 700	**15**	1374 ÷ 60	**16**	30 × 70
17	61 × 9000	**18**	2904 ÷ 8000	**19**	1664 ÷ 40	**20**	1698 ÷ 600
21	98 × 1000	**22**	161 × 300	**23**	50 × 60	**24**	8001 ÷ 90
25	266 × 8000	**26**	4536 ÷ 700	**27**	673 × 100	**28**	216 × 40
29	1472 ÷ 8000	**30**	955 × 800				

Exercise 2B

Write down the answer to each of the following problems. Do not use a calculator.

1	66 × 50	**2**	28 × 900	**3**	792 ÷ 60	**4**	54 × 3000
5	580 ÷ 20	**6**	57 × 700	**7**	46 × 1000	**8**	759 ÷ 30
9	672 ÷ 600	**10**	496 ÷ 2000	**11**	32 × 600	**12**	1100 ÷ 500
13	2332 ÷ 40	**14**	1715 ÷ 700	**15**	3100 ÷ 5000	**16**	1616 ÷ 80
17	49 × 60	**18**	95 × 1000	**19**	164 × 70	**20**	4284 ÷ 7000
21	3546 ÷ 90	**22**	269 × 300	**23**	788 × 800	**24**	4986 ÷ 60
25	7533 ÷ 900	**26**	483 × 40	**27**	704 × 700	**28**	1568 ÷ 700
29	750 × 400	**30**	108 × 8000				

3/ ORDERING DECIMALS

▶ Place in ascending order: 0.501, 0.6, 0.5, 0.4999.

   Compare the first decimal place, then the second decimal place, and so on.
   0.4999 (smallest), 0.5, 0.501, 0.6 (largest)

Exercise 3A

Place the decimals in ascending order.

1 0.64, 0.63, 0.69
2 0.19, 0.72, 0.33
3 0.6, 0.1, 0.3, 0.8
4 0.8, 0.4, 0.5
5 0.955, 0.949, 0.222, 0.345
6 0.4145, 0.9247, 0.3024, 0.8050
7 0.267, 0.035, 0.305
8 0.0333, 0.003, 0.3
9 0.6, 0.06, 0.006
10 0.044, 0.034, 0.059
11 4.008, 4.208, 4.048
12 0.204, 0.044, 0.064
13 0.99, 0.09, 0.9, 9.9
14 0.43, 0.34, 3.4, 4.3
15 34.432, 34.442, 34.234
16 3.0048, 3.008, 3.0078
17 0.0307, 0.0377, 0.007 77
18 5.550, 5.505, 5.055
19 8.07, 20.7, 8.7, 2.07
20 0.583, 0.576, 0.585, 0.567
21 8.909, 8.999, 8.099
22 3.652, 3.552, 4.558, 4.553
23 1.1, 1.11, 1.001, 1.101
24 0.2, 2.0, 0.02, 0.002
25 5.4, 4.0, 0.86, 0.04
26 5.53, 5.43, 6.63, 6.03
27 7.305, 7.307, 7.204, 7.202
28 0.235, 0.77, 0.727, 2.35
29 0.330, 0.033, 3.03, 3.0
30 99.5, 99.1, 9.90, 9.93

Exercise 3B

Place the decimals in ascending order.

1 0.03, 0.003, 0.3
2 0.6, 0.8, 0.4
3 0.042, 0.022, 0.202
4 0.7, 0.8, 0.5, 0.3
5 0.049, 0.124, 0.044
6 0.29, 0.92, 0.43
7 0.52, 0.51, 0.59
8 0.33, 0.941, 0.433, 0.684
9 7.049, 7.009, 7.109
10 0.243, 0.343, 0.023
11 0.9, 0.0999, 0.009
12 14.441, 14.124, 14.421
13 5.111, 5.011, 5.101
14 0.9143, 0.3254, 0.9242, 0.2053
15 7.009, 7.0069, 7.0089
16 8.088, 8.880, 8.808
17 3.1, 4.3, 0.43, 0.34
18 0.7, 7.7, 0.07, 0.77
19 5.0, 7.7, 0.05, 0.85
20 343.02, 342.49, 342.53
21 0.88, 1.85, 0.825, 0.425
22 0.0188, 0.008 88, 0.0108
23 6.403, 6.506, 6.303, 6.304
24 0.365, 0.352, 0.363, 0.325
25 0.022, 2.0, 2.02, 0.220
26 4.4, 4.07, 5.4, 4.04
27 0.006, 6.0, 0.6, 0.06
28 7.665, 7.667, 6.865, 6.734
29 9.714, 9.908, 9.9, 9.99
30 2.23, 22.2, 2.20, 22.4

4/ EVALUATING POWERS

$2^1 = 2$
$2^2 = 2 \times 2 = 4$
$2^3 = 2 \times 2 \times 2 = 8$
$2^4 = 2 \times 2 \times 2 \times 2 = 16$

EXAMPLE

▶ $6^n = 1296$. Find n.

$6 \times 6 \times 6 \times 6 = 1296$
So $6^4 = 1296$; $n = 4$

EXAMPLE

▶ Evaluate $2^3 \times 6^4$

$2^3 \times 6^4 = 8 \times 1296 = 10\,368$

Exercise 4A

Evaluate.

1 6^2	**2** 4^3	**3** 2^6	**4** 4^6	**5** 8^3
6 4^4	**7** 5^4	**8** 3^6	**9** 2^8	**10** 7^2
11 6^5	**12** 8^4	**13** 10^4	**14** 11^4	**15** 13^3

Find the number n.

16 $5^n = 25$	**17** $2^n = 128$	**18** $9^n = 729$
19 $7^n = 343$	**20** $4^n = 1024$	**21** $3^n = 729$

Evaluate.

22 $5^2 \times 3^3$	**23** $4^2 \times 9^2$	**24** $4^6 - 5^5$
25 $5^3 + 2^6$	**26** $2^7 + 3^5$	**27** $11^2 \times 10^3$
28 $6^4 \times 4^5$	**29** $3^6 \times 4^5$	**30** $13^2 \times 7^3$

Exercise 4B

Evaluate.

1 3^2	**2** 6^4	**3** 3^4	**4** 9^2	**5** 4^2
6 2^9	**7** 3^7	**8** 5^5	**9** 7^4	**10** 9^4
11 10^2	**12** 11^3	**13** 15^2	**14** 12^3	**15** 25^2

Find the number n.

16 $3^n = 27$	**17** $8^n = 64$	**18** $10^n = 1000$
19 $6^n = 216$	**20** $5^n = 125$	**21** $2^n = 1024$

Evaluate.

22 $3^4 \times 5^4$	**23** $12^2 \times 8^3$	**24** $2^5 \times 4^3$
25 $6^3 - 2^7$	**26** $3^6 \times 9^3$	**27** $8^2 \times 2^8$
28 $7^2 + 6^5$	**29** $9^3 - 5^4$	**30** $4^4 \times 3^7$

5/ EXPRESSING POSITIVE INTEGERS AS PRODUCTS OF PRIMES

A **prime number** is a number that has no factors other than 1 and itself. For example:
2, 3, 5, 7, 11, 13, ... (1 is not a prime number.)
Any number can be broken down into **prime factors** which, when multiplied together, will give that number.

EXAMPLE

▶ Write these numbers as products of prime factors.
   (a) 24   (b) 300   (c) 34

   Begin with the smallest prime number and divide into the numbers repeatedly where possible.

   (a) 2) 24   (b) 2) 300   (c) 2) 34
        2) 12   2) 150   17) 17
        2) 6   3) 75   1
        3) 3   5) 25
            1   5)   5
                                 1

   $24 = 2 \times 2 \times 2 \times 3$ $300 = 2 \times 2 \times 3 \times 5 \times 5$ $34 = 2 \times 17$
   $\quad\ = 2^3 \times 3$ $\quad\quad\ = 2^2 \times 3 \times 5^2$

Exercise 5A

Express each number as a product of primes.

1	8	**2**	105	**3**	18	**4**	175	**5**	50
6	12	**7**	135	**8**	98	**9**	30	**10**	539
11	20	**12**	153	**13**	210	**14**	242	**15**	112
16	121	**17**	627	**18**	63	**19**	72	**20**	44
21	36	**22**	75	**23**	162	**24**	78	**25**	24
26	130	**27**	2940	**28**	434	**29**	875	**30**	200

Exercise 5B

Express each number as a product of primes.

1	12	**2**	154	**3**	42	**4**	60	**5**	70
6	28	**7**	165	**8**	40	**9**	45	**10**	52
11	66	**12**	286	**13**	330	**14**	190	**15**	117
16	275	**17**	80	**18**	68	**19**	285	**20**	363
21	186	**22**	132	**23**	7700	**24**	14	**25**	297
26	124	**27**	169	**28**	176	**29**	7865	**30**	729

6/ ROUNDING TO DECIMAL PLACES

Decimal places (d.p.) can be used in rounding numbers.

$$4 \quad 3 \quad . \quad 0 \quad 5 \quad 7$$

$$\uparrow \quad \uparrow \quad \uparrow$$

1st   2nd   3rd decimal place

> **EXAMPLE**
>
> ▶ Round the number 3.8497 to (a) 1 d.p. (b) 2 d.p. (c) 3 d.p.
>
> (a) 3.8
> (b) 3.85   (The next number is 5 or more, so round up).
> (c) 3.850   (The last 0 is important, since it is the third decimal place.)

Exercise 6A

Round each of these decimal numbers to (a) 1 d.p. (b) 2 d.p. (c) 3 d.p.

1	0.9214	**2**	0.6397	**3**	0.5228	**4**	0.4429
5	5.8959	**6**	0.032 11	**7**	7.5249	**8**	0.619 06
9	0.986 15	**10**	9.0814	**11**	5.966 02	**12**	3.111 42
13	8.1773	**14**	0.269 13	**15**	0.1341	**16**	8.7064
17	12.1142	**18**	5.3524	**19**	4.690 54	**20**	12.1051
21	7.0459	**22**	7.713 91	**23**	2.744 65	**24**	0.4032
25	81.7932	**26**	12.2216	**27**	7.6187	**28**	0.2738
29	10.2821	**30**	34.1549				

Exercise 6B

Round each of these decimal numbers to (a) 1 d.p. (b) 2 d.p. (c) 3 d.p.

1	0.0146	**2**	0.4685	**3**	0.7912	**4**	0.6438
5	0.994 32	**6**	2.0773	**7**	0.801 51	**8**	0.8696
9	5.9239	**10**	0.100 55	**11**	1.2539	**12**	7.276 17
13	0.9598	**14**	4.8030	**15**	0.8925	**16**	0.3909
17	8.048 31	**18**	0.3118	**19**	8.342 63	**20**	10.0945
21	12.9389	**22**	13.7801	**23**	9.7416	**24**	13.7526
25	0.2588	**26**	0.8769	**27**	0.0025	**28**	0.3545
29	9.2955	**30**	7.2411				

7/ USING A CALCULATOR FOR CALCULATIONS

A calculator is a useful tool for performing calculations, but it must be used properly and accurately. The order in which a calculation is entered is important. Good use can be made of MEMORY and (PARENTHESES).

To be worked out first or separately:
  anything in brackets
  anything under a square root sign
  anything written as a denominator (the bottom part of a fraction).

EXAMPLE

▶ Evaluate (a) $\dfrac{8.91}{4.2} - \dfrac{8.15}{4.9}$ (b) $\dfrac{5.2 \times 7.9}{8.4 \times 0.2}$ (c) $\sqrt{\dfrac{(4.2)^3}{1.7 \times 2.5}} + 3.7$

(a) $\dfrac{8.91}{4.2} - \dfrac{8.15}{4.9}$ $= 2.1214 - 1.6633 = 0.4581$

Stage 1: Work out the two fractions separately.   *Stage 2*: Take away.

(You could store the second fraction in the memory first, then do 8.91 ÷ 4.2 = − MEMORY.)

(b) $\dfrac{5.2 \times 7.9}{8.4 \times 0.2}$ $= \dfrac{41.08}{1.68} = 24.452$

Stage 1: Work out the top and bottom separately.   *Stage 2*: Divide.

(You could store the bottom number in the memory then do 5.2 × 7.9 ÷ MEMORY.)

(c) $\sqrt{\dfrac{(4.2)^3}{1.7 \times 2.5}} + 3.7$ $= \sqrt{17.43247} + 3.7$ $= 4.17522 + 3.7 = 7.87522$

Stage 1: work out the top and bottom separately.   *Stage 2*: Do the square root.   *Stage 3*: Add the next term

(You could start by storing the answer to 1.7 × 2.5 in the memory and then do $(4.2)^3$ ÷ MEMORY then square root and add 3.7.)

It is important that you show all working out when using a calculator, as in these examples.

Exercise 7A

Use a calculator to work out the following. Give your answer correct to three decimal places.

1 $\dfrac{891.7}{5.91} - \dfrac{715.5}{32.9}$

2 $\sqrt{\dfrac{269 \times 42.8}{1090}}$

3 $\dfrac{472.4 \times 89.71}{4.89 \times 4.29}$

4 $\dfrac{693}{2.76 \times 14.5}$

5 $\dfrac{545.6}{8.9} - \dfrac{819.9}{71.91}$

6 $\dfrac{89.4}{14.6 \times 3.65}$

7 $\dfrac{693.5}{31.9} + \dfrac{391.5}{39.1}$

8 $\dfrac{121.5 \times 3.75}{4.29 \times 71.9}$

9 $\dfrac{293.5 \times 49.76}{79.73}$

10 $\left(\dfrac{3.4 + 2.7}{1.4}\right)^2$

11 $\dfrac{4.57}{2.4} + \sqrt{\dfrac{5.21}{4.5}}$

12 $\dfrac{241.7 \times 36.12}{41.75 \times 81.94}$

13 $\sqrt{\dfrac{8412}{21.7}} + 5.42$

14 $\dfrac{542.4}{23.7} + \dfrac{32.4}{3.7}$

15 $\sqrt{\dfrac{2120}{41.6 \times 2.97}}$

16 $\dfrac{47.89 \times 21.9}{4.21}$

17 $\left(\dfrac{17.2}{4.3}\right)^2 + 7.49$

18 $\dfrac{2976}{41.7 \times 1.895}$

19 $\sqrt{\dfrac{92.1}{214}} + 3.67$

20 $\dfrac{89.73}{29.7 \times 49.7}$

21 $\left(\dfrac{8.4}{2.7}\right)^2 + \left(\dfrac{13.7}{5.9}\right)^2$

22 $\left(\dfrac{82.6}{72.5}\right)^2 + 14.4$

23 $\dfrac{2.95^2 + 3.42^2}{4.1^2}$

24 $\sqrt{\dfrac{707}{2.40}} + 6.7^2$

25 $\dfrac{\sqrt{1084.5}}{35.2 \times 4.97}$

26 $\dfrac{21.4 \times 3.5}{4.2 \times 5.6 \times 7.9}$

27 $\dfrac{91.4 \times 3.4^2}{3.52 + 9.59 - 1.4}$

28 $\dfrac{2.19}{4.2} + \dfrac{5.4}{2.7} - \dfrac{9.4}{8.5}$

29 $\dfrac{21.3^2 - 8.7^2}{5.9^2 + 6.4^2}$

30 $\dfrac{43.97 \times 55.56 \times 30.5}{3.14 \times 18.9 \times 17.9}$

Exercise 7B

Use a calculator to work out the following. Give your answer correct to three decimal places.

1 $\dfrac{147.8 \times 57.63}{47.91 \times 8.55}$

2 $\dfrac{215.6}{9.8} - \dfrac{719.9}{71.91}$

3 $\sqrt{\dfrac{132 \times 42.8}{932}}$

4 $\dfrac{542.7 \times 3.127}{54.73}$

5 $\sqrt{\dfrac{4.96 + 0.81}{3.27}}$

6 $\dfrac{42.6}{8.27 \times 81.9}$

7 $\dfrac{7.08 \times 71.54}{0.35 \times 0.39}$

8 $\dfrac{89.7}{43.9} + \dfrac{54.27}{5.79}$

9 $\dfrac{14.98 \times 47.55}{89.75 \times 4.57}$

10 $\dfrac{545.6}{6.9} - \dfrac{617.6}{71.01}$

11 $\dfrac{812.3 \times 17.85}{4.95}$

12 $\dfrac{479.2^2 + 891.4^2}{8149 - 25.3^2}$

13 $\sqrt{\dfrac{546 \times 23.4}{15.4}}$

14 $\dfrac{17.13 \times 3.49}{12.34 \times 11.21}$

15 $\dfrac{41.21}{37.89 \times 4.55}$

16 $\dfrac{14.72}{42.97} + \sqrt{\dfrac{25.5}{1.08}}$

17 $\dfrac{3.25^2 + 9.4^2}{5.41^2}$

18 $\dfrac{59.76}{1.74} + \dfrac{94.5}{1.47}$

19 $\dfrac{142.9 \times 3.57^2}{29.87 \times 21.9}$

20 $\dfrac{82.55}{42.3 \times 46.8}$

21 $\left(\dfrac{3.07}{0.04}\right)^2 + \left(\dfrac{1.27}{0.516}\right)^2$

22 $\dfrac{476.3}{29.78} + \dfrac{897.6}{51.54} + \dfrac{913.6}{4.9}$

23 $\dfrac{\sqrt{5421}}{2.37 \times 20.51}$

24 $\dfrac{29.87}{1.97} + \dfrac{4.79}{2.8}$

25 $\sqrt{\dfrac{7}{14.95 \times 21.97}}$

26 $\dfrac{28.9 \times 89.7}{4.99 \times 32.3 \times 2.98}$

27 $\dfrac{1.2^2 + 3.4^2}{5.6^2 + 7.8^2}$

28 $\left(\dfrac{4.82}{0.127}\right)^2 - \left(\dfrac{5.97}{1.48}\right)^2$

29 $\dfrac{2.1^2 + 3.2^2}{\sqrt{5547}}$

30 $\dfrac{89.17}{4.9} - \dfrac{84.4}{42.9} + \dfrac{32.3}{9.4}$

8/ ROUNDING TO SIGNIFICANT FIGURES

Significant figures (s.f.) are also used to round numbers.

$$4 \quad 5 \quad . \quad 0 \quad 8 \quad 5$$
$$\uparrow \quad \uparrow \quad \quad \uparrow \quad \uparrow \quad \uparrow$$

1st   2nd   3rd   4th   5th significant figure

EXAMPLE

► Round 45.085 to (a) 3 s.f. (b) 4 s.f.

(a) 45.1 (round after the 1 as 1 is the 3rd significant figure)
(b) 45.09 (rounding up)

When rounding whole numbers the value of the significant figures that have a value of 1 or more is important.

EXAMPLE

► Round 229.45 to (a) 1 s.f. (b) 2 s.f. (c) 3 s.f.

(a) 200 (the first significant figure is to the nearest 100)
(b) 230 (the second significant figure is to the nearest 10)
(c) 229 (the third significant figure is to the nearest unit)

Exercise 8A

Round each of these numbers to (a) 1 s.f. (b) 2 s.f. (c) 3 s.f.

1	0.6953	**2**	0.7738	**3**	0.530 86	**4**	0.5554
5	0.901 01	**6**	0.600 204	**7**	3.3020	**8**	4.861
9	8.2298	**10**	5.4648	**11**	9.43161	**12**	8.2649
13	49.63	**14**	548.99	**15**	1.3478	**16**	21.521
17	125.40	**18**	7972.3	**19**	404.14	**20**	0.054 827
21	9.2096	**22**	190.501	**23**	0.1044	**24**	474.32
25	8103.9	**26**	390.98	**27**	98.052	**28**	0.834 64
29	628.58	**30**	10.182				

Exercise 8B

1	0.9837	**2**	0.1956	**3**	0.8571	**4**	0.473 15
5	0.276 89	**6**	2.8773	**7**	7.809 61	**8**	27.980
9	57.764	**10**	878.035	**11**	8.1049	**12**	697.1
13	4319.2	**14**	21.923	**15**	935.48	**16**	3828.1
17	6.1467	**18**	0.678 15	**19**	740.90	**20**	5531.05
21	0.026 070	**22**	184.097	**23**	8501.36	**24**	54.366
25	740.49	**26**	199.76	**27**	2.1090	**28**	414.06
29	426.21	**30**	2057.4				

9 / ESTIMATES FOR CALCULATIONS

To make an **estimate** of the answer to a calculation round each number to one significant figure. The sign '≈' means 'is approximately equal to'.

EXAMPLE

▶ Find an estimated answer to (a) 2.18×487 (b) $698.7 \div 22.95$ (c) $\dfrac{81.97 \times 127.9}{4.27 \times 81.1}$

(a) $2.18 \times 487 \approx 2 \times 500 = 1000$ Rounded to 1 s.f.

(b) $698.7 \div 22.95 \approx \dfrac{700}{20} = \dfrac{70}{2} = 35$

(c) $\dfrac{81.97 \times 127.9}{4.27 \times 81.1} \approx \dfrac{80 \times 100}{4 \times 80} = \dfrac{8000}{320} = \dfrac{800}{32} = 25$

Exercise 9A

Find an estimated answer to each of the following.

1 6.03×14.92

2 36×1.05

3 2.4×13.8

4 8.9×93.4

5 $\dfrac{470 \times 1.95}{4.7 \times 3.9}$

6 $\dfrac{36 \times 15}{4.5}$

7 $\dfrac{1.56 \times 90}{1.5 \times 2.4}$

8 $\dfrac{42 \times 12}{1.4}$

9 $\dfrac{12.4 \times 45}{18.7}$

10 $\dfrac{2.8}{2.1 \times 2.7}$

11 $\dfrac{164.6 \times 4.1}{8.23 \times 2.05}$

12 $\dfrac{12}{6 \times 16.4}$

13 $\dfrac{27.8 \times 12.3}{5.1}$

14 $\dfrac{46.5 \times 15.1}{5.2}$

15 $\dfrac{84.2 \times 13.4}{5.2 \times 1.2}$

16 $\dfrac{169.4 \times 57.6}{2.4 \times 8.2}$

17 $\dfrac{545.6 \times 91.88}{8.9 \times 5.4}$

18 $\dfrac{3290}{1.87 \times 2.43}$

19 $\dfrac{891.7 \times 815.5}{32.4 \times 4.97}$

20 $\dfrac{847 \times 208}{107.6 \times 17.6}$

21 $\dfrac{82.3 \times 205}{4.1 \times 16.46}$

22 $\dfrac{24 \times 8.3}{1.9 \times 1.2}$

23 $\dfrac{196.4 \times 87.6}{26.2 \times 22.5}$

24 $\dfrac{4955 \times 3.72 \times 8.971}{32.9 \times 31.4 \times 1.8}$

25 $\dfrac{4789 \times 121.9}{1375}$

26 $\dfrac{697.5 \times 491.5}{40.9 \times 24.1}$

27 $\dfrac{31.2 \times 704.4}{4.92 \times 17.3}$

28 $\dfrac{8.43 \times 7.84 \times 424}{40.5 \times 80.21}$

29 $\dfrac{507 \times 4.45}{8.42 \times 10.9 \times 4.2}$

30 $\dfrac{874.9 \times 427.9}{39.35 \times 87.75}$

Exercise 9B

Find an estimated answer to each of the following.

1 8.04×12.98

2 127×47.08

3 11.5×2.3

4 $\dfrac{12.2 \times 14.3}{44 \times 9.6}$

5 $\dfrac{55 \times 18}{33 \times 25}$

6 $\dfrac{11.32 \times 1.5}{1.0 \times 1.1}$

7 $\dfrac{14 \times 90.4}{6.2}$

8 $\dfrac{12.7 \times 3.7}{5.4 \times 10.1}$

9 $\dfrac{63 \times 41}{98 \times 1.8}$

10 $\dfrac{282.4 \times 34.2}{8.5 \times 13.2}$ **11** $\dfrac{15 \times 56}{27}$ **12** $\dfrac{36}{1.2 \times 5.3}$

13 $\dfrac{117.3 \times 38.4}{5.1 \times 4.2}$ **14** $\dfrac{2.37 \times 9.71}{1.93 \times 3.72}$ **15** $\dfrac{64.2 \times 1.49}{14.9 \times 3.21}$

16 $\dfrac{34 \times 1.32}{14.7 \times 8.5}$ **17** $\dfrac{26.7 \times 15.3}{4.1 \times 1.3}$ **18** $\dfrac{42 \times 4.2}{8 \times 4.5}$

19 $\dfrac{35 \times 12.4}{1.75 \times 2.3}$ **20** $\dfrac{42.7 \times 4.47}{11.2 \times 1.4}$ **21** $\dfrac{36.5 \times 84.8}{2.12 \times 1.825}$

22 $\dfrac{94 \times 153}{324 \times 20.5}$ **23** $\dfrac{152.4 \times 12.12}{1.56 \times 9.6}$ **24** $\dfrac{43.1^2}{6.4 \times 8.1}$

25 $\dfrac{63.7 \times 15.7}{1.5 \times 1.6}$ **26** $\dfrac{6.87 \times 30.4 \times 215}{3240}$ **27** $\dfrac{182.5 \times 21.2}{36.5 \times 5.48}$

28 $\dfrac{4955 \times 3.7 \times 8.9}{32.9 \times 3.1 \times 18.4}$ **29** $\dfrac{47.6}{2.4} \times \dfrac{897.6}{5.75}$ **30** $\dfrac{49.97 \times 5.56}{35.2 \times 1.8 \times 2.2}$

10/ MEASUREMENT TO HALF A UNIT

When a measurement is taken it is always **rounded** in some way. This could be as a result of the accuracy of the measuring instrument. The rounding is within half a unit.

For example, 11.5 cm could be measured as 12 cm, to the nearest centimetre, and values up to 12.5 cm would also be 12 cm to the nearest centimetre.

> **EXAMPLE**
> ▶ For each measurement write down the (i) minimum (ii) maximum possible value.
> (a) 38 km   (b) 2.4 mm   (c) 1.388 kg
>
>   (a) 38 km (i) minimum is 37.5 km (ii) maximum is 38.5 km
>   (b) 2.4 mm (i) minimum is 2.35 mm (ii) maximum is 2.45 mm
>   (c) 1.388 kg (i) minimum is 1.3875 kg (ii) maximum is 1.3885 kg

Exercise 10A

For each measurement write down the (a) minimum (b) maximum possible value.

1 41 cm	**2** 131 km	**3** 95 m	**4** 2.38 cm	**5** 10.8 t
6 0.414 m	**7** 43.2 cm	**8** 0.385 l	**9** 32 cm	**10** 2.444 m
11 56.6 cl	**12** 7.279 kg	**13** 0.54 cm	**14** 3.09 g	**15** 100 m.p.h.
16 3.288 cm	**17** 2.23 g	**18** 21.2 cm	**19** 57 m	**20** 5.49 l
21 23.6 kg	**22** 2.69 ml	**23** 5.316 cm	**24** 4.77 s	**25** 93 km
26 14.293 cm	**27** 16.8 t	**28** 0.215 m	**29** 1.11 t	**30** 4.148 km

Exercise 10B

For each measurement write down the (a) minimum (b) maximum possible value.

1 23 ml	**2** 47 g	**3** 237 t	**4** 1.73 kg	**5** 7.95 m
6 20.1 g	**7** 5.245 t	**8** 15.8 km	**9** 7.381 l	**10** 17.2 m

11 5.108 cm	**12** 10 m.p.h.	**13** 0.681 cl	**14** 37.6 s	**15** 7.222 m
16 0.001 *l*	**17** 0.668 cm	**18** 22 m	**19** 0.04 *l*	**20** 30.6 s
21 3.08 cm	**22** 3.331 kg	**23** 2.11 km	**24** 2.07 *l*	**25** 1.2005 m
26 84 cl	**27** 1.128 kg	**28** 1.22 s	**29** 2.6005 t	**30** 3.66 g

11/ **RATIO**

A **ratio** is a comparison of two numbers or quantities. Ratios are normally expressed in their simplest form, as whole numbers.

> **EXAMPLE**
>
> ▶ Simplify: (a) $4:14$ (b) $750\,g:1\,kg$ (c) $40p:£1$ (d) $2\frac{1}{3}:3\frac{5}{6}$
>
>   (a) $4:14 = 2:7$ (divide by 2)
>
>   (b) $750\,g:1\,kg = 750:1000$ (change to the same units: g)
> $= 3:4$ (cancel)
>
>   (c) $40p:£1:80p = 40:100:80$ (change to the same units: pence)
> $= 2:5:4$ (cancel)
>
>   (d) $2\frac{1}{3}:3\frac{5}{6} = 14:23$ (multiply by 6 because of the $\frac{1}{6}$)

Ratios expressed in the form $1:n$ are called **unitary ratios.** The number n could be a whole number, fraction or decimal.

> **EXAMPLE**
>
> ▶ Express in the form $1:n$ (a) $10:13$ (b) £1.50 : 30p.
>
>   (a) $10:13 = 1:13 \div 10 = 1:1.3$ or $1:1\frac{3}{10}$
>
>   (b) £1.50 : 30p $= 150:30 = 5:1 = 1:1 \div 5 = 1:0.2$ or $1:\frac{1}{5}$

Exercise 11A

Simplify.

1 $2:8$	**2** $18:27$	**3** $125:1000$	**4** $3:12$
5 $180:270$	**6** $32:40$	**7** $18:12$	**8** $415:215$
9 $\frac{3}{4}:\frac{1}{2}$	**10** $75p:£3.75$	**11** $35:25$	**12** $\frac{3}{4}:5$
13 $75\,cm:3.5\,m$	**14** $9:36$	**15** $725\,mg:1.5\,g$	**16** $800\,m:1.8\,km$
17 £2.25 : £3.75	**18** $40\,mm:2\,m:8\,cm$	**19** £3.25 : 125p : £2	
20 $25\,m:1000\,cm:1\,km$			

Express these ratios in the form $1:n$.

21 $5\,mm:3\,cm$	**22** $4.8\,kg:200\,g$	**23** $4:1$	**24** $3:15$	**25** $6:3$
26 $2:5$	**27** $5:6$	**28** $5:11$	**29** $3:4$	**30** $7:8$

Exercise 11B

Simplify.

1 $8:16$	**2** $10:15$	**3** $10:4$	**4** $36:6$	**5** $200:450$

6 36:54	**7** 15:21	**8** 21:28	**9** $\frac{1}{4}$: 5	**10** £1.50:£5
11 44:11	**12** 50 cm:1.75 m	**13** $\frac{1}{4}$: $\frac{1}{2}$	**14** 45:120	**15** 28:42
16 450 cm:3 m	**17** $\frac{5}{8}$: $\frac{1}{2}$	**18** 750 g:2 kg:0.5 kg		
19 16 mm:2 cm:3.6 cm		**20** 1 m:25 cm:150 cm		

Express these ratios in the form 1 : *n*.

21 30 cm:2 m	**22** 24p:£1	**23** 7:14	**24** 4:5	**25** 4:10
26 9:3	**27** 5:12	**28** 5:3	**29** 6:4	**30** 13:7

12/ USING RATIOS

EXAMPLE

▶ Find the value of *x* when (a) 3:4 = 9:*x* (b) *x*:3 = 8:12.7 − 12 = −5

    (a) 3:4 = 9:*x*   (b) *x*:3 = 8:12
       (3→9 multiplied by 3)   (3→12 multiplied by 4)
       So 3:4 = 9:12   2:3 = 8:12 (work backwards)
         So *x* = 12   So *x* = 2

EXAMPLE

▶ In an office the ratio of men : women is 2 : 3. There are 21 women who work in the office. How many men work there?

    2:3 = *x*:21 (multiply by 7)
    2:3 = 14:21
    Number of men is 14.

Exercise 12A

Find the missing number in each question.

1 12:4 = 3:*x*	**2** 7:*x* = 1:3	**3** 2:*x* = 10:15	**4** 5:2 = *x*:8
5 24:14 = 12:*x*	**6** 3:1 = *x*:5	**7** 1:5 = *x*:25	**8** 5:2 = *x*:8
9 16:8 = *x*:1	**10** 2:3 = 18:*x*		

11 The speed of two cars is in the ratio 9:4. The speed of the first car is 45 km/h. What is the speed of the second car?

12 The ratio of boys to girls in a class is 3:4. There are 16 girls in the class. How many boys are there?

13 Two lengths of wood are in the ratio 4:7. The longer length is 35 cm. What is the shorter length?

14 A garden centre sells tables and chairs in the proportion of 1:5. In one week it sells 35 chairs. How many tables would they expect to have sold?

15 Two lengths are in the ratio 7:3. The smaller length is 42 cm. Find the larger length.

16 The total number of guests staying at two hotels was in the ratio 2:7. There were 54 guests staying at the smaller hotel. How many guests were staying at the larger hotel?

17 In a day a cafe sold cheese and ham sandwiches in the ratio 4:5. It has sold 30 ham sandwiches. How many cheese sandwiches has it sold?

18 Two soap packets contain powder in the ratio 3 : 10. The smaller contains 1 kg of powder. What weight of powder does the larger packet contain?

19 The ratio of swimmers to non-swimmers on an outward bound course is 9 : 2. Four people cannot swim. What is the total number of people on the outward bound course?

20 The ratio of men to women on a bus is 3 : 7. There are 15 men on the bus. What is the total number of people on the bus?

Exercise 12B

Find the missing number in each question.

1 $40 : x = 1 : 2$ **2** $2 : x = 1 : 4$ **3** $36 : 9 = x : 1$ **4** $x : 3 = 18 : 27$

5 $x : 6 = 2 : 3$ **6** $64 : 24 = x : 3$ **7** $7 : x = 35 : 40$ **8** $10 : 4 = 5 : x$

9 $4 : 9 = 20 : x$ **10** $7 : x = 21 : 90$

11 In a town the ratio of the number of males to the number of females is 70 : 77. The number of males is 91 280. How many females are there?

12 In a rectangle the ratio of the width to the length is 5 : 12. The length is 30 cm. Find the width.

13 The ratio of the number of red flowers to yellow flowers in a garden is 6 : 11. There are 132 red flowers. How many yellow flowers are there?

14 An alloy contains iron and copper in the ratio 5 : 1. A block of this alloy contains 8 kg of copper. What weight of iron does it contain?

15 In a survey the ratio of people who prefer to write in blue and black ink is 4 : 5. If 60 people preferred to write in blue ink, how many preferred to write in black ink?

16 A machine makes electrical components, of which 2 in 35 are faulty. If it has made 16 faulty components, how many good ones has it made?

17 A junction is controlled by traffic lights. The ratio of the number of seconds red is showing, compared to green, is 12 : 7. The green light was showing for 84 seconds. For how long would the red light show?

18 The ratio of the number of cats to the number of dogs owned by the children in a particular year group in a school is 5 : 4. There are 75 cats. How many dogs are there?

19 Of all the people on a course, the ratio of right-handed writers to left-handed writers was 5 : 2. Eight people were left-handed. How many people were on the course?

20 The ratio of the number of people attending a school play on Friday and Saturday was 4 : 5. On Friday 180 people attended. What was the total attendance over the two nights?

13/ DIVISION USING A RATIO

Ratios can be used to divide numbers or quantities into parts.

EXAMPLE

▶ Bill and Ben are directors of a company. They are to share a £14 000 profit in the ratio 3 : 4. How much will they each receive?

3 : 4 is 7 parts in total.
1 part is £14 000 ÷ 7 = £2000
So 3 parts is £2000 × 3 = £6000 for Bill
   4 parts is £2000 × 4 = £8000 for Ben

Check: £6000 + £8000 = £14 000

Exercise 13A

Divide the following numbers and quantities in the ratio given.

1 54; 2 : 1	**2** 330; 5 : 6	**3** 80; 5 : 3	**4** 70; 3 : 2
5 224; 4 : 3	**6** 125; 12 : 13	**7** 80p; 3 : 7	**8** 187; 5 : 6
9 30.78 m; 4 : 5	**10** £2.25; 4 : 5	**11** £25.60; 12 : 20	**12** £12.40; 2 : 3
13 £16.80; 3 : 5	**14** 38.0 kg; 3 : 5	**15** 46.8 *l*; 1 : 5	**16** £7.56; 3 : 4
17 54 kg; 12 : 6	**18** £170.52; 1 : 4 : 7	**19** 80p; 1 : 4 : 5	**20** £42.24; 1 : 3 : 4
21 471; 4 : 1 : 1	**22** 31.05 kg; 1 : 4 : 4	**23** 600 m; 2 : 3 : 3	
24 60.72 km; 1 : 3 : 3 : 4	**25** £130.87; 2 : 5 : 7 : 9		

Exercise 13B

Divide the following numbers and quantities in the ratio given.

1 100; 3 : 2	**2** 35; 3 : 2	**3** 374; 5 : 6	**4** 40; 5 : 3
5 £4.50; 4 : 5	**6** 3 m; 1 : 4	**7** 12 ml; 1 : 4	**8** 9 m; 5 : 1
9 54 kg; 2 : 1	**10** £24.75; 20 : 25	**11** £14.91; 2 : 5	**12** £12.80; 3 : 5
13 £30.24; 3 : 4	**14** 47.16 m; 4 : 5	**15** 46.8 g; 1 : 5	**16** £138.32; 5 : 8
17 72; 9 : 8 : 7	**18** £12; 2 : 3 : 3	**19** £31.56; 1 : 2 : 3	**20** £4.50; 2 : 3 : 4
21 67.0 kg; 1 : 2 : 7	**22** 336 kg; 1 : 2 : 4	**23** 46.17 m; 1 : 2 : 6	
24 42.24 km; 1 : 2 : 4 : 5	**25** £23.29; 2 : 3 : 5 : 7		

14/ DIRECT PROPORTION

Direct proportion is when two quantities are directly related; an increase in one will result in a proportionately similar increase in the other.

> **EXAMPLE**
>
> ▶ Three car tyres cost £165. How much will four tyres cost?
>
> First find the cost of *one* tyre; then the cost of any quantity of tyres can be found.
> 3 tyres cost £165
> 1 tyre costs £165 ÷ 3 = £55
> 4 tyres cost £55 × 4 = £220

Exercise 14A

Assume the same rate is maintained in each question.

1 Ten packets of sweets of the same kind cost £3.50. Find the cost of four boxes.
2 The cost of printing a book with 220 pages is £5.50. What would be the cost of printing a book with 180 pages?
3 A dozen cakes of soap made in a cottage factory weigh $1\frac{1}{2}$ kg. What will be the weight of 27 cakes?
4 Nine pens cost £1.44. What is the cost of eight pens?
5 An aeroplane travels 4800 km in 6 hours. How far will it travel in 8 hours?
6 Six chairs cost £84. What is the cost of five of these chairs?
7 Seven tickets for a concert cost £59.50. How much would five tickets cost?

8   Twelve books cost £90. Find the cost of 15 books.

9   In a garden 32 seedling trees need 24 cm^2 of space. How much space is needed for 48 seedlings?

10 A 23 kilometre journey by train costs £5.75. How much will a 128 kilometre journey cost?

11 A 4 kg bag of sugar costs £2.12. How much will a 7 kg bag cost?

12 Helen takes 36 minutes to iron 12 kg of clothes. How long will she take to iron 9 kg of clothes?

13 A boiler uses 500 kg of coal in 4 weeks. How long will 2 tonnes last?

14 Four metres of shelving is needed for 112 books. How many books would go on seven metres of shelving?

15 A hiker covers 16 km in four hours. How long will it take the hiker to cover 12 km?

16 A machine in a soft drinks factory fills 870 bottles in six hours. How many could it fill in five hours?

17 A pile of 500 sheets of paper is 6 cm thick. How thick is a pile of 200 sheets of paper?

18 It takes 22 minutes to empty a tank holding 272.8 litres of liquid. How much liquid is removed in just 14 minutes?

19 A train takes 4 hours to go 320 km. How long would it take to go 200 km?

20 Wiring costs £1.20 per 1.8 metre length. How much would 15 metres cost?

Exercise 14B

Assume the same rate is maintained in each question.

1   A motorcycle will travel 72 km on 6 litres of petrol. How far would it go on 10 litres?

2   Twenty children use 640 litres of water per day. How much will be used by nine children?

3   A clock gains 30 seconds in five days. How much does it gain in seven days?

4   A carpet of area 12 m^2 costs £96. What is the cost of a carpet of area 18 m^2?

5   A hotel charges £186 for a stay of six days. How much would they charge for ten days at the same rate?

6   Ten packets of sweets cost £4.50. Find the cost of 25 packets.

7   The average rainfall in a town is 19.6 cm in four weeks. How much rain falls, on average, in 17 days?

8   A 44-seater coach costs £363 to hire. How much would a 56-seater coach cost, if the charge per passenger is the same?

9   Seven pencils cost 56p. How much will five pencils cost?

10 It costs £222.75 to turf a lawn of area 45 m^2. How much will it cost to turf a lawn of area 68 m^2?

11 A helicopter travels 288 km in $2\frac{1}{4}$ hours. How far will it travel in 30 minutes?

12 You can buy 37 toy figures for £44.40. Find the cost of buying 31 figures.

13 If 1440 brass plates can be packed in 16 boxes, how many boxes are needed to pack 450 brass plates?

14 Eight eggs from a farm cost 48p. Find the cost of a dozen eggs.

15 On six pages of a book there are 2100 words. How many words would you expect to find on eight pages?

16 You can buy 25 metres of cloth for £40. How many metres of the same material could you buy for £56?

17 Six dogs eat 24 kg of food in a week. How much will five similar dogs eat in a week?

18 A plane travels 5100 km in six hours. How far will it travel in 3 h 36 min?

19 An electric fire uses $8\frac{1}{4}$ units of electricity in three hours. How many units will it use in eight hours?

20 Four packets of cereal have a total weight of 2000 g. What is the weight of nine packets?

15/ INVERSE PROPORTION

With **inverse proportion**, two quantities are inversely related. A decrease in one will result in a proportionately similar increase in the other.

> **EXAMPLE**
>
> ▶ It takes 9 men 30 days to complete a contract. How long would it take 15 men?
>
>   Total time taken = 9 × 30 = 120 man-days
>   So 120 ÷ 15 = 8 days

Exercise 15A

In this exercise assume that all rates remain constant.

1   A farmer employs 12 men to harvest a crop. They take 9 days to do the job. If he had employed 8 men how long would it have taken them?

2   A man can pay off a loan in 15 weekly instalments of £15. How many weeks will it take if the instalments are reduced to £12.50?

3   Flagstones are arranged to make a terrace 30 metres by 20 metres. The same number of flagstones is rearranged to make a terrace 24 metres wide. What is the length of the terrace?

4   Eggs are packed into boxes. With 6 eggs per box, 15 boxes are needed. How many boxes would be needed if 9 eggs could fit into a box?

5   You buy 30 pens at 36p each. If the price rises to 40p, how many pens could you buy for the same amount of money?

6   Gail has bought enough material to make eight curtains, each 3 metres wide. How wide would the curtains have been if she had made six curtains?

7   A secretary typed 3690 words in $4\frac{1}{2}$ hours. How long would it take her to type 5535 words?

8   Ten men produce 500 articles in 6 days. How long would it take 15 men to produce the same amount?

9   At a speed of 30 km/h a car takes 6 hours to complete a journey. On the way back the car is driven at 36 km/h. How long does it take to get back?

10   Eleven taps fill a tank in three hours. How long would it take to fill the tank if only six taps are working?

11   It takes 9 men 20 days to mend a road. How long would the job take 15 men?

12   Travelling at 30 m.p.h. it takes a car four hours for a journey. How long would the journey take at a speed of 40 m.p.h.?

13   A farm has sufficient feed to last 189 cows for 33 days. How long would the same quantity feed 231 cows?

14   Vases are packed in 25 cases, each of which contains 12 vases. If the same batch was packed in boxes containing 10 vases, how many boxes would there be?

15   The length of an article in a newspaper is 174 lines with an average of 14 words per line. If it is set out with 12 words per line, how many lines would there be?

16   When a bag of counters is shared out 8 children receive 9 counters each. If there were 12 children, how many counters would each receive?

17   Four men can paint a bridge in 10 days. How long would it take five men?

18   Five pumps can empty the bilges in a boat in 6 hours. How long would it take four pumps?

19   A gardener has space for 160 plants spaced 9 cm apart. How many plants could fit in the space if they were 15 cm apart?

20   Three dogs eat a bag of biscuits every 16 days. How long will it take four dogs to eat a bag of biscuits?

Exercise 15B

In this exercise assume that all rates remain constant.

1   Nine men put up a fence in 10 days. How long would 12 men take?

2   To complete a harvest a farmer needs three combine harvesters for five days. How long would it take if he had six combine harvesters?

3   Bill takes 4 hours to cycle a route at an average speed of 6 m.p.h. On the return journey his average speed was 8 m.p.h. How long did the return journey take?

4   A scarf is knitted with a length of 18 cm, and a width of 48 stitches. It is unpicked and reknitted with a width of 54 stitches. What is its new length?

5   A large tin of chocolates is shared between a group of nine children. They get eight each. If there were 12 children, how many would each get?

6   Twenty men produce 3000 electronic components in 12 days. How long will it take 15 men to make a further 3000 components?

7   A truck can carry 3240 blocks, each of weight 1.25 kg. The truck can also carry 2700 of a second type of brick. How heavy is this second type of brick?

8   A builder can put up a temporary warehouse in nine weeks using four men. If an additional two men are employed, how long will it take to build the warehouse?

9   A coach travels at 80 km/h, and takes 3 hours to make a journey. A slower coach makes the same journey at 60 km/h. How long did it take?

10   A bag of bird seed will feed six birds for 14 days. How long will the bag feed seven birds?

11   Four men can do a piece of work in 30 hours. How many would be required to do the work in 6 hours?

12   A field of grass feeds 24 cows for six days. How long would the same field feed 36 cows?

13   There are seven boxes of orange cordial bottles, each box containing 12 bottles. Only six larger boxes are needed for all the bottles. How many bottles will fit into a larger box?

14   Working for 7 hours a day a man completes a job in 24 days. How long would it take him if he worked for 6 hours a day?

15   A farmer needs two combine harvesters for 9 days on his farm. How long would the same job take if he had three combine harvesters?

16   Six machines are used to do a job in eight hours. How long would it take if only four machines were used?

17   A car travels at 30 km/h, and takes 6 hours to cover a certain distance. How long would it take at a speed of 36 km/h?

18   A man pays £15 for 14 weeks to pay off a loan. If he paid £10.50 how long would it take to pay off the loan?

19   Five men prepare the foundations on a building site in 14 days. How long would seven men take to repeat the job?

20   A man can carry eight 32 kg sacks on his truck. How many 64 kg sacks could he carry?

REVISION

Exercise A

1   Evaluate the following *without* the aid of a calculator.
    (a) 31 × 20   (b) 1320 ÷ 8000   (c) 29 × 500   (d) 2478 ÷ 700
    (e) 57 × 4000   (f) 3726 ÷ 90

2   State the value of the digit underlined in each number.
    (a) 14.<u>5</u>78   (b) 2.36<u>9</u>   (c) 37.8<u>4</u>1   (d) 2<u>3</u>7.514

3 Write each list of decimals in order, starting with the smallest.
(a) 2.101, 2.011, 2.111, 2.01, 2.11, 2.1   (b) 3.87, 3.78, 3.9, 3.8, 3.007
(c) 5.1, 5.9, 5.009, 5.01, 5.09, 5.11

4 Evaluate: (a) 3^5 (b) 7^0 (c) 5^3 (d) 10^5
(e) $3^2 \times 2^4$ (f) $4^2 + 5^3$ (g) $8^2 \div 2^5$

5 Express the following numbers as a product of prime factors.
(a) 48   (b) 108   (c) 390

6 Round these numbers correct to the number of decimal places given in brackets.
(a) 1.417 (1)   (b) 17.3554 (3)   (c) 6.666 666 (3)   (d) 3.199 (2)

7 Evaluate. Give your answer correct to 3 decimal places.

(a) $\dfrac{12.54 \times 84.27}{3.24 \times 2.89}$ (b) $\sqrt{\dfrac{14.2^2}{5.37 \times 1.89}}$ (c) $\dfrac{5.42}{1.97} + \dfrac{3.52}{1.42} + \dfrac{7.43}{2.64}$

8 Round these numbers correct to the number of significant figures given in brackets.
(a) 5.4792 (2)   (b) 333.383 (3)   (c) 109.4 (2)   (d) 52 200 (1)

9 Work out an estimate of the answer for each expression.

(a) 34.23 − 13.75   (b) $\dfrac{23.4 \times 14.3}{1.32 \times 1.97}$ (c) $\left(\dfrac{210 + 179}{4.5 \times 24.7}\right)^2$

10 Simplify.
(a) $4:6$ (b) $3:15$ (c) $8:6$ (d) $\frac{1}{4}:5$
(e) $\frac{3}{4}:\frac{1}{2}$ (f) $20\,\text{min}:3\,\text{h}$ (g) $50\text{p}:£3$ (h) $600\,\text{g}:1.8\,\text{kg}$

11 Express these ratios in the form $1:n$.
(a) $6:3$ (b) $2:5$ (c) $8:6$ (d) $8:4$

12 (a) If $x:y = 3:4$ find the value of x when $y = 20$.
(b) If $a:b = 5:9$ find the value of b when $a = 30$.

13 Divide the quantity in the ratio stated.
(a) £12.40; $2:3$ (b) 23.4 m; $1:5$ (c) 67 kg; $1:2:7$

Exercise AA

1 For each measurement write down the (i) minimum (ii) maximum it could be.
(a) 23 m   (b) 5.75 g   (c) 1.542 l (d) 0.029 km

2 A man spends £10 on petrol and £2 on oil. Write the ratio of money spent on petrol to money spent on oil.

3 A triangle has sides of length 12 cm, 30 cm, and 48 cm. Write the ratio of the three sides in its simplest form.

4 The ratio of girls to boys in a year group is $5:4$. There are 80 boys in the year group. How many girls are there?

5 The ratio of cats to dogs in a village is $5:6$. There are 30 cats. How many dogs are there?

6 The ratio of wet days to dry days during a holiday season is $3:4$. The holiday season was 84 days. How many days were wet?

7 The ratio of boys to girls in a youth club is $4:9$. There are 91 members of the club. How many were boys?

8 A 28 kg bag of oats costs £4.20 How much will a 98 kg bag cost, at the same rate?

9 Five identical wooden statues weigh 8 kg. What will be the weight of 19 such statues?

10 A car uses four litres of petrol to travel 75 km. How much petrol is needed to travel 60 km?

11 Three men can paint a house in 20 days. How long would it take five men?

12 Two secretaries can type a document between them in nine hours. How long would it take three secretaries working together?

13 Eggs are packed in 100 boxes, each containing 6 eggs. If the eggs were to be packed in new boxes containing 8 each, how many boxes would be needed?

16/ CANCELLING FRACTIONS

Fractions can be simplified by cancelling the numbers top and bottom. This can be done by dividing top and bottom numbers by any common factors.

EXAMPLES

▶ Cancel these fractions to their lowest terms.

$$\frac{18}{24} = \frac{3}{4} \quad (\div 6) \qquad \frac{27}{39} = \frac{9}{13} \quad (\div 3)$$

Note: Check your cancelled fraction to make sure you can't cancel it again.

Exercise 16A

Cancel these fractions to their lowest terms.

1 $\frac{15}{20}$	**2** $\frac{6}{9}$	**3** $\frac{14}{21}$	**4** $\frac{40}{64}$	**5** $\frac{18}{63}$	**6** $\frac{80}{90}$
7 $\frac{24}{54}$	**8** $\frac{40}{48}$	**9** $\frac{25}{30}$	**10** $\frac{15}{25}$	**11** $\frac{39}{65}$	**12** $\frac{21}{56}$
13 $\frac{56}{84}$	**14** $\frac{75}{80}$	**15** $\frac{36}{54}$	**16** $\frac{25}{30}$	**17** $\frac{15}{24}$	**18** $\frac{28}{49}$
19 $\frac{80}{126}$	**20** $\frac{39}{52}$	**21** $\frac{54}{60}$	**22** $\frac{45}{60}$	**23** $\frac{192}{448}$	**24** $\frac{48}{72}$
25 $\frac{45}{105}$	**26** $\frac{48}{84}$	**27** $\frac{60}{156}$	**28** $\frac{252}{308}$	**29** $\frac{105}{189}$	**30** $\frac{85}{100}$

Exercise 16B

Cancel these fractions to their lowest terms.

1 $\frac{14}{24}$	**2** $\frac{5}{15}$	**3** $\frac{15}{20}$	**4** $\frac{76}{92}$	**5** $\frac{3}{9}$	**6** $\frac{9}{12}$
7 $\frac{10}{15}$	**8** $\frac{35}{49}$	**9** $\frac{39}{51}$	**10** $\frac{27}{45}$	**11** $\frac{18}{24}$	**12** $\frac{27}{36}$
13 $\frac{18}{21}$	**14** $\frac{35}{42}$	**15** $\frac{96}{216}$	**16** $\frac{8}{10}$	**17** $\frac{20}{25}$	**18** $\frac{35}{50}$
19 $\frac{15}{45}$	**20** $\frac{54}{72}$	**21** $\frac{24}{27}$	**22** $\frac{24}{32}$	**23** $\frac{36}{45}$	**24** $\frac{77}{121}$
25 $\frac{32}{48}$	**26** $\frac{42}{105}$	**27** $\frac{63}{728}$	**28** $\frac{168}{480}$	**29** $\frac{24}{60}$	**30** $\frac{275}{325}$

17/ CONVERTING TO AND FROM MIXED NUMBERS

Mixed numbers are numbers that have a 'whole number' part and a 'fraction' part. A mixed number can be changed to an improper fraction.

EXAMPLE

▶ Change to single fractions: (a) $2\frac{3}{4}$ (b) $2\frac{5}{6}$.

(a) $2\frac{3}{4} = 2 + \frac{3}{4} = \frac{8}{4} + \frac{3}{4} = \frac{11}{4}$ (b) $2\frac{5}{6} = 2 + \frac{5}{6} = \frac{12}{6} + \frac{5}{6} = \frac{17}{6}$

Improper fractions can be changed to mixed numbers if the top part of the fraction is larger than the bottom part. They might also need cancelling.

EXAMPLE

▶ Change to mixed numbers: (a) $\frac{41}{6}$ (b) $\frac{97}{16}$.

(a) $\frac{41}{6}$: $6\overline{)41}^{\,6r5}$ $\frac{41}{6} = 6\frac{5}{6}$ (b) $\frac{97}{16}$: $16\overline{)97}^{\,6r1}$ $\frac{97}{16} = 6\frac{1}{16}$

Exercise 17A

Change these mixed numbers to fractions.

1 $2\frac{1}{2}$	**2** $4\frac{2}{3}$	**3** $8\frac{3}{7}$	**4** $6\frac{4}{5}$	**5** $4\frac{1}{2}$	**6** $2\frac{2}{3}$
7 $7\frac{2}{5}$	**8** $7\frac{8}{11}$	**9** $2\frac{2}{3}$	**10** $3\frac{7}{10}$	**11** $7\frac{4}{5}$	**12** $18\frac{11}{12}$
13 $4\frac{3}{4}$	**14** $15\frac{5}{8}$	**15** $5\frac{3}{5}$	**16** $3\frac{4}{7}$	**17** $3\frac{4}{9}$	**18** $8\frac{3}{5}$
19 $10\frac{7}{8}$	**20** $13\frac{7}{11}$	**21** $12\frac{13}{15}$	**22** $12\frac{1}{9}$	**23** $6\frac{11}{20}$	**24** $15\frac{14}{15}$
25 $8\frac{5}{12}$	**26** $3\frac{11}{15}$	**27** $7\frac{8}{15}$	**28** $4\frac{11}{14}$	**29** $5\frac{14}{15}$	**30** $2\frac{5}{16}$

Exercise 17B

Change these mixed numbers to fractions.

1 $7\frac{1}{2}$	**2** $9\frac{1}{4}$	**3** $4\frac{3}{4}$	**4** $3\frac{1}{3}$	**5** $8\frac{2}{3}$	**6** $2\frac{5}{6}$
7 $6\frac{3}{5}$	**8** $17\frac{5}{6}$	**9** $7\frac{9}{11}$	**10** $9\frac{2}{3}$	**11** $8\frac{5}{6}$	**12** $4\frac{4}{5}$
13 $1\frac{5}{9}$	**14** $10\frac{3}{7}$	**15** $9\frac{5}{8}$	**16** $2\frac{3}{7}$	**17** $12\frac{4}{13}$	**18** $7\frac{4}{5}$
19 $8\frac{8}{15}$	**20** $5\frac{1}{20}$	**21** $8\frac{13}{21}$	**22** $6\frac{3}{20}$	**23** $7\frac{19}{25}$	**24** $8\frac{7}{20}$
25 $9\frac{11}{20}$	**26** $11\frac{7}{12}$	**27** $18\frac{7}{15}$	**28** $6\frac{9}{19}$	**29** $9\frac{4}{9}$	**30** $3\frac{7}{11}$

Exercise 17C

Change these fractions to mixed numbers.

1 $\frac{7}{4}$	**2** $\frac{4}{3}$	**3** $\frac{17}{2}$	**4** $\frac{11}{6}$	**5** $\frac{9}{2}$	**6** $\frac{14}{5}$
7 $\frac{9}{4}$	**8** $\frac{49}{8}$	**9** $\frac{39}{7}$	**10** $\frac{89}{5}$	**11** $\frac{49}{10}$	**12** $\frac{29}{7}$
13 $\frac{63}{12}$	**14** $\frac{46}{10}$	**15** $\frac{91}{8}$	**16** $\frac{37}{10}$	**17** $\frac{57}{6}$	**18** $\frac{24}{5}$
19 $\frac{27}{8}$	**20** $\frac{20}{9}$	**21** $\frac{95}{3}$	**22** $\frac{36}{10}$	**23** $\frac{47}{5}$	**24** $\frac{83}{25}$

25 $\frac{101}{9}$		**26** $\frac{96}{5}$		**27** $\frac{97}{14}$		**28** $\frac{107}{10}$		**29** $\frac{33}{15}$		**30** $\frac{217}{25}$

Exercise 17D

Change these fractions to mixed numbers.

1 $\frac{16}{5}$	**2** $\frac{17}{8}$	**3** $\frac{13}{2}$	**4** $\frac{17}{5}$	**5** $\frac{7}{3}$	**6** $\frac{19}{7}$
7 $\frac{23}{5}$	**8** $\frac{27}{19}$	**9** $\frac{7}{2}$	**10** $\frac{8}{3}$	**11** $\frac{49}{4}$	**12** $\frac{57}{9}$
13 $\frac{11}{6}$	**14** $\frac{22}{5}$	**15** $\frac{29}{3}$	**16** $\frac{89}{12}$	**17** $\frac{53}{10}$	**18** $\frac{77}{12}$
19 $\frac{47}{3}$	**20** $\frac{31}{7}$	**21** $\frac{77}{10}$	**22** $\frac{110}{6}$	**23** $\frac{86}{10}$	**24** $\frac{104}{5}$
25 $\frac{99}{16}$	**26** $\frac{89}{10}$	**27** $\frac{147}{11}$	**28** $\frac{173}{20}$	**29** $\frac{89}{11}$	**30** $\frac{114}{12}$

18/ ADDITION OF SIMPLE FRACTIONS

When fractions with the same denominators are added do *not* add the denominators. Always cancel an answer to its simplest form.

EXAMPLES

▶ $\frac{2}{7} + \frac{1}{7} = \frac{3}{7}$ 　　　　　　　 $\frac{3}{5} + \frac{4}{5} = \frac{7}{5} = 1\frac{2}{5}$

When fractions of **different denominators** are added, change one of the fractions into an equivalent fraction so that the two fractions then have a **common denominator** (the denominators will be the same).

EXAMPLES

▶ $\frac{1}{4} + \frac{5}{12}$ 　　　　　　 $\frac{5}{6} + \frac{7}{12}$ 　　　　　　 $1\frac{2}{3} + 2\frac{5}{6}$

$= \frac{3}{12} + \frac{5}{12}$ 　　　　 $= \frac{10}{12} + \frac{7}{12}$ 　　　 $= 3 + \frac{2}{3} + \frac{5}{6}$

$= \frac{8}{12} = \frac{2}{3}$ 　　　　 $= \frac{17}{12} = 1\frac{5}{12}$ 　　 $= 3 + \frac{4}{6} + \frac{5}{6}$

Explanation: 　　　　　　　　　　　　　　 $= 3 + \frac{9}{6} = 3 + 1\frac{3}{6} = 4\frac{1}{2}$

$\frac{1}{4}\frac{\times 3}{\times 3} = \frac{3}{12}$ 　　　 $\frac{5}{6}\frac{\times 2}{\times 2} = \frac{10}{12}$ 　　 Note: The whole numbers are dealt with separately.

Note: addition of fractions with two different denominators that do not share a common factor is dealt with at a higher level.

Exercise 18A

1 $\frac{5}{8} + \frac{3}{8}$	**2** $\frac{4}{5} + \frac{2}{5}$	**3** $\frac{6}{7} + \frac{5}{7}$	**4** $\frac{5}{9} + \frac{8}{9}$	**5** $\frac{1}{2} + \frac{3}{8}$
6 $\frac{1}{2} + \frac{3}{16}$	**7** $\frac{3}{4} + \frac{1}{8}$	**8** $\frac{1}{8} + \frac{5}{16}$	**9** $\frac{9}{16} + \frac{5}{32}$	**10** $\frac{3}{8} + \frac{1}{16}$

11 $\frac{3}{8} + \frac{3}{32}$		**12** $\frac{5}{16} + \frac{1}{32}$		**13** $\frac{5}{16} + \frac{5}{32}$		**14** $\frac{7}{8} + \frac{15}{16}$		**15** $\frac{9}{16} + \frac{1}{2}$
16 $\frac{1}{8} + \frac{15}{16}$		**17** $\frac{9}{16} + \frac{19}{32}$		**18** $\frac{3}{8} + \frac{11}{16}$		**19** $\frac{3}{4} + \frac{15}{16}$		**20** $\frac{1}{2} + \frac{3}{8}$
21 $\frac{1}{5} + \frac{13}{20}$		**22** $\frac{1}{2} + \frac{5}{8}$		**23** $\frac{5}{6} + \frac{11}{12}$		**24** $3\frac{4}{7} + 6\frac{5}{7}$		**25** $2\frac{7}{9} + 2\frac{4}{9}$
26 $6\frac{2}{3} + 2\frac{1}{3}$		**27** $8\frac{2}{7} + 1\frac{3}{7}$		**28** $5\frac{3}{4} + 2\frac{3}{8}$		**29** $3\frac{7}{9} + 2\frac{2}{3}$		**30** $\frac{15}{32} + 3\frac{1}{2}$

Exercise 18B

1 $\frac{7}{10} + \frac{3}{10}$	**2** $\frac{7}{9} + \frac{4}{9}$	**3** $\frac{4}{7} + \frac{6}{7}$	**4** $\frac{7}{9} + \frac{4}{9}$	**5** $\frac{1}{4} + \frac{1}{8}$
6 $\frac{1}{4} + \frac{3}{16}$	**7** $\frac{1}{4} + \frac{7}{16}$	**8** $\frac{3}{4} + \frac{3}{16}$	**9** $\frac{1}{2} + \frac{7}{8}$	**10** $\frac{1}{8} + \frac{5}{32}$
11 $\frac{1}{4} + \frac{5}{32}$	**12** $\frac{1}{4} + \frac{7}{8}$	**13** $\frac{1}{2} + \frac{9}{16}$	**14** $\frac{1}{4} + \frac{15}{16}$	**15** $\frac{3}{4} + \frac{9}{16}$
16 $\frac{7}{8} + \frac{11}{32}$	**17** $\frac{7}{8} + \frac{3}{16}$	**18** $\frac{15}{16} + \frac{21}{32}$	**19** $4\frac{3}{4} + 1\frac{1}{4}$	**20** $\frac{3}{5} + \frac{1}{10}$
21 $\frac{2}{3} + \frac{1}{24}$	**22** $\frac{1}{2} + \frac{3}{4}$	**23** $4\frac{3}{4} + 2\frac{1}{4}$	**24** $5\frac{1}{4} + 2\frac{7}{8}$	**25** $1\frac{7}{8} + 3\frac{1}{8}$
26 $2\frac{5}{9} + 1\frac{5}{9}$	**27** $5\frac{2}{7} + 3\frac{6}{7}$	**28** $1\frac{3}{5} + 2\frac{9}{10}$	**29** $3\frac{5}{16} + 2\frac{3}{4}$	**30** $5\frac{1}{2} + 1\frac{11}{12}$

19/ SUBTRACTION OF SIMPLE FRACTIONS

When a fraction is taken away from a whole number, remember that the fraction is a fraction of a 'whole one'.

EXAMPLES

▶ $1 - \frac{3}{7}$

$= \frac{7}{7} - \frac{3}{7}$

$= \frac{4}{7}$

$5 - \frac{5}{8}$

$= 4 + 1 - \frac{5}{8}$

$= 4 + \frac{8}{8} - \frac{5}{8} = 4\frac{3}{8}$

Subtraction of fractions involves the same process as in adding fractions.

EXAMPLES

▶ $\frac{9}{10} - \frac{2}{5}$

$= \frac{9}{10} - \frac{4}{10} = \frac{5}{10} = \frac{1}{2}$

$4\frac{3}{4} - 2\frac{3}{8}$

$= 2 + \frac{6}{8} - \frac{3}{8} = 2\frac{3}{8}$

Note: Subtraction of fractions with two different denominators that do not share a common factor is dealt with at a higher level.

Exercise 19A

1 $1 - \frac{1}{4}$	**2** $1 - \frac{13}{16}$	**3** $4 - \frac{7}{8}$	**4** $3 - \frac{1}{8}$	**5** $6 - \frac{7}{8}$
6 $1 - \frac{1}{32}$	**7** $4\frac{3}{4} - 1\frac{1}{4}$	**8** $10\frac{2}{7} - 3\frac{1}{7}$	**9** $\frac{1}{2} - \frac{1}{8}$	**10** $\frac{3}{4} - \frac{3}{8}$

11 $\frac{5}{8}-\frac{1}{4}$		**12** $\frac{3}{5}-\frac{1}{10}$		**13** $\frac{9}{16}-\frac{1}{2}$		**14** $\frac{11}{12}-\frac{3}{4}$		**15** $\frac{7}{8}-\frac{1}{16}$	
16 $\frac{1}{4}-\frac{3}{16}$		**17** $\frac{3}{4}-\frac{3}{16}$		**18** $\frac{25}{32}-\frac{3}{4}$		**19** $\frac{13}{15}-\frac{2}{3}$		**20** $\frac{15}{16}-\frac{3}{4}$	
21 $7\frac{9}{16}-1\frac{1}{8}$		**22** $\frac{11}{24}-\frac{1}{3}$		**23** $\frac{5}{8}-\frac{11}{24}$		**24** $4\frac{7}{12}-1\frac{1}{3}$		**25** $8\frac{11}{18}-\frac{1}{9}$	
26 $\frac{3}{4}-\frac{5}{12}$		**27** $5\frac{3}{4}-2\frac{1}{2}$		**28** $7\frac{3}{4}-6\frac{11}{16}$		**29** $2\frac{1}{2}-1\frac{3}{8}$		**30** $6\frac{5}{8}-4\frac{3}{16}$	

Exercise 19B

1 $1-\frac{1}{8}$	**2** $2-\frac{1}{4}$	**3** $6-\frac{1}{2}$	**4** $1-\frac{11}{16}$	**5** $7-\frac{7}{8}$
6 $3-\frac{13}{16}$	**7** $9\frac{2}{3}-8\frac{1}{3}$	**8** $8\frac{4}{5}-7\frac{1}{5}$	**9** $\frac{1}{2}-\frac{1}{10}$	**10** $\frac{1}{2}-\frac{1}{4}$
11 $\frac{4}{5}-\frac{3}{10}$	**12** $\frac{1}{2}-\frac{3}{8}$	**13** $\frac{3}{4}-\frac{5}{8}$	**14** $\frac{5}{16}-\frac{1}{4}$	**15** $\frac{31}{32}-\frac{1}{2}$
16 $\frac{7}{8}-\frac{3}{4}$	**17** $\frac{7}{8}-\frac{27}{32}$	**18** $\frac{11}{18}-\frac{1}{2}$	**19** $2\frac{7}{10}-\frac{2}{5}$	**20** $6\frac{4}{5}-2\frac{3}{10}$
21 $3\frac{11}{12}-\frac{3}{4}$	**22** $1\frac{8}{15}-\frac{2}{5}$	**23** $4\frac{13}{18}-\frac{5}{9}$	**24** $4\frac{5}{6}-1\frac{1}{3}$	**25** $4\frac{1}{2}-\frac{7}{18}$
26 $\frac{9}{16}-\frac{1}{2}$	**27** $5\frac{7}{8}-1\frac{1}{2}$	**28** $4\frac{1}{2}-1\frac{7}{16}$	**29** $5\frac{7}{8}-4\frac{11}{16}$	**30** $2\frac{7}{8}-1\frac{1}{2}$

20/ SIMPLE MULTIPLICATION OF FRACTIONS

When multiplying fractions first multiply the top numbers, then multiply the bottom numbers. Cancelling top and bottom numbers first might make the problem easier to solve.

EXAMPLE

▶ $\frac{3}{4} \times \frac{1}{5} = \frac{3 \times 1}{4 \times 5} = \frac{3}{20}$

EXAMPLE

▶ $\frac{2}{3} \times \frac{5}{6} = \frac{\cancel{2}^1 \times 5}{3 \times \cancel{6}_3}$ (Cancel the 2 and the 6)

$= \frac{1 \times 5}{3 \times 3} = \frac{5}{9}$

EXAMPLE

▶ $\frac{3}{8} \times 20 = \frac{3 \times \cancel{20}^5}{\cancel{8}_2} = \frac{3 \times 5}{2} = \frac{15}{2} = 7\frac{1}{2}$

Exercise 20A

1 $\frac{4}{7} \times \frac{1}{3}$	**2** $\frac{2}{3} \times \frac{2}{5}$	**3** $\frac{1}{3} \times \frac{6}{7}$	**4** $\frac{2}{7} \times \frac{1}{3}$	**5** $\frac{5}{6} \times \frac{5}{7}$
6 $\frac{6}{7} \times \frac{5}{12}$	**7** $\frac{5}{12} \times \frac{3}{10}$	**8** $\frac{3}{7} \times \frac{14}{15}$	**9** $\frac{4}{5} \times \frac{10}{7}$	**10** $\frac{2}{3} \times \frac{9}{10}$
11 $\frac{7}{8} \times 16$	**12** $\frac{4}{7} \times \frac{7}{8}$	**13** $\frac{1}{4} \times \frac{1}{8}$	**14** $\frac{10}{30} \times \frac{14}{7}$	**15** $\frac{7}{16} \times \frac{8}{9}$
16 $\frac{5}{2} \times \frac{1}{2}$	**17** $\frac{2}{3} \times 27$	**18** $\frac{6}{25} \times \frac{35}{54}$	**19** $\frac{5}{2} \times \frac{1}{4}$	**20** $\frac{26}{30} \times \frac{5}{13}$
21 $\frac{8}{5} \times \frac{5}{2}$	**22** $\frac{2}{5} \times 10$	**23** $\frac{15}{4} \times \frac{8}{5}$	**24** $\frac{7}{8} \times \frac{1}{2}$	**25** $\frac{4}{9} \times 3$
26 $\frac{11}{4} \times \frac{9}{2}$	**27** $\frac{5}{6} \times 24$	**28** $\frac{3}{4} \times \frac{9}{16}$	**29** $\frac{5}{3} \times \frac{7}{2}$	**30** $\frac{7}{5} \times \frac{4}{3}$

Exercise 20B

1 $\frac{2}{5} \times \frac{1}{3}$	**2** $\frac{2}{3} \times \frac{10}{3}$	**3** $\frac{2}{7} \times \frac{1}{5}$	**4** $\frac{4}{5} \times \frac{3}{8}$	**5** $\frac{3}{5} \times \frac{1}{2}$
6 $\frac{5}{12} \times \frac{7}{15}$	**7** $\frac{3}{8} \times \frac{2}{3}$	**8** $\frac{4}{5} \times \frac{3}{8}$	**9** $\frac{7}{8} \times \frac{16}{21}$	**10** $\frac{3}{7} \times \frac{14}{15}$
11 $\frac{9}{10} \times \frac{11}{18}$	**12** $\frac{6}{7} \times \frac{2}{3}$	**13** $\frac{8}{9} \times 27$	**14** $\frac{15}{16} \times \frac{4}{5}$	**15** $\frac{4}{3} \times \frac{1}{5}$
16 $\frac{15}{21} \times \frac{7}{5}$	**17** $\frac{4}{5} \times 6$	**18** $\frac{6}{35} \times \frac{35}{54}$	**19** $\frac{3}{4} \times 40$	**20** $\frac{9}{16} \times \frac{1}{2}$
21 $\frac{3}{7} \times 21$	**22** $\frac{9}{5} \times \frac{11}{9}$	**23** $\frac{3}{4} \times 7$	**24** $\frac{5}{2} \times \frac{1}{4}$	**25** $\frac{7}{8} \times \frac{3}{4}$
26 $\frac{7}{10} \times 25$	**27** $\frac{3}{4} \times \frac{5}{8}$	**28** $36 \times \frac{3}{8}$	**29** $\frac{3}{2} \times \frac{5}{2}$	**30** $\frac{5}{2} \times \frac{3}{4}$

21/ SIMPLE DIVISION OF FRACTIONS

When dividing fractions an 'inverse' property can be used to change the division problem into a multiplication problem. For example:

$\frac{3}{5} \div \frac{1}{2}$ is the same as $\frac{3}{5} \times \frac{2}{1}$

(Using the inverse second fraction and the inverse of division, which is multiplication.)

So $\frac{4}{5} \div \frac{3}{4} = \frac{4}{5} \times \frac{4}{3} = \frac{16}{15} = 1\frac{1}{15}$

EXAMPLE

▶ $\frac{7}{8} \div 5 = \frac{7}{8} \times \frac{1}{5} = \frac{7}{40}$

Exercise 21A

1 $\frac{3}{5} \div 2$	**2** $\frac{4}{9} \div \frac{2}{3}$	**3** $\frac{1}{2} \div \frac{2}{3}$	**4** $\frac{2}{3} \div 3$	**5** $\frac{1}{2} \div 8$
6 $\frac{2}{5} \div \frac{3}{4}$	**7** $\frac{3}{7} \div 2$	**8** $\frac{8}{15} \div \frac{4}{9}$	**9** $\frac{9}{16} \div \frac{1}{2}$	**10** $\frac{3}{8} \div \frac{1}{4}$
11 $\frac{13}{14} \div \frac{13}{15}$	**12** $\frac{11}{12} \div \frac{3}{4}$	**13** $\frac{6}{7} \div \frac{3}{5}$	**14** $\frac{21}{25} \div \frac{14}{15}$	**15** $\frac{7}{2} \div \frac{7}{4}$
16 $\frac{14}{3} \div \frac{7}{6}$	**17** $\frac{9}{17} \div 3$	**18** $\frac{21}{2} \div \frac{9}{4}$	**19** $\frac{24}{5} \div \frac{16}{3}$	**20** $\frac{27}{2} \div \frac{21}{4}$

Exercise 21B

1 $\frac{9}{16} \div \frac{3}{4}$	**2** $\frac{3}{4} \div 2$	**3** $\frac{1}{4} \div \frac{2}{5}$	**4** $\frac{8}{15} \div \frac{9}{20}$	**5** $\frac{4}{5} \div 5$
6 $\frac{5}{8} \div 4$	**7** $\frac{9}{16} \div \frac{2}{3}$	**8** $\frac{3}{8} \div \frac{2}{3}$	**9** $\frac{7}{10} \div 3$	**10** $\frac{13}{14} \div \frac{2}{7}$
11 $\frac{5}{12} \div \frac{1}{6}$	**12** $\frac{9}{16} \div \frac{3}{14}$	**13** $\frac{5}{9} \div \frac{5}{6}$	**14** $\frac{13}{14} \div \frac{4}{7}$	**15** $\frac{15}{4} \div \frac{15}{2}$
16 $\frac{8}{3} \div \frac{12}{5}$	**17** $\frac{8}{15} \div 16$	**18** $\frac{28}{9} \div \frac{14}{3}$	**19** $\frac{9}{2} \div \frac{15}{4}$	**20** $\frac{9}{4} \div \frac{15}{8}$

To convert a fraction to a decimal divide the top number by the bottom number, then add on any whole numbers.

EXAMPLE

▶ Convert $3\frac{5}{8}$ to a decimal.

$5 \div 8 = 0.625$

$3\frac{5}{8} = 3 + 0.625 = 3.625$

To convert a decimal to a fraction write the decimal part over a denominator, cancel if possible, and add on any whole numbers. The denominator is decided by the length of the decimal as shown below.

EXAMPLE

▶ Convert (a) 1.32 (b) 0.0325 to fractions.

(a) $0.32 = \frac{32}{100} = \frac{8}{25}$

So $1.32 = 1\frac{8}{25}$

(b) $0.0325 = \frac{325}{10\,000} = \frac{13}{400}$

Exercise 22A

Convert the following fractions to decimals.

1	$\frac{3}{4}$	**2**	$\frac{7}{8}$	**3**	$\frac{3}{16}$	**4**	$\frac{2}{5}$	**5**	$\frac{1}{32}$
6	$\frac{9}{10}$	**7**	$4\frac{2}{25}$	**8**	$4\frac{81}{100}$	**9**	$9\frac{3}{5}$	**10**	$\frac{11}{20}$
11	$3\frac{11}{25}$	**12**	$2\frac{1}{10}$	**13**	$\frac{11}{16}$	**14**	$8\frac{11}{25}$	**15**	$7\frac{3}{100}$
16	$5\frac{49}{50}$	**17**	$3\frac{5}{16}$	**18**	$2\frac{3}{25}$	**19**	$3\frac{1}{20}$	**20**	$1\frac{1}{50}$

In the following questions give your answers correct to 4 decimal places.

21	$\frac{13}{30}$	**22**	$\frac{5}{9}$	**23**	$\frac{3}{7}$	**24**	$\frac{2}{9}$	**25**	$\frac{5}{12}$
26	$\frac{1}{3}$	**27**	$\frac{6}{11}$	**28**	$\frac{2}{11}$	**29**	$\frac{4}{9}$	**30**	$\frac{3}{11}$

Exercise 22B

Convert the following fractions to decimals.

1	$\frac{5}{8}$	**2**	$\frac{3}{5}$	**3**	$\frac{7}{16}$	**4**	$\frac{1}{10}$	**5**	$3\frac{7}{10}$
6	$7\frac{1}{2}$	**7**	$\frac{7}{20}$	**8**	$2\frac{1}{5}$	**9**	$2\frac{9}{40}$	**10**	$1\frac{9}{10}$
11	$3\frac{4}{5}$	**12**	$\frac{17}{20}$	**13**	$3\frac{4}{25}$	**14**	$3\frac{13}{25}$	**15**	$2\frac{13}{40}$
16	$1\frac{15}{16}$	**17**	$\frac{13}{32}$	**18**	$4\frac{1}{16}$	**19**	$3\frac{17}{25}$	**20**	$7\frac{49}{50}$

In the following questions give your answers correct to 4 decimal places.

21 $\frac{5}{11}$	**22** $\frac{10}{11}$	**23** $\frac{19}{30}$	**24** $\frac{2}{3}$	**25** $\frac{4}{7}$
26 $\frac{5}{9}$	**27** $\frac{1}{11}$	**28** $\frac{8}{9}$	**29** $\frac{7}{12}$	**30** $\frac{1}{12}$

Exercise 22C

Convert the following decimals to fractions expressed in their lowest terms.

1 0.13	**2** 0.1	**3** 0.75	**4** 0.45	**5** 0.2
6 0.09	**7** 0.625	**8** 0.377	**9** 0.06	**10** 0.08
11 0.44	**12** 0.001	**13** 0.55	**14** 0.93	**15** 0.006
16 0.675	**17** 0.88	**18** 0.84	**19** 1.36	**20** 0.895
21 3.8125	**22** 7.4	**23** 0.025	**24** 0.76	**25** 5.05
26 0.755	**27** 8.875	**28** 0.24	**29** 4.52	**30** 3.6125

Exercise 22D

Convert the following decimals to fractions expressed in their lowest terms.

1 0.3	**2** 0.57	**3** 0.15	**4** 0.32	**5** 0.9
6 0.425	**7** 0.999	**8** 9.3	**9** 0.16	**10** 0.47
11 0.103	**12** 0.825	**13** 0.275	**14** 0.52	**15** 0.435
16 7.8	**17** 0.08	**18** 5.04	**19** 0.36	**20** 0.875
21 2.2125	**22** 0.815	**23** 2.175	**24** 4.9375	**25** 0.28
26 0.715	**27** 0.855	**28** 2.09375	**29** 0.325	**30** 2.8125

23/ CONVERTING BETWEEN DECIMALS AND PERCENTAGES

To convert a decimal to a percentage multiply by 100.
To convert a percentage to a decimal divide by 100.

EXAMPLE

▶ Convert (a) 0.73 (b) 0.625 (c) 0.1425 to percentages.

(a) $0.73 \times 100 = 73\%$ (b) $0.625 \times 100 = 62.5\%$ or $62\frac{1}{2}\%$

(c) $0.1425 \times 100 = 14.25\%$ or $14\frac{1}{4}\%$

EXAMPLE

▶ Convert (a) 87% (b) $32\frac{1}{2}\%$ (c) $58\frac{1}{3}\%$ (d) 4.7% to decimals.

(a) $87 \div 100 = 0.87$ (b) $32\frac{1}{2} \div 100 = 32.5 \div 100 = 0.325$

(c) $58\frac{1}{3} \div 100 = 58.33 \div 100 = 0.5833$ (d) $4.7 \div 100 = 0.047$

Exercise 23A

Convert the following decimals to percentages.

1 0.2	**2** 0.125	**3** 0.23	**4** 0.38	**5** 0.4
6 0.145	**7** 0.93	**8** 0.8	**9** 0.255	**10** 0.46

11	0.13	12	0.78	13	0.215	14	0.48	15	0.665
16	0.165	17	0.86	18	0.0475	19	0.1725	20	0.64
21	0.65	22	0.125	23	0.455	24	0.0225	25	0.0025
26	0.015	27	0.6525	28	0.9275	29	0.045	30	0.7575

Exercise 23B

Convert the following decimals to percentages.

1	0.425	2	0.5	3	0.355	4	0.17	5	0.53
6	0.6	7	0.98	8	0.39	9	0.9	10	0.66
11	0.355	12	0.21	13	0.56	14	0.835	15	0.2925
16	0.7775	17	0.61	18	0.655	19	0.83	20	0.95
21	0.45	22	0.835	23	0.09	24	0.825	25	0.035
26	0.0075	27	0.735	28	0.0425	29	0.1975	30	0.5525

Exercise 23C

Convert the following percentages to decimals.

1	31%	2	85%	3	10%	4	42%	5	16%
6	50%	7	57%	8	2%	9	96%	10	41%
11	18%	12	$21\frac{3}{4}$%	13	$86\frac{1}{2}$%	14	44%	15	$15\frac{1}{4}$%
16	62%	17	$32\frac{1}{4}$%	18	79%	19	$31\frac{3}{4}$%	20	$49\frac{1}{2}$%
21	$33\frac{1}{2}$%	22	18%	23	$48\frac{3}{4}$%	24	$68\frac{1}{2}$%	25	94.5%
26	12.7%	27	85.42%	28	22.1%	29	19.9%	30	44.35%

Exercise 23D

Convert the following percentages to decimals.

1	86%	2	60%	3	31%	4	3%	5	53%
6	30%	7	82%	8	42%	9	8%	10	90%
11	$54\frac{1}{4}$%	12	4%	13	$17\frac{1}{2}$%	14	$29\frac{3}{4}$%	15	69%
16	59%	17	$51\frac{3}{4}$%	18	72%	19	$80\frac{1}{4}$%	20	$59\frac{1}{2}$%
21	$13\frac{1}{2}$%	22	$42\frac{1}{4}$%	23	$9\frac{1}{2}$%	24	$\frac{3}{4}$%	25	14.5%
26	73.7%	27	84.8%	28	14.35%	29	92.55%	30	14.94%

24/ CONVERTING BETWEEN FRACTIONS AND PERCENTAGES

To convert a fraction to a percentage, divide the top number by the bottom number (to change it to a decimal) then multiply by 100.

EXAMPLE

▶ Convert these fractions to percentages: (a) $\frac{11}{20}$ (b) $\frac{5}{8}$.

(a) $11 \div 20 \times 100 = 55\%$

(b) $5 \div 8 \times 100 = 62.5\%$ or $62\frac{1}{2}\%$

To convert a percentage to a fraction, write the percentage over 100, and cancel. If necessary, any fractional percentages must be removed before cancelling.

EXAMPLE

▶ Convert the following percentages to fractions: (a) 40% (b) $37\frac{1}{2}$%.

(a) $\frac{40}{100} = \frac{4}{10} = \frac{2}{5}$

(b) $\frac{37\frac{1}{2}}{100} = \frac{75}{200}$ (× 2 to remove fractions) $= \frac{3}{8}$

Exercise 24A

Convert the following fractions to percentages.

1 $\frac{2}{5}$		**2** $\frac{9}{20}$		**3** $\frac{7}{25}$		**4** $\frac{1}{40}$		**5** $\frac{18}{25}$		**6** $\frac{17}{100}$
7 $\frac{4}{25}$		**8** $\frac{13}{20}$		**9** $\frac{31}{50}$		**10** $\frac{11}{40}$		**11** $\frac{1}{200}$		**12** $\frac{19}{20}$
13 $\frac{1}{3}$		**14** $\frac{3}{20}$		**15** $\frac{17}{25}$		**16** $\frac{1}{8}$		**17** $\frac{3}{400}$		**18** $\frac{48}{300}$
19 $\frac{2}{9}$		**20** $\frac{13}{40}$		**21** $\frac{9}{50}$		**22** $\frac{3}{5}$		**23** $\frac{11}{25}$		**24** $\frac{19}{25}$
25 $\frac{21}{80}$		**26** $\frac{59}{80}$		**27** $\frac{5}{8}$		**28** $\frac{8}{9}$		**29** $\frac{7}{12}$		**30** $\frac{11}{12}$

Exercise 24B

Convert the following fractions to percentages.

1 $\frac{4}{5}$		**2** $\frac{1}{2}$		**3** $\frac{16}{25}$		**4** $\frac{11}{20}$		**5** $\frac{11}{100}$		**6** $\frac{14}{25}$
7 $\frac{17}{20}$		**8** $\frac{21}{25}$		**9** $\frac{7}{20}$		**10** $\frac{3}{40}$		**11** $\frac{23}{40}$		**12** $\frac{17}{200}$
13 $\frac{2}{3}$		**14** $\frac{7}{40}$		**15** $\frac{1}{20}$		**16** $\frac{104}{200}$		**17** $\frac{12}{25}$		**18** $\frac{1}{6}$
19 $\frac{3}{80}$		**20** $\frac{4}{9}$		**21** $\frac{3}{25}$		**22** $\frac{9}{40}$		**23** $\frac{7}{80}$		**24** $\frac{63}{80}$
25 $\frac{39}{40}$		**26** $\frac{5}{6}$		**27** $\frac{7}{9}$		**28** $\frac{7}{8}$		**29** $\frac{1}{12}$		**30** $\frac{5}{12}$

Exercise 24C

Convert the following percentages to fractions.

1 20%		**2** 7%		**3** 50%		**4** 70%		**5** 29%		**6** 95%
7 57%		**8** 90%		**9** 11%		**10** 36%		**11** 15%		**12** 72%
13 45%		**14** 16%		**15** 52%		**16** $\frac{1}{3}$%		**17** $47\frac{1}{2}$%		**18** $1\frac{1}{4}$%
19 $32\frac{1}{2}$%		**20** $66\frac{2}{3}$%		**21** $67\frac{1}{2}$%		**22** $95\frac{1}{2}$%		**23** $46\frac{1}{4}$%		**24** $89\frac{3}{4}$%
25 $78\frac{1}{3}$%		**26** $34\frac{2}{3}$%		**27** $14\frac{1}{8}$%		**28** $64\frac{2}{3}$%		**29** $21\frac{3}{4}$%		**30** $32\frac{1}{3}$%

Exercise 24D

Convert the following percentages to fractions.

1	40%	**2**	9%	**3**	37%	**4**	45%	**5**	51%	**6**	12%
7	85%	**8**	19%	**9**	24%	**10**	5%	**11**	32%	**12**	35%
13	48%	**14**	95%	**15**	65%	**16**	$14\frac{2}{7}$%	**17**	$41\frac{2}{3}$%	**18**	$\frac{3}{4}$%
19	$6\frac{1}{5}$%	**20**	$33\frac{1}{3}$%	**21**	$39\frac{1}{2}$%	**22**	$5\frac{1}{2}$%	**23**	$41\frac{3}{4}$%	**24**	$87\frac{1}{4}$%
25	$14\frac{3}{8}$%	**26**	$81\frac{1}{3}$%	**27**	$6\frac{2}{3}$%	**28**	$36\frac{5}{8}$%	**29**	$40\frac{1}{2}$%	**30**	$24\frac{2}{3}$%

25/ FRACTIONAL CHANGES

One method of increasing a quantity by a fraction is to calculate the fraction of that quantity, and add it to the original quantity.

EXAMPLE

▶ Increase £42 by $\frac{1}{6}$.

$\frac{1}{6}$ of £42 is $42 \times \frac{1}{6} = \frac{42}{6} = 7$

The increased amount is therefore £42 + £7 = £49

EXAMPLE

▶ Decrease £200 by $\frac{3}{4}$.

$\frac{3}{4}$ of £200 = $\frac{3}{4} \times 200 = £150$

The decreased amount is therefore £200 − £150 = £50

Exercise 25A

1 Increase 16 by $\frac{1}{4}$.

2 Increase 30 by $\frac{1}{3}$.

3 Decrease 21 by $\frac{4}{7}$.

4 Increase 56 by $\frac{1}{8}$.

5 Decrease 40 by $\frac{5}{8}$.

6 Decrease 18 by $\frac{2}{3}$.

7 Decrease 50 l by $\frac{3}{10}$.

8 Increase 20 by $\frac{4}{5}$.

9 Decrease 14 by $\frac{2}{7}$.

10 Increase 35 by $\frac{3}{7}$.

11 Decrease 20 m by $\frac{1}{5}$.

12 Increase 64 by $\frac{1}{4}$.

13 Decrease 80 by $\frac{3}{8}$.

14 Decrease 36 by $\frac{2}{3}$.

15 Decrease 48 g by $\frac{3}{16}$.

16 Decrease 63 m by $\frac{1}{9}$.

17 Increase 35 km by $\frac{5}{7}$.

18 Decrease 121 by $\frac{2}{11}$.

19 Increase 18 km by $\frac{5}{9}$.

20 Increase £2 by $\frac{1}{4}$.

21 Increase 88 kg by $\frac{5}{8}$.

22 Decrease 16 m by $\frac{3}{8}$.

23 Increase 15 kg by $\frac{2}{3}$.

24 Decrease £1 by $\frac{3}{10}$.

25 Increase $45 by $\frac{5}{9}$.

26 Decrease 180 by $\frac{1}{12}$.

27 Increase 60p by $\frac{5}{12}$.

28 Increase 48 by $\frac{5}{12}$.

29 Increase £38.25 by $\frac{4}{9}$.

30 Decrease £27.36 by $\frac{5}{6}$.

Exercise 25B

1 Increase 10 by $\frac{1}{2}$.

2 Increase 21 by $\frac{5}{7}$.

3 Decrease 30 by $\frac{2}{5}$.

4 Decrease 64 by $\frac{3}{4}$.

5 Decrease 20 by $\frac{4}{5}$.

6 Decrease 16 by $\frac{3}{4}$.

7 Decrease 18 by $\frac{1}{3}$.

8 Decrease 36 by $\frac{2}{3}$.

9 Increase 14 by $\frac{6}{7}$.

10 Decrease 40 by $\frac{7}{8}$.

11 Decrease 30 by $\frac{2}{3}$.

12 Increase 56 by $\frac{5}{8}$.

13 Increase 48 by $\frac{1}{16}$.

14 Decrease 80 by $\frac{1}{8}$.

15 Increase 16 by $\frac{1}{8}$.

16 Increase $8 by $\frac{3}{4}$.

17 Increase 50 l by $\frac{1}{10}$.

18 Decrease $45 by $\frac{4}{9}$.

19 Decrease 35 m by $\frac{6}{7}$.

20 Increase £88 by $\frac{7}{8}$.

21 Decrease £1 by $\frac{7}{10}$.

22 Increase £20 by $\frac{2}{5}$.

23 Increase 18 t by $\frac{7}{9}$.

24 Decrease 48 g by $\frac{11}{12}$.

25 Increase 45 m by $\frac{8}{9}$.

26 Decrease 63 cm by $\frac{2}{9}$.

27 Increase 121 g by $\frac{9}{11}$.

28 Increase 15 cm by $\frac{1}{3}$.

29 Increase £60 by $\frac{7}{12}$.

30 Decrease £52.71 by $\frac{5}{7}$.

26/ ONE NUMBER AS A FRACTION OF ANOTHER

EXAMPLE
▶ Write £15 as a fraction of £150.

$$\frac{15}{150} = \frac{1}{10}$$

EXAMPLE
▶ A computer costs £900. A computer game costs £120. Write the cost of the game as a fraction of the cost of the computer.

$$\frac{£120}{£900} = \frac{12}{90} = \frac{4}{30} = \frac{2}{15}$$

Remember to write the fraction in its lowest terms by cancelling where possible.

Exercise 26A

Write the first as a fraction of the second.

1 10p, 130p

2 18 ml, 50 ml

3 5 g, 40 g

4 30 km, 130 km

5 15 cm, 120 cm

6 25p, 35p

7 40 t, 80 t

8 35 kg, 85 kg

9 30 mm, 130 mm

10 10 g, 35 g

11 15 miles, 75 miles

12 50p, 54p

13 40, 75

14 $55, $120

15 45 s, 165 s

16 £1.20 for parking one morning, compared with £2.80 for a day.

17 16 passengers on a bus at 6 a.m., compared with 50 on the bus at 8 a.m.

18 The distance of one pen pal who lives 48 miles away, written as a fraction of the 130 miles distance of a second pen pal.

19 60p for a small loaf, written as a fraction of £1.80 for a large loaf.

20 An 80 mark test result, written as a fraction of a 200 mark test result.

Exercise 26B

Write the first as a fraction of the second.

1	20p, 60p	**2**	15 mm, 85 mm	**3**	10 kg, 60 kg
4	45 cm, 90 cm	**5**	10 km, 35 km	**6**	60 ml, 140 ml
7	32p, 144p	**8**	24 g, 144 g	**9**	30 t, 120 t
10	60p, £1.30	**11**	70p, £1.40	**12**	20 kg, 75 kg
13	10 miles, 111 miles	**14**	15 g, 35 g	**15**	40p, £1.20

16 A bolt weighing 15 kg written as a fraction of the weight of the 135 kg part it screws into.

17 The 45 people on a ferry compared with the 195 people on a ferry one hour later.

18 The 70p cost of one diary compared with the £1.75 cost of another.

19 The 80 cows in one field written as a fraction of the 120 cows in the next field.

20 The 55 letters received by one house written as a fraction of the 150 letters received by another house.

27/ PERCENTAGE CHANGE

A **percentage change** can be either an *increase* or a *decrease* by a percentage. There are two common methods used to calculate a percentage change.

EXAMPLE

▶ Decrease 120 by 45%.

Method 1
Find the percentage of the quantity and take away from the original quantity:
45% of 120 = $120 \times \frac{45}{100}$ = 54
A decrease requires a subtraction: 120 − 54 = 66

Method 2
Find the actual percentage change first.
A decrease of 45% is a reduction from 100% to 55%.
55% of 120 = $120 \times \frac{55}{100}$ = 66

EXAMPLE

▶ A new fridge costs £249 plus VAT at $17\frac{1}{2}$%. Find the total cost.

Method 1
Find the percentage of the quantity and add to the original quantity.
$17\frac{1}{2}$% of £249 = $249 \times \frac{17.5}{100}$ = 43.575 = £43.58 (rounded to the nearest penny)
An increase requires an addition: £249 + £43.58 = £292.58

Method 2
Find the actual percentage change first.
An increase of $17\frac{1}{2}$% means 100% will become $117\frac{1}{2}$%:
£249 $\times \frac{117.5}{100}$ = 292.575 = £292.58 (rounded to the nearest penny)

Exercise 27A

1 Increase 640 by 25%.
2 Increase £10 by 5%.
3 Decrease £40 by 15%.
4 Decrease 300 by 5%.
5 Increase 975 by 36%.
6 Decrease £60 by $\frac{1}{2}$%.
7 Decrease £480 by 9%.
8 Increase 32 km by $37\frac{1}{2}$%.
9 Increase 4.5 km by 30%.
10 Increase 400 g by 77%.
11 Decrease £4.50 by 35%.
12 Decrease 280 ml by 45%.
13 Increase 640 g by $12\frac{1}{2}$%.
14 Increase 900 km by 43%.
15 Decrease 250 g by 5%.
16 Decrease £48 by 9%.
17 Increase 96 ml by $6\frac{1}{4}$%.
18 Decrease £2.50 by 3%.
19 Decrease £2.00 by 17.5%
20 Increase 800 m by 57%.
21 Increase £7.50 by 37%.
22 Increase £15.50 by 25%.
23 Decrease £300 by 20%.
24 Decrease £7.60 by 7.5%.
25 Increase £5.25 by $17\frac{1}{2}$%.
26 A telephone bill is £80.60 plus $17\frac{1}{2}$% VAT. What is cost of the total bill?
27 A £36 coat is reduced by $12\frac{1}{2}$%. How much will it now cost?
28 How much will a £270 television set cost, if its price is increased by 8%?
29 A garage offers 12.5% off a service normally costing £160. How much will the service cost?
30 A man has been offered a discount of $22\frac{1}{2}$% on a £9670 motorbike. How much will he now have to pay for it?

Exercise 27B

1 Increase 500 by 16%.
2 Decrease 350 by 20%.
3 Decrease £1 by 20%.
4 Increase £240 by 4%.
5 Decrease £240 by 5%.
6 Decrease £41 by $7\frac{1}{2}$%.
7 Increase £1.25 by 68%.
8 Decrease £40 by $\frac{1}{8}$%.
9 Decrease 3000 ml by 73%.
10 Increase £460 by 60%.
11 Decrease £32 by 10.5%.
12 Decrease 80 km by 40%.
13 Decrease 600 cm by 36%.
14 Increase 880 mm by 75%.
15 Increase 48 g by $18\frac{3}{4}$%.
16 Increase 800 kg by 70%.
17 Decrease £1.80 by $37\frac{1}{2}$%.
18 Decrease £6.40 by $6\frac{1}{4}$%.
19 Increase £14.60 by 12.5%.
20 Increase £15 by $12\frac{1}{2}$%.
21 Decrease £6.40 by 75%.
22 Increase £85 by $7\frac{1}{2}$%.
23 Decrease 50p by 2%.
24 Increase £2.42 by 17.5%.
25 Decrease £2.80 by $17\frac{1}{2}$%.
26 Typewriters cost £129.99 plus $17\frac{1}{2}$% VAT. What is the total cost of buying a typewriter?
27 A pair of trainers would normally cost £43.60. They are to be sold at a reduction of 35% in a closing down sale. What is the sale price?
28 A lawnmower costs £125.80 plus $17\frac{1}{2}$% VAT. What is the total cost of the lawn mower?
29 The price of a holiday is increased by 5.5% from £850. How much will it now cost?
30 The population of a village was 6100. Its population reduced by 5% in a year. What is the new population?

EXAMPLE

▶ Express (a) 27 as a percentage of 90 (b) 15 as a percentage of 40.

(a) $\frac{27}{90} \times 100 = 30\%$ (b) $\frac{15}{40} \times 100 = 37.5\%$ or $37\frac{1}{2}\%$

EXAMPLE

▶ Of a batch of 120 eggs, 102 are brown and the rest are white. What percentage are (a) brown (b) white?

(a) $\frac{102}{120} \times 100 = 85\%$ (b) $100\% - 85\% = 15\%$

Remember: whenever comparisons are made between two numbers they should always have the same units.

Exercise 28A

Write the first number as a percentage of the second.

1	3, 60	**2**	40, 100	**3**	150, 400
4	60, 100	**5**	40, 200	**6**	116, 725
7	232, 725	**8**	30 cm, 1 m	**9**	72 mm, 225 mm
10	17 cm, 85 cm	**11**	£12, £300	**12**	49 ml, 350 ml
13	4.8 km, 12 km	**14**	6p, £1.50	**15**	£37.50, £125
16	15 mm, 6 cm	**17**	12.5 cm, 2 m	**18**	20p, £1.60
19	35p, £10.50	**20**	£17, £62.50	**21**	£5, £30
22	£2.25, £7.50	**23**	250 g, 400 g	**24**	£21, £56
25	15 km, 75 km				

26 Of the 150 pupils in a year group, 36 go home for lunch. What percentage of pupils go home for lunch?

27 A packet of stamps contains 30 second-class and 10 first-class stamps. What percentage of the packet are first-class stamps?

28 Jomo gains 28 marks out of 30 for a Technology test. Write this as a percentage.

29 A class had 209 attendances out of 220. What is the percentage attendance of the class?

30 After spending £75 on lottery tickets a woman wins a prize of £10. Write this as a percentage of the money she has spent.

Exercise 28B

Write the first number as a percentage of the second.

1	2, 200	**2**	375, 500	**3**	270, 400
4	20, 50	**5**	650 mm, 1 m	**6**	63, 420
7	£24, £300	**8**	350, 1250	**9**	2.4 km, 12 km
10	9 miles, 20 miles	**11**	900 mm, 1.5 m	**12**	27 m, 250 m
13	19 g, 20 g	**14**	50 mm, 75 cm	**15**	£17.50, £25
16	£4.20, £12	**17**	5p, 80p	**18**	£1.75, £10

19 £12.50, £30   **20** 45, 200   **21** £2.10, £12
22 £18.50, £50   **23** 5p, 75p   **24** 1.3 kg, 1.5 kg
25 6 mm, 48 mm
26 100 g of butter is to be cut from a pack of 250 g. What percentage is this of the whole pack?
27 Ashraf gained 63 marks out of 70 for a French test. Write this as a percentage.
28 A population has increased by 360 from 1800. What is the percentage increase?
29 In a school year group there are 46 boys and 54 girls. Find the percentage of the year group who are girls.
30 In a survey 105 out of 240 vehicles were cars. What percentage is this?

REVISION

Exercise B

1 Simplify.
   (a) $\frac{24}{32}$ (b) $\frac{25}{55}$ (c) $\frac{72}{90}$ (d) $\frac{75}{200}$ (e) $\frac{42}{105}$

2 Change these mixed numbers to fractions.
   (a) $7\frac{3}{4}$ (b) $4\frac{6}{7}$ (c) $5\frac{3}{5}$ (d) $9\frac{4}{9}$

3 Change these fractions to mixed numbers.
   (a) $\frac{73}{10}$ (b) $\frac{23}{3}$ (c) $\frac{11}{5}$ (d) $\frac{48}{7}$

4 Work out.
   (a) $\frac{2}{3} + \frac{5}{6}$ (b) $\frac{5}{8} + \frac{1}{32}$ (c) $6\frac{2}{3} + 2\frac{7}{9}$ (d) $\frac{3}{4} - \frac{5}{28}$ (e) $4\frac{3}{4} - 3\frac{3}{16}$

5 Work out.
   (a) $\frac{2}{5} \times \frac{7}{8}$ (b) $\frac{2}{7} \times 28$ (c) $\frac{15}{4} \times \frac{3}{2}$ (d) $\frac{7}{10} \div \frac{2}{5}$ (e) $\frac{4}{9} \div 8$

6 Change the following to decimals.
   (a) $\frac{3}{20}$ (b) $2\frac{9}{25}$ (c) 37%   (d) $17\frac{1}{2}$%

7 Change the following to fractions.
   (a) 0.375   (b) 1.3125   (c) 56%   (d) $37\frac{1}{2}$%

8 Change the following to percentages.
   (a) 0.39   (b) 0.815   (c) $\frac{21}{50}$ (d) $\frac{7}{8}$

9 Work out.
   (a) 16% of 1275 g   (b) 35% of £42

10 Increase (a) 18 by $\frac{2}{3}$ (b) 900 km by 31%.

11 Decrease (a) 35 m by $\frac{3}{7}$ (b) £2.80 by $17\frac{1}{2}$%.

Exercise BB

1 Find the cost of a car exhaust system priced at £86 plus $17\frac{1}{2}$% VAT.
2 A £25 train ticket is to be increased in price by $5\frac{1}{2}$%. What will be its new price?
3 A £425 washing machine has its price reduced by 15% in a sale. Find its sale price.
4 A £12 998 car has its price reduced by 18%. What will be its new price?

5 A clarinet costs £150 plus $17\frac{1}{2}$% VAT. What is its total cost?

6 A village population of 2700 reduces by 8% in a year. What is the new village population?

7 A newspaper boy delivers 32 papers. He is asked to deliver an extra 4 papers. What is this as a percentage increase?

8 Paul gained 18 marks out of 72 for a Physics test. Write this as a percentage.

9 Sixteen out of 24 learner drivers passed their test. What percentage failed?

10 A class had 187 attendances out of 200. What was the percentage attendance of the class?

11 A car salesman receives 6% commission on the sale of a £6000 car. How much is this?

12 A man in a shop earns £1.80 per hour and commission of 8% on sales. Find how much is he paid for 38 hours work, and sales of £500 during the week.

13 Martin is quoted a cash price of £946 for a new boiler. The terms for a credit agreement are 15% deposit, and 24 monthly instalments of £39.50 Find (a) the total price on credit (b) the difference between the cash price and the credit agreement.

14 A new kitchen costs £254 cash. The credit price is 12% deposit plus 16 weekly instalments of £17.35 Find (a) the total price on credit (b) the difference between the cash price and the credit agreement.

15 A second-hand car is advertised at a price of £3300. The credit agreement would be a 24% deposit, plus 36 monthly instalments of £86.30 Find (a) the total price on credit (b) the difference between the cash price and the credit agreement (c) this difference written as a percentage of the cash price.

Algebra

29/ CONTINUING A NUMBER SEQUENCE

Number sequences can follow a pattern. There are many different types of number pattern in sequences. The most common patterns in number sequences can be investigated using a **difference method.**

EXAMPLE

▶ State the next two terms in the sequence: 1, 5, 12, 25, 47.

```
 1      5      12      25      47
    4      7      13      22      ◀——— 1st difference line
       3      6      9      ◀——— 2nd difference line
          3      3      ◀——— 3rd difference line
```

Write down the difference between each pair of numbers in the sequence.
The second row gives the pattern: add on increasing multiples of 3 each time.
The next two numbers in the second difference line are therefore
22 + 12 = **34**, 34 + 15 = **49**.
The next two numbers in the sequence are 47 + 34 = **81**, 81 + 49 = **130**.

Exercise 29A

State the next two terms in each sequence.

1 2, 10, 18, 26, ..., ...
2 14, 25, 36, 47, ..., ...
3 42, 36, 30, 24, ..., ...
4 50, 41, 32, 23, ..., ...
5 31, 33, 36, 40, ..., ...
6 12, 13, 16, 21, ..., ...
7 9, 9, 11, 15, ..., ...
8 6, 11, 17, 24, ..., ...
9 15, 19, 27, 39, ..., ...
10 22, 21, 19, 16, ..., ...
11 35, 30, 24, 17, ..., ...
12 19, 22, 28, 37, ..., ...
13 10, 11, 12, 14, 17, ..., ...
14 4, 8, 10, 14, 16, ..., ...
15 16, 21, 26, 30, 36, ..., ...
16 32, 30, 26, 20, ..., ...
17 6, 8, 12, 19, 30, ..., ...
18 1, 19, 34, 46, ..., ...
19 4, 4, 7, 13, ..., ...
20 7, 6, 8, 7, 9, ..., ...
21 8, 17, 25, 32, ..., ...
22 19, 26, 36, 49, ..., ...
23 33, 33, 30, 24, ..., ...
24 4, 9, 18, 31, ..., ...
25 7, 4, 6, 3, 5, ..., ...
26 9, 10, 14, 23, 39, ..., ...
27 5, 9, 8, 12, 11, ..., ...
28 6, 7, 8, 10, 14, ..., ...
29 2, 14, 31, 52, 76, ..., ...
30 9, 12, 18, 28, 43, ..., ...

Exercise 29B

State the next two terms in each sequence.

1 3, 10, 17, 24, ..., ...
2 14, 23, 32, 41, ..., ...
3 29, 24, 19, 14, ..., ...
4 44, 36, 28, 20, ..., ...
5 8, 13, 19, 26, ..., ...
6 12, 14, 18, 24, ..., ...
7 6, 11, 21, 36, ..., ...
8 7, 23, 37, 49, ..., ...
9 4, 4, 7, 13, ..., ...
10 20, 18, 15, 11, ..., ...
11 14, 16, 20, 28, 44, ..., ...
12 41, 38, 33, 26, ..., ...
13 8, 13, 16, 21, 24, ..., ...
14 11, 13, 15, 18, 23, ..., ...
15 14, 16, 19, 21, 24, ..., ...
16 23, 23, 21, 17, ..., ...
17 9, 13, 19, 28, 41, ..., ...
18 7, 7, 9, 9, 11, ..., ...
19 4, 2, 5, 3, 6, ..., ...
20 5, 8, 13, 21, 33, ..., ...
21 2, 12, 20, 26, ..., ...

22	6, 9, 14, 21, ..., ...	23	8, 28, 45, 59, ..., ...	24	11, 16, 15, 20, 19, ..., ...
25	7, 30, 48, 61, ..., ...	26	4, 7, 12, 20, 32, ..., ...	27	5, 11, 6, 12, 7, ..., ...
28	8, 9, 12, 18, 28, ..., ...	29	12, 22, 30, 36, ..., ...	30	14, 16, 18, 21, 26, ..., ...

30/ MAKING PREDICTIONS AND GENERALISING IN NUMBER SERIES

A **rule** is a short cut that helps you to calculate later terms in the series more easily.

EXAMPLE

▶ A sequence of numbers is: 4th: 12   5th: 14   6th: 16   7th: 18.
(a) Find a rule in words to describe this series.
(b) Write the rule using n to represent the nth term.
(c) Use the rule to find the 15th and 20th term in the series.

(a) It is helpful to write the series in a table:

Term (n)	4	5	6	7
Number	12	14	16	18

$4 \rightarrow 12$ In each case the first number
$5 \rightarrow 14$ has been multiplied by 2,
$6 \rightarrow 16$ and 4 has been added.
$7 \rightarrow 18$ The rule is 'Times 2 and add 4'.

(b) In symbols: $n \times 2 + 4$ becomes $2n + 4$.

(c) The rule is $2n + 4$. The 15th number is $(15 \times 2) + 4 = 34$.
                    The 20th number is $(20 \times 2) + 4 = 44$.

EXAMPLE

▶ A sequence of numbers is: 1st: 2   2nd: 6   3rd: 12   4th: 20   5th: 30
(a) Find a rule in words to describe this series.
(b) Write the rule using n to represent the nth term.
(c) Use the rule to find the 20th and 50th term in the series.

(a)

Term (n)	1	2	3	4	5
Number	2	6	12	20	30

Since the differences between the numbers in the table (bottom row) do not remain the same there is probably an n^2 in the rule. It is sometimes useful to add this row to the table:

Term^2 (n^2)	1	4	9	16	25

$1 \rightarrow 1 + 1 = 2$
$2 \rightarrow 2 + 4 = 6$ The rule that works is
$3 \rightarrow 3 + 9 = 12$ 'Add the term to the
etc.   square of the term'.

(b) The rule is: term^2 + term or $n^2 + n$.

(c) The 20th number is therefore $(20 \times 20) + 20 = 420$.
    The 50th number is therefore $(50 \times 50) + 50 = 2550$.

Exercise 30A

In each question there are four terms of a series of numbers.
(a) Write down a description (in words) of the rule for the series.
(b) Write down the rule using n to represent the nth term.
(c) Find the terms indicated.

1	1st: 1	2nd: 4	3rd: 7	4th: 10		State the 10th and 15th terms.
2	2nd: 1	3rd: 3	4th: 5	5th: 7		State the 10th and 15th terms.
3	2nd: 1	3rd: 4	4th: 7	5th: 10		State the 10th and 15th terms.
4	1st: 8	2nd: 13	3rd: 18	4th: 23		State the 10th and 15th terms.
5	1st: 9	2nd: 13	3rd: 17	4th: 21		State the 15th and 20th terms.
6	1st: 6	2nd: 9	3rd: 12	4th: 15		State the 15th and 20th terms.
7	3rd: 1	4th: 3	5th: 5	6th: 7		State the 15th and 20th terms.
8	1st: 3	2nd: 7	3rd: 11	4th: 15		State the 10th and 20th terms.
9	1st: 7	2nd: 10	3rd: 13	4th: 16		State the 10th and 20th terms.
10	1st: 1	2nd: 6	3rd: 11	4th: 16		State the 15th and 20th terms.
11	1st: 7	2nd: 11	3rd: 15	4th: 19		State the 15th and 20th terms.
12	1st: 3	2nd: 8	3rd: 13	4th: 18		State the 15th and 20th terms.
13	1st: 0	2nd: 4	3rd: 8	4th: 12		State the 10th and 20th terms.
14	1st: 5	2nd: 11	3rd: 17	4th: 23		State the 10th and 20th terms.
15	1st: 6	2nd: 11	3rd: 16	4th: 21		State the 10th and 15th terms.
16	1st: 8	2nd: 14	3rd: 20	4th: 26		State the 10th and 15th terms.
17	1st: 29	2nd: 28	3rd: 27	4th: 26		State the 15th and 20th terms.
18	2nd: 0	3rd: 3	4th: 6	5th: 9		State the 10th and 15th terms.
19	1st: 9	2nd: 14	3rd: 19	4th: 24		State the 10th and 15th terms.
20	1st: 48	2nd: 46	3rd: 44	4th: 42		State the 15th and 20th terms.
21	1st: 5	2nd: 8	3rd: 13	4th: 20	5th: 29	State the 10th and 20th terms.
22	1st: 0	2nd: 3	3rd: 8	4th: 15	5th: 24	State the 10th and 20th terms.
23	1st: 4	2nd: 7	3rd: 12	4th: 19	5th: 28	State the 10th and 20th terms.
24	1st: 5	2nd: 14	3rd: 27	4th: 44	5th: 65	State the 10th and 20th terms.
25	1st: 3	2nd: 8	3rd: 15	4th: 24	5th: 35	State the 10th and 20th terms.
26	1st: 3	2nd: 9	3rd: 19	4th: 33	5th: 51	State the 10th and 20th terms.
27	1st: 4	2nd: 14	3rd: 30	4th: 52	5th: 80	State the 15th and 20th terms.
28	1st: 4	2nd: 6	3rd: 10	4th: 16	5th: 24	State the 15th and 20th terms.
29	1st: 2	2nd: 7	3rd: 14	4th: 23	5th: 34	State the 15th and 20th terms.
30	1st: 6	2nd: 12	3rd: 20	4th: 30	5th: 42	State the 15th and 20th terms.

Exercise 30B

In each question there are four terms of a series of numbers.
(a) Write down a description (in words) of the rule for the series.
(b) Write the rule down using n to represent the nth term.
(c) Find the terms indicated.

1	1st: 5	2nd: 9	3rd: 13	4th: 17	State the 10th and 15th terms.
2	1st: 2	2nd: 7	3rd: 12	4th: 17	State the 10th and 15th terms.
3	1st: 0	2nd: 2	3rd: 4	4th: 6	State the 10th and 15th terms.
4	1st: 11	2nd: 13	3rd: 15	4th: 17	State the 10th and 15th terms.
5	1st: 10	2nd: 14	3rd: 18	4th: 22	State the 10th and 15th terms.

6	1st: 9	2nd: 11	3rd: 13	4th: 15	State the 15th and 20th terms.	
7	1st: 8	2nd: 12	3rd: 16	4th: 20	State the 15th and 20th terms.	
8	1st: 7	2nd: 12	3rd: 17	4th: 22	State the 15th and 20th terms.	
9	1st: 6	2nd: 10	3rd: 14	4th: 18	State the 10th and 20th terms.	
10	4th: 1	5th: 3	6th: 5	7th: 7	State the 10th and 20th terms.	
11	1st: 2	2nd: 5	3rd: 8	4th: 11	State the 10th and 20th terms.	
12	1st: 2	2nd: 6	3rd: 10	4th: 14	State the 15th and 20th terms.	
13	1st: 5	2nd: 8	3rd: 11	4th: 14	State the 15th and 20th terms.	
14	1st: 7	2nd: 15	3rd: 23	4th: 31	State the 15th and 20th terms.	
15	1st: 9	2nd: 12	3rd: 15	4th: 18	State the 10th and 20th terms.	
16	1st: 4	2nd: 9	3rd: 14	4th: 19	State the 15th and 20th terms.	
17	1st: 9	2nd: 15	3rd: 21	4th: 27	State the 15th and 20th terms.	
18	1st: 24	2nd: 23	3rd: 22	4th: 21	State the 10th and 20th terms.	
19	1st: 10	2nd: 12	3rd: 14	4th: 16	State the 15th and 20th terms.	
20	1st: 43	2nd: 41	3rd: 39	4th: 37	State the 10th and 20th terms.	
21	2nd: 3	3rd: 7	4th: 11	5th: 15	State the 15th and 20th terms.	
22	1st: 4	2nd: 7	3rd: 12	4th: 19	5th: 28	State the 10th and 20th terms.
23	2nd: 2	3rd: 7	4th: 14	5th: 23	6th: 34	State the 10th and 20th terms.
24	1st: 7	2nd: 10	3rd: 15	4th: 22	5th: 31	State the 10th and 20th terms.
25	1st: 1	2nd: 6	3rd: 15	4th: 28	5th: 45	State the 10th and 20th terms.
26	1st: 5	2nd: 12	3rd: 21	4th: 32	5th: 45	State the 15th and 20th terms.
27	1st: 6	2nd: 15	3rd: 30	4th: 51	5th: 78	State the 15th and 20th terms.
28	1st: 3	2nd: 10	3rd: 21	4th: 36	5th: 55	State the 15th and 20th terms.
29	1st: 0	2nd: 4	3rd: 10	4th: 18	5th: 28	State the 15th and 20th terms.
30	1st: 4	2nd: 9	3rd: 16	4th: 25	5th: 36	State the 15th and 20th terms.

31/ SERIES FROM DIAGRAMS

Number patterns can also be found in diagrams.

> **EXAMPLE**
>
> ▶ This diagram shows how a pattern develops. It shows the first three stages in the pattern. Write down a rule, using symbols, that will help you calculate the number of sticks in each stage of the diagram.

You can summarise this information in a table.

Diagram stage	1	2	3	
Number of sticks	4	6	8	

Comparing the top row with the bottom row, as before in number patterns, helps state the rule: $2n + 2$

Exercise 31A

In each question a diagram shows the first three stages in a pattern. Write down a rule for each question.

1 The number of blocks.

   1   2   3

2 The number of 'x' points.

   1   2   3

3 The number of sticks.

   1   2   3

4 The perimeter of each shape.

   1   2   3

5 The number of sticks.

   1   2   3

6 The number of 'x' points.

   1   2   3

7 The number of sticks.

   1   2   3

8 The number of white slabs.

   1   2   3

9 The number of sticks.

   1   2   3

10 The number of regions within each shape.

   1   2   3

11 The number of dots.

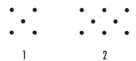

   1   2   3

12 The number of blocks.

   1   2   3

13 The number of faces showing.

   1   2   3

14 The number of blocks.

   1   2   3

15 The area of each shape.

1   2   3

Exercise 31B

In each question a diagram shows the first three stages in a pattern. Write down a rule for each question.

1 The number of dots.

1   2   3   4

2 The number of sticks.

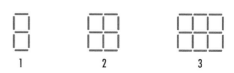

1   2   3

3 The number of dotted lines in each shape.

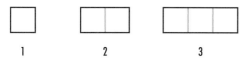

1   2   3

4 The number of 'x' points.

1   2   3

5 The number of '+' points.

1   2   3

6 The number of 'x' points.

1   2   3

7 The number of sticks.

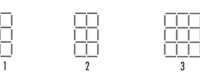

1   2   3

8 The number of dots.

1   2   3

9 The number of 'x' points.

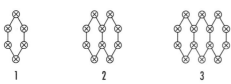

1   2   3

10 The perimeter of each shape.

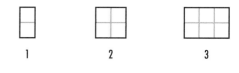

1   2   3

11 The number of white slabs.

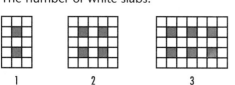

1   2   3

12 The number of sticks.

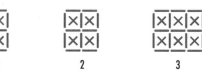

1   2   3

13 The number of faces showing.

1   2   3

14 The number of blocks.

1   2   3

15 The number of blocks.

1   2   3

32/ COLLECTING LIKE TERMS

When combining algebraic expressions, only those expressions with like terms can be combined.

$a + a + a + a + a = 5a$

$6x - 5x = x$

$abc + abc = 2abc$

$3ab^2c + 4abc^2 + ab^2c = 4ab^2c + 4abc^2$

$b + b + b + 2b = 5b$

$a + 2b + 2a - 3c = 3a + 2b - 3c$

$x^2 + 2x^2 = 3x^2$

EXAMPLE

▶ Simplify (a) $2a + 7b - 3b + 2a$ (b) $4pqr + 2pq^2r - 2pqr + pqr^2$

    (a) $2a + 7b - 3b + 2a$
          $= 4a + 4b$

    (b) $4pqr + 2pq^2r - 2pqr + pqr^2$
          $= 2pqr + 3pqr^2$

Exercise 32A

Simplify.

1 $6a + 2b + b - 4a$

2 $6c + a + b - 2c + a$

3 $c + 5b + 7a - 2b - 2a$

4 $6a + 3b - 2a - 3b$

5 $7m + n - 2m - 4m + 3n$

6 $3a + b + 2a + c - b$

7 $8x - 4x + y + 5y - 4x - 4y$

8 $5c + 3b - 3c - 3b + 2a$

9 $a + b + a - b + c$

10 $3e + 2f - e + g - 2f - g$

11 $4a + b + c - a - b - a$

12 $3ab + 2ab + 3b + 2a$

13 $xy + 3cd + 3xy - cd$

14 $3x^2 + 4x^3 - 2x^2$

15 $4x + 2y + 3y^2 - y$

16 $9cd^2 + 4cd^2 - 5cd^2$

17 $10a^3 + 3a^3 - 5a^3$

18 $a^3y^2 + 4a^2y^2 + 3a^3y^2$

19 $5a + a^2 + 2a^3 - 3a$

20 $8abc + 7ab + a - 5ab$

21 $9xyuv - 3xyuv - 5xyuv$

22 $8t^2 + 3t^2 + 5t^3 - 2t^2$

23 $4a^2 + 3a^2 - 6a^2 + 2a^2$

24 $5pqr + 6pqr - 8pqr$

25 $5a + 4a^5 + 3a^2 - 4a$

26 $8a^3 + 5a^2 - a^4 - a^2$

27 $4x^2 + 2x - 2 + 3x - 2x^2$

28 $8g^3 + 7g^2 - 3 + 3g^2$

29 $3x^3 - 2x^2 + 3x^3 - x^2$

30 $a^3 + 2a^4 + 3a^5 + a^2 + a^3$

Exercise 32B

Simplify.

1 $5b + c - 3b + 2a$

2 $6a + 5b + c - 5b - a$

3 $4c + 2b - c + b - 2a$

4 $a + 3b + a - c$

5 $y + 2w - y + 3w + 2y$

6 $8x + 3y + w - 2x - y$

7 $8a + b - 6a + 2c - b$	**8** $5a + 3b - b + 3a - b - 5a$	**9** $2m + n + p - 2m + 3n$
10 $a + b + c - a + 2b - c$	**11** $5a + 3b - 2a - 3b - 3a$	**12** $x + xy + y + 2xy + y$
13 $cd + 3cd + d - 2cd$	**14** $4x^2 + x + 2x^2$	**15** $5x^3 + 3x^2 - 4x^3 - 3x^2$
16 $7x^2 + 5y + 4y^2 - 2x^2$	**17** $c^2d^3 + 5c^3d^3 + 3c^2d^3$	**18** $8st^2 + 2st^2 - 4st^2$
19 $4xyuv - 2xyuv + 3xyuv$	**20** $9a^2 + 3a^2 - 5a^2 - 3a^2$	**21** $7pqr + 4pq + p - 4pq$
22 $6a + 3a^2 + 4a^3 - 2a$	**23** $7w^2 + 2w^3 - 3w^2 + 3w^3$	**24** $2pqr + 5pqr - 6pqr$
25 $2a + a^4 + 3a^2 - a$	**26** $2x^2 - 3x^5 - 2x^3 - x^2$	**27** $4x^3 - 6 + 2x^3 - x^2$
28 $2t^2 + 3 + 5t^3 - t^2 + 2$	**29** $6a^3 + 5a^2 - a^4 - 2a^2$	**30** $6x^2 + 4x - 3 + 5x - 2x^2$

33/ MULTIPLICATION OF TERMS

When terms are multiplied together the letters are arranged in alphabetical order; when like terms are multiplied together the indices are added.

EXAMPLES

▶ $3 \times p \times 5 \times q \times r = 15pqr$ $a \times a \times a \times a \times a = a^5$

$x^4 \times x^3 = x^7$ $4y^2 \times 3y^2 \times 2y^3 = 24y^7$

Exercise 33A

Simplify.

1 $5 \times m \times 4 \times n$	**2** $4 \times a \times 2 \times b \times 3 \times c$	**3** $2 \times a \times 5 \times b \times 3 \times c$
4 $4x \times 5y$	**5** $2c \times 4b \times 5a$	**6** $2 \times 2 \times a \times a \times a$
7 $7 \times 7 \times q \times q$	**8** $a \times b \times a \times b \times 5$	**9** $3 \times 3 \times xy \times xy$
10 $2 \times 3 \times cd \times cd \times c$	**11** $x^3 \times x^4$	**12** $t^3 \times t^7$
13 $y^4 \times y^5$	**14** $n^2 \times n^2 \times n^2$	**15** $d^3 \times d^4 \times d^5$
16 $3x^2 \times 2x^6$	**17** $7f^5 \times 3f^4$	**18** $5y^2 \times 6y^9$
19 $2c^4 \times 3c^4 \times 2c^5$	**20** $4x^6 \times 2x^4 \times 3x^3$	**21** $3a \times 3a$
22 $gh \times hi$	**23** $3yw \times w$	**24** $4cd \times 4c$
25 $2hk \times 3km$	**26** $2d^2 \times 2e^2$	**27** $3xyw \times 3xw$
28 $10a \times 10a \times 10a$	**29** $y \times 2y \times y \times 2y$	**30** $3xy \times 2y \times y$

Exercise 33B

Simplify.

1 $7 \times 3 \times q \times r$	**2** $4 \times p \times 4 \times q \times 2$	**3** $4 \times a \times 3 \times c \times d$
4 $2a \times 3b \times 4c$	**5** $5t \times 3n \times 5w$	**6** $y \times y \times y \times y \times y$
7 $x \times x \times x \times x \times y \times y$	**8** $2 \times 2 \times a \times a \times b$	**9** $5 \times 5 \times a \times y \times y \times y$
10 $4 \times 4 \times g \times g \times g$	**11** $a \times a \times b \times b \times b$	**12** $3 \times 3 \times a \times a \times b$
13 $x^7 \times x^2$	**14** $e^{10} \times e^9$	**15** $m^4 \times m^{12}$
16 $4y^2 \times 3y^3$	**17** $5g^7 \times 4g^4$	**18** $4d^2 \times 3d^2 \times 2d^2$
19 $2x^9 \times 3x^{10}$	**20** $4e^4 \times 3e^4 \times 2e^6$	**21** $2w^4 \times w^5 \times 4w^4$
22 $4d \times 4d$	**23** $st \times ts$	**24** $ab \times 2a$
25 $ef \times eg$	**26** $3ab \times 4ac$	**27** $5gh \times 4gh$
28 $3ab \times 2ab$	**29** $2a^2 \times 3ab$	**30** $a \times ab \times a \times ab \times a$

34/ DIVISION OF TERMS

When terms are divided common factors top and bottom are cancelled. When like terms are divided the indices are taken away.

EXAMPLES

▶ $12e \div 3 = \dfrac{12e}{3} = 4e$
$\qquad\qquad k \div k^2 = \dfrac{k}{k^2} = \dfrac{1}{k}$

$\dfrac{8a^7}{4a^5} = 2a^2$

Exercise 34A

Simplify.

1 $6f \div 6$	**2** $8m \div 4$	**3** $k \div k$
4 $6r \div 9$	**5** $m^2 \div m$	**6** $k^2m^2 \div km$
7 $14x \div 7$	**8** $16a \div 4a$	**9** $15ab \div 5ab$
10 $12a^2b \div 4ab$	**11** $x^4 \div x^3$	**12** $y^{12} \div y^4$
13 $g^{18} \div g^7$	**14** $10x^7 \div 2x^3$	**15** $27m^{10} \div 9m^3$
16 $28t^{15} \div 7t^7$	**17** $15m^2 \div 3m^2$	**18** $8a^9b^7 \div 4a^4b^3$
19 $8a^2 \div 16a$	**20** $24p^7q^{10} \div 8p^5q^9$	**21** $8ab \div 10b$
22 $6pqr^2 \div 9pqr$	**23** $14a^7b^{10} \div 7a^5b^5$	**24** $25h^2k \div 5h^3$
25 $16abc \div 6bcd$	**26** $5xy \div 10y$	**27** $8xy \div 12x^2$
28 $6stu^2 \div 4s^2u$	**29** $12p^4q^3r \div 8pqr$	**30** $3x^3y^2 \div 6x^2y^3$

Exercise 34B

Simplify.

1 $12g \div 8$	**2** $5p \div 5$	**3** $cd \div ce$
4 $f \div fg$	**5** $mn \div m$	**6** $8a^7 \div 4a^5$
7 $12p \div 6$	**8** $12q \div q$	**9** $18c \div 9$
10 $x^{10} \div x^3$	**11** $k^{10} \div k^4$	**12** $t^6 \div t^2$
13 $w^{10} \div w^4$	**14** $12y^8 \div 4y^3$	**15** $30b^{12} \div 15b^4$
16 $4a^4b^3 \div 2a^2b^2$	**17** $18xy \div 9y$	**18** $28p^2q \div 7q$
19 $16abc \div 8c$	**20** $16x^5y^7 \div 8x^3y^4$	**21** $12fgh \div 6gh$
22 $8a^{10}b^4 \div 2a^8b^2$	**23** $a^2 \div abc$	**24** $m^2n \div 2mn$
25 $27c^3d^3 \div 9c^2d^2$	**26** $12p^4q^3r \div 8pqr$	**27** $4m^2n^2 \div 6mn^2$
28 $2p^8q \div 6p^7q$	**29** $x^2y \div xy^2$	**30** $a^2bc^2 \div ab^2c^3$

35/ BRACKETS

Multiplying out brackets frequently leaves terms which can then be collected together or simplified further. If you multiply a bracket by a negative term, the negative sign outside the bracket has the effect of changing all the signs inside the bracket.

> **EXAMPLE**
>
> ▶ Multiply out and simplify $3(2x - 1) + 4(x + 3)$.
>
> $$3(2x - 1) + 4(x + 3) = 6x - 3 + 4x + 12$$
> $$= 10x + 9$$

> **EXAMPLE**
>
> ▶ Multiply out and simplify $2a(2c + 5d) + 3c(2a - 3d)$.
>
> $$2a(2c + 5d) + 3c(2a - 3d) = 4ac + 10ad + 6ac - 9cd$$
> $$= 10ac + 10ad - 9cd$$

> **EXAMPLE**
>
> ▶ Multiply out and simplify $10 - 4(a - 3)$.
>
> $$10 - 4(a - 3) = 10 - 4a + 12 \quad \text{Note: } -4 \times -3 \text{ gives } + 12 \text{ since } - \times - = +$$
> $$= 22 - 4a$$

Exercise 35A

Multiply out and simplify.

1 $2(4b - 3) + 3(b - 1)$	**2** $5(c + 4) + 2(3c - 8)$	**3** $2(4x + 3y) - 3(2x + y)$
4 $3(y - x) + 4(x - y)$	**5** $4(d - 2) - 3(d + 1)$	**6** $3(p + q) - 6(q - p)$
7 $y(2y + x) - x(y - x)$	**8** $3(2x + 4) - 5(3 - x)$	**9** $a(a + 2b) - b(a - b)$
10 $2x(4x - 5) - 5(x - 2)$	**11** $5(3c - 2) - (4 + 5c)$	**12** $6(1 - 3t) + (t - 5)$
13 $2x(3y + 4w) + 3x(y - 2w)$	**14** $7w(2x + y) + 3w(y - 4x)$	**15** $5a(b + 4c) + 2a(b - 10c)$
16 $a + (a + b)$	**17** $p + (q + p)$	**18** $4(a - b) + 3(b - a)$
19 $mp + 3p(m - 2n)$	**20** $3(p + q) - 6(q - p)$	**21** $y(2y + x) - x(y - x)$
22 $3p(m - 2n) + 2n(4p - m)$	**23** $x(y + 2w) + y(x - w)$	**24** $2a - (3 + a)$
25 $8 - (3 + 2a)$	**26** $4x - 2(x - 4)$	**27** $8 - 3(x - 7)$
28 $2y + y(2y + 5)$	**29** $3 + 4(5 - 2x)$	**30** $3t - t(t - 4)$

Exercise 35B

Multiply out and simplify.

1 $4(r - t) + 3(r - t)$	**2** $3(x + 7) + 2(x - 3)$	**3** $3(a + 4) + (a - 1)$
4 $4(k + m) - 3(k + 2m)$	**5** $x(x + 2y) - y(x - y)$	**6** $3(x + 1) + 2(x - 1)$
7 $2(t - y) + 4(y - t)$	**8** $x(x + 2) + 3(x - 4)$	**9** $d(c + 2d) - c(d - 3c)$
10 $2c(c + 3d) - 3d(2c + d)$	**11** $3x(3x - 2y) + 2y(3x - 2y)$	**12** $a(a + b) + b(a + b)$
13 $5f(2g + 5h) + 2f(g - 10h)$	**14** $3a(4b + 2c) + a(c - 8b)$	**15** $5a(2 - 3b) + b(10a + 3)$
16 $3a + (a + b)$	**17** $2a + (3 + a)$	**18** $2(4x + 3y) - 3(2x + y)$
19 $5(x - y) - 4(x + y)$	**20** $3(f + 1) + 2(f - 1)$	**21** $x(y - w) + y(w - x)$

22 $4(4 + a) - 3(a - 3)$	**23** $7c - 2(c - d)$	**24** $3x - (x + y)$
25 $8x - 3(2x - 1)$	**26** $7 - 2(3x - 5)$	**27** $13 - 4(2x + 3)$
28 $5a - a(a - 2)$	**29** $6w - w(2w - 4)$	**30** $2p - 3p(2p - 1)$

REVISION

Exercise C

1 Simplify.
(a) $a + 2b - a + 3b + 2a$
(b) $8x - 3x + y + 4y - 3x - 3y$
(c) $2x^2 + 3x^3 - x^2 + x^3$
(d) $3abc + 2bc - abc + ad + 3bc$
(e) $3 \times a \times 4 \times b$
(f) $3d \times 3d$
(g) $st \times tu$
(h) $c \times cd \times c \times cd \times c$
(i) $5ab \times 2abc$
(j) $xy \times 3xy \times 5y$
(k) $y^4 \div y$
(l) $15pq^2 \div 3pq$
(m) $27s^3t^2 \div 9s^2t^3$
(n) $12p^4q^3r \div 8p^2qr$

2 Multiply out and simplify.
(a) $a(a + 3b) - b(2a + b)$
(b) $2(3b - 2) + 3(b - 2)$
(c) $ab + 2a(b - d)$
(d) $2t - (2 - t)$
(e) $9 - 2(x - 3)$
(f) $4f - f(f - 3)$

Exercise CC

1 Find the next two terms in each number series.
(a) $7, 11, 15, 19, ..., ...$
(b) $1, 10, 18, 25, ..., ...$
(c) $4, 5, 6, 8, 12, ..., ...$
(d) $7, 10, 8, 11, 9, ..., ...$

2 In each question there are four terms of a series of numbers.
(i) Write down a description (in words) of the rule for the series.
(ii) Write the rule down using algebraic symbols.
(iii) Find the terms indicated.

(a) 1st: 5	2nd: 9	3rd: 13	4th: 17	State the 10th and 15th terms.
(b) 1st: 1	2nd: 4	3rd: 7	4th: 10	State the 15th and 20th terms.
(c) 1st: 2	2nd: 5	3rd: 10	4th: 17	State the 10th and 15th terms.
(d) 1st: 4	2nd: 10	3rd: 20	4th: 34	State the 12th and 15th terms.

3 In each question a diagram shows the first three stages in a pattern. Write down a rule for each question.
(a) Find a rule linking the number of dots with the diagram number.

1   2   3

(b) Find a rule linking the diagram number with
(i) the number of squares
(ii) the perimeter.

1   2   3

(c) Find a rule linking the diagram number with the number of lines in the diagram.

1   2   3

When finding the **coordinates** of a point, give the *x* value (to the left or right) first and the *y* value (up or down) second.

EXAMPLE

▶ State the coordinates of the points in the diagram.

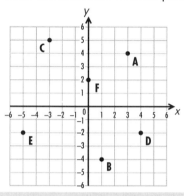

A = (3, 4)   B = (1, −4)   C = (−3, 5)
D = (4, −2)   E = (−5, −2)   F = (0, 2)

Exercise 36A

Write down the coordinates of the points in each diagram.

1

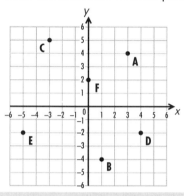

2

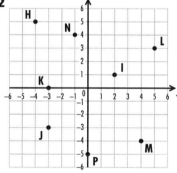

3

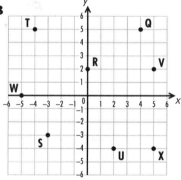

4

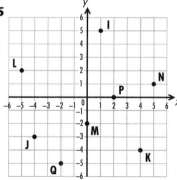

5

6

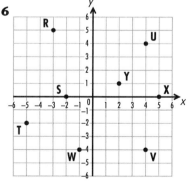

Exercise 36B

Write down the coordinates of the points in each diagram.

1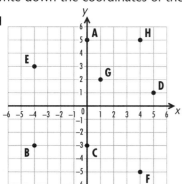

2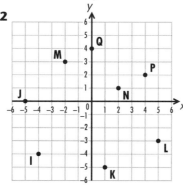

3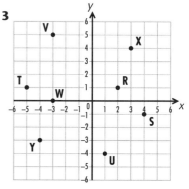

4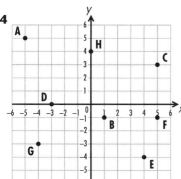

5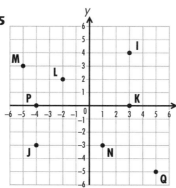

6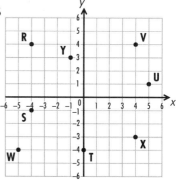

37/ PLOTTING POINTS IN ALL FOUR QUADRANTS

For these questions you will need to draw axes from –6 to +6 for each question, on squared paper.

EXAMPLE

▶ Plot and label the points:

A = (–4, 3)   B = (2, –3)   C = (0, 5)
D = (–3, –5)   E = (–2, 0)   F = (4, 2)

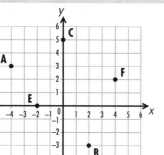

Exercise 37A

Draw axes from –6 to +6 for each question. Plot and label the points.

1 A = (–4, 2), B = (2, –5), C = (–3, –3), D = (–2, 5), E = (3, 2), F = (4, 0)

2 I = (–1 ,3), J = (–3, –2), K = (4, –3), L = (0, –5), M = (3, 3), N = (–5, 1)

3 P = (–3, 4), Q = (–5, –4), R = (5, 1), S = (–4, 0), T = (4, –5), U = (2, 2)

4 A = (–5, 3), B = (–3, –4), C = (5, 1), D = (2, 4), E = (0,–3), F = (5, –4)

Draw axes from –6 to +6 for each question. Plot the points and join them together in the order stated to draw various shapes.

5 (–3, 5), (–3, 0), (3, 5), (–3, 0), (–3, –5), (–3, 0), (3, –5)

6 (–2, 5), (5, –2), (5, –5), (2, –5), (–5, 2), (–5, 5), (–2, 5)

7 (–5, 5), (0, 2), (5, 5), (4, 0), (5, –5), (0, –2), (–5, –5), (–4, 0), (–5, 5)

8 (–5, –1), (–4, –3), (3, 4), (4, 3), (–3, –4), (–1, –5), (–5, –5), (–5, –1)

Exercise 37B

Draw axes from –6 to +6 for each question. Plot and label the points.

1 A = (3, –3), B = (2, 4), C = (–5, 2), D = (5, 2), E = (–4, –3), F = (–1, 0)

2 G = (–5, –1), H = (5, 1), I = (1, –5), J = (–4, 4), K = (3, 3), L = (0, 2)

3 M = (–4, –3), N = (5, –1), P = (2, 4), Q = (–5, 0), R = (2, –4), S = (–3, 1)

4 T = (–5, 3), U = (–4, –2), V = (3, –5), W = (5, 4), X = (5, –1), Y = (0, 1)

Draw axes from –6 to +6 for each question. Plot the points and join them together in the order stated to draw various shapes.

5 (–4, 5), (1, 5), (2, 3), (1, 1), (–4, 1), (1, 1), (3, –1), (3, –3), (1, –5), (–4, –5), (–4, 5)

6 (–4, 5), (4, 5), (2, 2), (2, –3), (4, –6), (–4, –6), (–2, –3), (–2, 2), (–4, 5)

7 (6, 1), (4, –4), (0, –5), (–4, –4), (–6, 1), (–5, 4), (–1, 5), (1, 5), (5, 4), (6, 1)

8 (3, 4), (4, 3), (1, 0), (4, –3), (3, –4), (0, –1), (–3, –4), (–4, –3), (–1, 0), (–4, 3), (–3, 4), (0, 1), (3, 4)

38/ DRAWING GRAPHS

A simple **function** takes one number and changes it into another number, according to a series of **operations**, or instructions. The way it does this can be shown as a graph. But first you need a table of values to provide some coordinates for the graph.

> **EXAMPLE**
> ▶ (a) Complete the table of values for the function $y = 2x – 3$.
> (b) Draw the graph of $y = 2x – 3$.
>
> (a) When $x = -2$, $y = (2 \times -2) -3 = -7$
> When $x = -1$, $y = (2 \times -1) -3 = -5$
> When $x = 0$, $y = (2 \times 0) -3 = -3$
> When $x = 1$, $y = (2 \times 1) -3 = -1$, and so on.
>
> Table of values:
>
> | x | –2 | –1 | 0 | 1 | 2 | 3 | 4 |
> |---|---|---|---|---|---|---|---|
> | $y = 2x – 3$ | –7 | –5 | –3 | –1 | 1 | 3 | 5 |

(b) These points can be plotted on a grid and joined to make a straight-line graph.

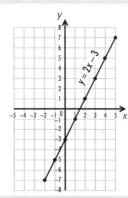

▶ (a) Complete the table of values for the function $y = 12 - 3x$.
(b) Draw the graph of $y = 12 - 3x$.

(a) Table of values:

x	0	2	4	6	8
$y = 12 - 3x$	12	6	0	−6	−12

(b) As the numbers in the table are large, choose the *scale* on the graph carefully.

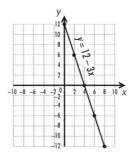

Exercise 38A

(a) Copy and complete the table of values for the function shown.
(b) On graph or squared paper draw and label the graph of the function.

1

x	−3	−2	−1	0	1	2	3
$y = 2x$	−6					4	

2

x	−3	−2	−1	0	1	2	3
$y = x + 2$		0				4	

3

x	−2	−1	0	1	2	3	4
$y = 2x - 2$				0	2		

4

x	−2	−1	0	1	2	3	4
$y = 4x - 5$		−9			3		

5

x	-2	-1	0	1	2	3	4
$y = 2x + 3$	-1			5			

6

x	-2	-1	0	1	2	3	4
$y = 3x - 4$		-7		-1			

7

x	-3	-2	-1	0	1	2	3
$y = 7 - x$	10						4

8

x	-3	-2	-1	0	1	2	3
$y = -3x$				0			-9

9

x	-2	-1	0	1	2	3	4
$y = 3x - 3$		-6		0			

10

x	-1	0	1	2	3	4	5
$y = 2x - 4$					2	4	

11

x	-3	-2	-1	0	1	2	3
$y = 2x - 1$	-7			-1			

12

x	-2	-1	0	1	2	3	4
$y = 5 - x$				4	3		

13

x	-4	-2	0	2	4	6	8
$y = \frac{1}{2}x - 4$	-6					-1	

14

x	-1	0	1	2	3	4	5
$y = 10 - 2x$		10			4		

15

x	-6	-4	-2	0	2	4	6
$y = \frac{1}{2}x + 3$	0		2				

Exercise 38B

(a) Copy and complete the table of values for the function shown.
(b) On graph or squared paper draw and label the graph of the function.

1

x	-3	-2	-1	0	1	2	3
$y = 4x$	-12			0			

2

x	-3	-2	-1	0	1	2	3
$y = 2x - 1$		-5			1		

3

x	-2	-1	0	1	2	3	4
$y = x - 3$			-3			0	

4

x	−3	−2	−1	0	1	2	3
$y = -2x$		4					−6

5

x	−2	−1	0	1	2	3	4
$y = 3x - 5$					1	4	

6

x	−3	−2	−1	0	1	2	
$y = 3x + 3$		−3	0				

7

x	−3	−2	−1	0	1	2	3
$y = -x$	3						−3

8

x	−3	−2	−1	0	1	2
$y = 2x + 6$					8	10

9

x	−2	−1	0	1	2	3	4
$y = 8 - x$		9				5	

10

x	−2	−1	0	1	2	3	4
$y = 3x - 2$				1	4		

11

x	−2	−1	0	1	2	3
$y = 4x - 2$	−10			2		

12

x	−2	−1	0	1	2	3	4
$y = 8 - 2x$		10					0

13

x	−6	−4	−2	0	2	4	6
$y = \frac{1}{2}x + 1$			0	1			

14

x	−1	0	1	2	3	4	5
$y = 7 - 3x$		7				−5	

15

x	−4	−2	0	2	4	6	8
$y = \frac{1}{2}x - 2$					0	1	

39/ SOLVING EQUATIONS

To solve equations:
(a) expand brackets if necessary
(b) collect numbers on one side of the equation, and terms involving the unknown on the other side
(c) gather number and/or algebra terms, if necessary
(d) multiply or divide both sides to ensure the unknown is on its own.

EXAMPLES

▶ $4x + 2 = 14$
$4x = 14 - 2$
$4x = 12$
$x = 12 \div 4 = 3$

$6x - 3 = 21$
$6x = 21 + 3$
$6x = 24$
$x = 24 \div 6 = 4$

$3(2x + 6) = 33$
$6x + 18 = 33$
$6x = 33 - 18$
$6x = 15$
$x = 15 \div 6 = 2\frac{1}{2}$

$3x + 3 = x + 7$
$2x - x = 7 - 3$
$x = 4$

$2x - 2 = 18 - 3x$
$2x + 3x = 18 + 2$
$5x = 20$
$x = 4$

$x + x + 7 = 21 - 2x$
$x + x + 2x = 21 - 7$
$4x = 14$
$x = 14 \div 4 = 3\frac{1}{2}$

Exercise 39A

Solve the equations.

1	$3x + 2 = 11$	**2**	$5x - 4 = 6$	**3**	$2x - 4 = 6$	**4**	$3x - 10 = 8$
5	$7x - 8 = 20$	**6**	$3x + 2 = 5$	**7**	$2x - 4 = 14$	**8**	$5x - 4 = 11$
9	$5x + 1 = 21$	**10**	$4x - 3 = 3$	**11**	$4x + 10 = 30$	**12**	$6x - 7 = 8$
13	$2x + 7 = 19$	**14**	$8x - 12 = 48$	**15**	$2x - 5 = 13$	**16**	$2(x + 2) = 14$
17	$4(3x - 2) = 40$	**18**	$3(2x + 3) = 27$	**19**	$3(x - 4) = 9$	**20**	$3(2x - 2) = 3$
21	$4(5x + 3) = 92$	**22**	$5(7x + 5) = 95$	**23**	$2(x - 2) = 8$	**24**	$4(3x - 2) = 16$
25	$7(x - 2) = 7$	**26**	$5(x + 5) = 55$	**27**	$4(2x + 9) = 48$	**28**	$6(x - 4) = 9$
29	$2(6x - 1) = 82$	**30**	$9(2x - 7) = 0$				

Exercise 39B

Solve the equations.

1	$4x + 5 = 21$	**2**	$2x + 7 = 9$	**3**	$3x - 6 = 12$	**4**	$9x - 4 = 14$
5	$3x - 12 = 9$	**6**	$3x + 9 = 33$	**7**	$4x - 2 = 10$	**8**	$6x + 2 = 35$
9	$4x - 16 = 0$	**10**	$6x - 8 = 7$	**11**	$5x - 15 = 5$	**12**	$5x + 8 = 13$
13	$8x + 9 = 49$	**14**	$4x + 15 = 29$	**15**	$7x + 4 = 32$	**16**	$3(x + 1) = 15$
17	$5(2x + 3) = 25$	**18**	$6(2x - 1) = 18$	**19**	$3(3x + 1) = 57$	**20**	$3(x + 3) = 24$
21	$2(x - 2) = 2$	**22**	$4(2x + 5) = 76$	**23**	$5(3x - 2) = 50$	**24**	$4(x + 3) = 34$
25	$6(5x - 6) = 9$	**26**	$4(3x + 6) = 54$	**27**	$9(x - 3) = 45$	**28**	$7(2x + 5) = 77$
29	$3(x + 2) = 24$	**30**	$4(6x + 3) = 72$				

Exercise 39C

Solve the equations.

1	$4x - 4 = x + 2$	**2**	$3x + 5 = 12 + 2x$	**3**	$4x - 5 = 4 + 3x$
4	$4x - 3 = 37 - x$	**5**	$4x - 2x + 7 = 11$	**6**	$5x - 4x + 15 = 21$

7 $2x - 7 = 5 - 2x$	**8** $3x - x + 3 = 11$	**9** $2x + 5 = 19 - 5x$
10 $2x + x + 5 = 20$	**11** $x - 15 = 1 - x$	**12** $5x + 2 = 7 + 2x$
13 $3x + 2x + 4 = 34$	**14** $5x + 5x - 6 = 2x + 18$	**15** $5x + 6 = 36 - 2x$
16 $5x + 9 = 25 + x$	**17** $3x + 1 = 64 - 2x$	**18** $4x + 2x - 9 = 26 - x$
19 $3x + x + 5 = 49$	**20** $2x + 2x + 7 = 25$	**21** $5x - 2 = 25 + 2x$
22 $4x - 2 = 38 - x$	**23** $4x - 2 = x + 19$	**24** $4x + 2x - 12 = 2 - 2x$
25 $5x - 4 = 3 + 4x$	**26** $6x - 4 = 1 + 4x$	**27** $3x + x - 3 = 42 - x$
28 $4x + 3x - 6 = 50$	**29** $2x - 8 = 9 - 2x$	**30** $3x + x - 8 = 27 - 3x$

Exercise 39D

Solve the equations.

1 $3x + 5 = x + 11$	**2** $4x - 3 = 2x + 7$	**3** $3x + 2 = 2x + 8$
4 $x + 5 = 11 - 2x$	**5** $3x + 2x - 4 = 16$	**6** $x + 2x - 2 = 7$
7 $5x - 5 = 16 + 2x$	**8** $5x - 4x - 12 = 4$	**9** $3x - 1 = 19 - 2x$
10 $3x + 14 = 16 + 2x$	**11** $5x + 3 = 3x + 13$	**12** $2x + x + 10 = 19$
13 $4x + 3 = 2x + 8$	**14** $x - 1 = 39 - 4x$	**15** $3x - 6 = 4 - 2x$
16 $4x + 4 = x + 25$	**17** $2x + x - 2 = 7$	**18** $x - 4 = 41 - 4x$
19 $2x + 2x + 2 = 26 + x$	**20** $5x - 1 = 14 + 2x$	**21** $3x + x - 9 = 4$
22 $5x - 5 = 7 + 3x$	**23** $2x + 7 = 43 - x$	**24** $4x + 9 = 19 - 4x$
25 $3x + x - 2 = 4$	**26** $6x - 4 = 3x + 41$	**27** $5x + 4 = 22 + 3x$
28 $5x - 10 = x + 1$	**29** $3x + x - 15 = 25 - x$	**30** $3x + 2x - 10 = 2x + 11$

40/ WRITING EQUATIONS

Sometimes the answer to a practical problem may be obvious, or can be found by trial and error. An equation is a way of describing a situation *mathematically*. It can be solved to find the answer to a problem.

EXAMPLE

▶ When a number is trebled and 2 taken away, the result is 10.
Find the number.

Let x be the number.

Then $3x - 2 = 10$
$3x = 10 + 2$
$3x = 12$
$x = 4$

EXAMPLE

▶ Barry has x stamps. Ahmed has twice as many stamps as Barry. Leon has 20 more stamps than Barry. Altogether they have 340 stamps. Find the value of x.

Barry: x stamps; Ahmed: $2x$ stamps; Leon: $x + 20$ stamps

$x + 2x + x + 20 = 340$
$4x + 20 = 340$
$4x = 340 - 20$
$4x = 320$
$x = 80$

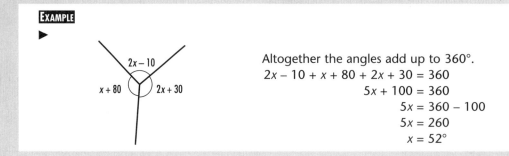

Altogether the angles add up to 360°.
$$2x - 10 + x + 80 + 2x + 30 = 360$$
$$5x + 100 = 360$$
$$5x = 360 - 100$$
$$5x = 260$$
$$x = 52°$$

Exercise 40A

Write down an equation for each of the following problems and solve it.

1 A number is doubled, and 9 is added. The result is 17.

2 A number has 9 added to it; the answer is then multiplied by 3. The result is 42.

3 A number has 5 added to it. The answer is multiplied by 3. The result is 19.

4 A number is multiplied by 4, and 5 is taken away. The result is 19.

5 A number is multiplied by 8, and 6 is taken away. The result is 38.

6 A number is multiplied by 7, and 9 is taken away. The result is 40.

7 A number has 4 taken away, and the answer is then multiplied by 3. The result is 24.

8 A number is multiplied by 9, and 7 is then taken away. The result is 29.

9 Doubling a number and adding 20 gives the same answer as multiplying the number by 6, and taking 4 away. Find the number.

10 A number has 2 taken away, and the answer multiplied by 5. This gives the same result as when 6 is added to the number, and the result multiplied by 3. What is the number?

11 Alan's age is x years. His brother is 5 years older. Their combined age is 31 years. Find x.

12 Julie and her three children want to go to the cinema. The cost of a child's ticket is £x. An adult ticket is twice the cost of a child's ticket. The cost for the family is £15. Find x.

13 Mary has three times as much money as Ann. They have £18 altogether. How much money has Ann?

14 After cutting 3 pieces of tape from a piece 94 cm long there is 28 cm left. How long is each smaller piece?

15 A number is x. The next number is $x + 1$. The sum of these two numbers is 93. Find the two numbers.

16 Three boys go on a trip. Ali has 3 times as much money as Alan. Azghar has 4 times as much money as Alan. They have £32 altogether. How much has Alan?

17 In a competition Ann scored 3 points more than Ali, and 5 points more than Jomo. Their combined marks come to 64. Find their individual marks.

18 Simon is 6 years older than his brother Alex. Simon's sister is 8 years younger than Alex. All their ages add up to 37 years. How old is Simon?

19 Clare has 4 more sums wrong than Janet. William has 2 more wrong than Clare. They have 16 wrong together. How many did Janet get wrong?

20 Jeremy has 12 more stamps than Jomo. Jane has 15 more than Jomo. They have 63 stamps altogether. How many stamps has Jomo?

Write down an equation for each of the following diagrams, and use it to find the value of x.

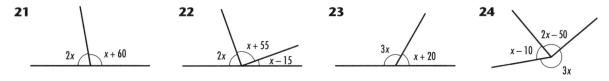

21 $2x$ $x + 60$

22 $2x$ $x + 55$ $x - 15$

23 $3x$ $x + 20$

24 $2x - 50$ $x - 10$ $3x$

25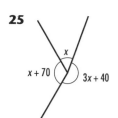

26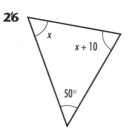

27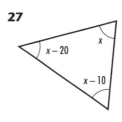

28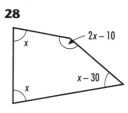

29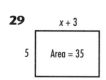

30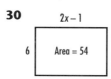

Exercise 40B

Write down an equation for each of the following problems, and solve it.

1 A number is multiplied by 3, and 5 is added. The result is 17.

2 A number has 12 taken away from it. The result is 13.

3 A number is multiplied by 6, and 18 is added. The result is 39.

4 A number is multiplied by 5, and 3 is added. The result is 48.

5 A number is multiplied by 7, and 2 is added. The result is 37.

6 A number is multiplied by 3, and 2 is taken away. The result is 25.

7 A number is multiplied by 6, and 7 is taken away. The result is 29.

8 A number is multiplied by 4, and 5 is added. The result is 29.

9 A number is multiplied by 5, and 6 is taken away. The result is 24.

10 Six is taken from a number and the answer is doubled. The same result is found if the number is divided by 2. What is the number?

11 Shirley is 3 years younger than Shreena. The sum of their ages is 25 years. How old is Shirley?

12 The perimeter of a rectangle is 42 cm. The length is x cm. The width is 3 cm shorter than the length. Find x.

13 Sadiah is 3 years older than Melanie. Their ages add up to 27. How old is Melanie?

14 Mary's father is 4 times older than she is. Their ages add up to 65 years. How old is Mary?

15 A number is x. The next number is $x + 1$. The sum of the two numbers is 93. Find the two numbers.

16 The two longest sides of a triangle are the same. The short side is half of a long side. All three sides add up to 30 cm. What is the length of a short side?

17 Martin gives 5 sweets to Mark. Martin then had 26 sweets. Mark had half this number. How many sweets did Mark start with?

18 Three boys had a number of marbles to share. They first gave 9 marbles to another boy, and were left with 6 marbles each. How many marbles did they start with?

19 Raji has a number of books. Kashif has 3 more books than Raji. Sadiah has 4 less books than Kashif. They have 29 books altogether. How many has Raji?

20 Tom has a number of records. Azhar has 4 more than Tom. Kevin has 3 less than Tom. They have 22 altogether. How many has Tom?

Write down an equation for each of the following diagrams, and use it to find the value of x.

21 **22** **23** **24**

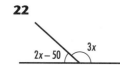
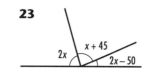

25

x + 50

3x + 30   4x

26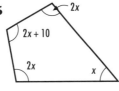

2x

2x + 10

2x   x

27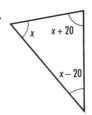

x   x + 20

x − 20

28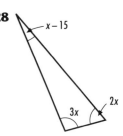

x − 15

3x   2x

29

3x + 2

4   Area = 20

30

x − 4

7   Area = 14

41/ TRIAL AND IMPROVEMENT

'Trial and improvement' is a recognised method of solving equations. Try a possible answer; if it is not an exact answer, then try an answer which might be more accurate.

> **EXAMPLE**
>
> ▶ Find a solution to the equation $x^2 - x = 4$.
>
> Try $x = 1$: $1^2 - 1 = 0$
> Try $x = 2$: $2^2 - 2 = 2$
> Try $x = 3$: $3^2 - 3 = 6$
>
> A solution seems to be between $x = 2$ and $x = 3$, about in the middle.
>
> Try $x = 2.5$: $2.5^2 - 2.5 = 3.75$ — too small
> Try $x = 2.6$: $2.6^2 - 2.6 = 4.16$ — too big
>
> The solution would appear to be between $x = 2.5$ and $x = 2.6$, so next try $x = 2.55$.
>
> Try $x = 2.55$: $2.55^2 - 2.55 = 3.9525$ — very close
> Try $x = 2.56$: $2.56^2 - 2.56 = 3.9936$ — closer
> Try $x = 2.57$: $2.57^2 - 2.57 = 4.0349$ — too large
>
> Of the two results, 3.9936 is closer to 4 than 4.0349, so the solution, to two decimal places, is 2.56.

The second solution to the quadratic equation can be found in the same way.

Exercise 41A

Solve these equations, to 2 decimal places, using the 'trial and improvement' process. Equations with x^2 will have two solutions, whilst equations with x^3 will have one solution.

1 $6x^2 + x = 15$	**2** $x^2 + x = 1$	**3** $x^2 - 2x = 5$	**4** $3x^2 + 2x = 5$
5 $6x^2 - 3x = 7$	**6** $3x^2 + 2x = 4$	**7** $x^3 + 3 = 10$	**8** $3x^2 + 5x = 7$
9 $2x^2 - 7x = -4$	**10** $2x^2 + 8x = 1$	**11** $3x^2 - 6x = 2$	**12** $x^2 - 8x = -2$
13 $5x^2 - 9x = -1$	**14** $x^3 - 8 = 7$	**15** $x^2 + 4x = 1$	**16** $x^3 + 7 = 19$
17 $x^2 - 6x = -2$	**18** $x^3 - 9 = 18$	**19** $2x^2 - 3x = 4$	**20** $3x^2 + 12x = 3$

Exercise 41B

Solve these equations, to 2 decimal places, using the 'trial and improvement' process. Equations with x^2 will have two solutions, whilst equations with x^3 will have one solution.

1 $8x^2 - 6x = 9$	**2** $x^2 + 2x = 5$	**3** $5x^2 + x = 3$	**4** $x^2 - x = 1$
5 $x^2 - 10x = -18$	**6** $x^3 - 5 = 4$	**7** $4x^2 - 8x = 9$	**8** $x^3 + 4 = 40$
9 $2x^2 + 6x = 1$	**10** $2x^2 + 3x = 4$	**11** $x^2 - 6x = -2$	**12** $x^2 - 4x = 3$
13 $x^3 + 11 = 30$	**14** $3x^2 - 10x = 4$	**15** $x^2 + 6x = -3$	**16** $4x^2 + 12x = -9$
17 $x^3 - 8 = 24$	**18** $x^2 + 7x = -2$	**19** $x^2 - 6x = 3$	**20** $2x^2 - 15x = 3$

42/ SOLVING SIMULTANEOUS EQUATIONS BY ALGEBRAIC METHODS

EXAMPLE

► Solve the simultaneous equations

(a) $x + y = 5$
$x - y = 1$

(b) $3x + 11y = 20$
$3x + y = 10$

(c) $4x + y = 2$
$5x - 2y = 9$

(d) $4x + 3y = 5$
$10x - 2y = 3$

(a) $x + y = 5$
$\underline{x - y = 1}$ Add equations.
$2x = 6$
$x = 3$

Take $x = 3$ and substitute in one of the equations, $x + y = 5$: $3 + y = 5$
$y = 2$

Solution is $x = 3$, $y = 2$.

(b) $3x + 11y = 20$
$\underline{3x + y = 10}$ Take away to remove the xs.
$10y = 10$
$y = 1$

Substitute $y = 1$ into the second (easier) equation: $3x + 1 = 10$
$3x = 9$
$x = 3$

Solution is $x = 3$, $y = 1$.

(c) Multiply the top equation by 2 to get the same number of ys:
$8x + 2y = 4$
$\underline{5x - 2y = 9}$ Add to remove the ys.
$13x = 13$
$x = 1$

Substitute $x = 1$ into $4x + y = 2$: $4 + y = 2$
$y = 2$

Solution is $x = 1$, $y = 2$.

(d) To get the same number of xs and ys the equations need to be multiplied by two *different* numbers:

$$4x + 3y = 5 \times 2 \quad \rightarrow \quad 8x + 6y = 10$$
$$10x - 2y = 3 \times 3 \quad \rightarrow \quad \underline{30x - 6y = 9}$$
$$38x = 19 \qquad \text{Add.}$$
$$x = \tfrac{1}{2}$$

Substitute into equation $4x + 3y = 5$: $\quad (4 \times \tfrac{1}{2}) + 3y = 5$
$$3y = 3$$
$$y = 1$$

Solution is $x = \tfrac{1}{2}$, $y = 1$.

Exercise 42A

Solve the simultaneous equations.

1 $x + y = 6$
$x - y = 2$

2 $x + y = 6$
$x - y = 4$

3 $x + y = 9$
$x - y = 3$

4 $x + 2y = 5$
$x + 3y = 7$

5 $x + 5y = 12$
$x + 2y = 6$

6 $x + 3y = 11$
$x + y = 5$

7 $x + y = 5$
$2x - y = 7$

8 $3x + y = 23$
$x - y = 5$

9 $4x + y = 21$
$x - y = 4$

10 $x + 2y = 13$
$x - y = 4$

11 $5x - y = 9$
$4x + y = 9$

12 $4x - 2y = 18$
$5x + 2y = 27$

13 $7x + 8y = 12$
$7x + 11y = 6$

14 $2x + 3y = 7$
$5x - 3y = 7$

15 $5x + 7y = 10$
$3x - 7y = 6$

16 $3x + 2y = 5$
$4x + y = 5$

17 $4x + 3y = 10$
$x + y = 3$

18 $3x + y = 4$
$4x + 2y = 6$

19 $x + 3y = 11$
$2x - y = 8$

20 $5x + 2y = 6$
$3x - 10y = 26$

21 $x + 3y = 5$
$5x + 2y = 12$

22 $x + 5y = 8$
$3x + 2y = 11$

23 $9x - 2y = 4$
$6x - 8y = 6$

24 $3x + 2y = 13$
$2x + 5y = 16$

25 $3y + 5x = 9$
$7x - 2y = 25$

26 $2x + 3y = 11$
$3x + 5y = 17$

27 $12x + 9y = 30$
$8x + 12y = 32$

28 $5x + 9y = 8$
$4x + 12y = 8$

29 $2x + 8y = 10$
$5x + 6y = 18$

30 $6x + 2y = 1$
$9x - 6y = 6$

Exercise 42B

Solve the simultaneous equations.

1 $x + y = 13$
$x - y = 1$

2 $x + y = 11$
$x - y = 5$

3 $x + y = 7$
$x - y = 1$

4 $x + 2y = 8$
$x + 3y = 11$

5 $x + 6y = 9$
$x + y = 4$

6 $x + 3y = 6$
$x - y = 2$

7 $2x - y = 13$
$x + y = 11$

8 $4x + y = 40$
$x - y = 5$

9 $3x - y = 10$
$x + y = 6$

10 $2x + y = 12$
$x - y = 3$

11 $5x + 6y = 17$
$5x + 5y = 15$

12 $x + y = 8$
$x - y = 2$

13 $3x + 2y = 17$
$3x + y = 10$

14 $2x + 3y = 19$
$2x + y = 9$

15 $7x - y = 6$
$5x - y = 4$

16 $2x + y = 9$
$3x + 2y = 14$

17 $2x + 3y = 4$
$4x - y = 1$

18 $x + y = 5$
$3x + 2y = 16$

19 $5x - 3y = 3$
$7x - y = 1$

20 $11x + 9y = 6$
$5x + 3y = 6$

21 $x + 2y = 5$
$3x + y = 5$

22 $8x + 3y = 27$
$2x - 5y = 1$

23 $5x - 6y = 2$
$10x + 2y = 11$

24 $3x - 2y = 5$
$4x - 3y = 6$

25 $5x - 4y = 8$
$7x + 3y = 37$

26 $7x + 3y = 21$
$5x + 2y = 15$

27 $7x - 2y = 11$
$12x + 5y = 2$

28 $4x + 3y = 5$
$10x - 2y = 3$

29 $7x + 2y = -6$
$11x - 3y = 9$

30 $3x - 8y = 5$
$5x - 12y = 9$

EXAMPLE

▶ Two pens and three rulers cost 56p. One pen and four rulers cost 58p. Find the cost of each pen and each ruler.

$$2p + 3r = 56$$
$$\underline{1p + 4r = 58} \quad \text{Double the second equation.}$$
$$2p + 3r = 56$$
$$\underline{2p + 8r = 116} \quad \text{Take top from bottom.}$$
$$5r = 60$$
$$r = 12$$

Substitute in $p + 4r = 58$: $\quad p + 48 = 58$
$$p = 10$$

Solution is pens are 10p, rulers 12p.

Exercise 42C

For each problem write down a pair of simultaneous equations, and solve them to find the solution to the question.

1 Two pens and three rulers cost 65p. Three pens and two rulers cost 60p. Find the price of each.

2 The rail fare for 10 adults and 2 children (half price) is £44. For 3 adults and 50 children it is £112. What is the fare for one child?

3 The total weight of 3 large and 7 small boxes is 48.3 kg. The total weight of 4 large and 5 small boxes is 46.2 kg. Find the weight of each type of box.

4 Three apples and two oranges weigh 200 g. Four apples and four oranges weigh 300 g. Find the weight of each.

5 Three magazines and four newspapers cost 65p. Half as many newspapers and three times as many magazines cost £1.45. Find the cost of six of each.

6 Twelve bottles and three cartons have a capacity of 30 litres. Eight bottles and twelve cartons have a capacity of 32 litres. Find the capacity of each.

7 Two numbers have a sum of 27 and a difference of 9. Find the two numbers.

8 The sum of two numbers is 5. Twice the second number added to the first is 8. Find the two numbers.

9 Six tins of dog food and three tins of cat food cost £4.35. Four tins of dog food and one tin of cat food cost £2.65. Find the cost of each.

10 Two cotton shirts and one satin shirt cost £50. Three cotton and four satin shirts cost £125. Find the cost of each.

11 Three bags and two boxes of seed weigh 12 kg. One bag and six boxes of seed also weigh 12 kg. Find the weight of each.

12 Four cups and three saucers cost £2.70. Three cups and five saucers cost £2.85. Find the cost of each.

13 The total of 5 large coins and 3 small coins is 13p. The total of 3 large coins and 2 small coins is 8p. What is the value of each of the two coins?

14 Five bottles and eight glasses have a total capacity of 9 pints. Three bottles and five glasses have a total capacity of $5\frac{1}{2}$ pints. Find the capacity of both a bottle and a glass.

15 Two cars and a motorbike have a total length of 11 metres. Three cars and seven motorbikes have a total length of 19 metres. Find the length of each type of vehicle.

Exercise 42D

For each problem write down a pair of simultaneous equations and solve them to find the solution to the question.

1 A motorbike and a mountain bike cost £4000. Two motorbikes and three mountain bikes cost £9600. Find the cost of each.

2 The wages of 10 mechanics and 4 assistants amount to £2000 a day, while 5 mechanics and 6 assistants earn £1400. What is the daily wage of each?

3 Five oranges and two lemons cost 46p; three oranges and one lemon cost 26p. Find the price of each.

4 The sum of two numbers is 12. The difference between the numbers is 6. Find the two numbers.

5 Laid side by side two large and three smaller coins make a row 11 cm long. Four large and one smaller coins make a row 12 cm long. Find the width of each of the coins.

6 Four goldfish and one carp cost £10. Three goldfish and one carp cost £9. Find the cost of each.

7 Two chocolate bars and one ice-cream cost £1. Three chocolate bars and one ice-cream cost £1.40. Find the cost of each.

8 Two D-type video tapes and one C-type have a total running time of 10 hours. Three D-type and two C-type have a total running time of 18 hours. What is the running time of each type of tape?

9 A farmer can buy 3 cows and 4 sheep for £1120. Six cows and 4 sheep will cost £1840. Find the cost of each.

10 Two rulers and a compass cost 80p. A ruler and three compasses cost 90p. Find the cost of each.

11 Three red and four blue stamps cost £15. Two red and three blue stamps cost £11. Find the cost of each type of stamp.

12 Two knives and three forks cost £1.20. Three knives and five forks cost £1.90. Find the cost of each.

13 Five large glasses and four smaller glasses have a total capacity of 7 pints. Two of each type of glass have a total capacity of 3 pints. Find the capacity of each type of glass.

14 Three boxes and eight bags of sweets weigh 11 lb. One box and four bags of sweets weigh 4 lb. Find the weight of each of a box and a bag of sweets.

15 Four small boxes and two large boxes laid end to end have a total length of 20 feet. Seven small boxes and three large boxes have a total length of 32 feet. Find the length of each of the boxes.

43/ SOLVING SIMULTANEOUS EQUATIONS BY GRAPHICAL METHODS

EXAMPLE

▶ Find the solution to the simultaneous equations
$y = x + 1$
$2y = 8 - x$

The diagram shows the graphs of the lines
$y = x + 1$ and $2y = 8 - x$.
The solution to the simultaneous equations is where the two graphs cross at the point (2,3).
The solution is $x = 2$, $y = 3$.

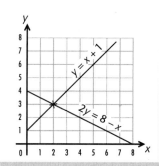

Exercise 43A

Write down the solution to the simultaneous equations, which are shown as straight line graphs.

1 $y = 8 - x$
$y = x - 2$

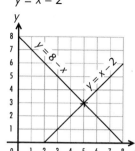

2 $y = 2x - 1$
$2y = 13 - x$

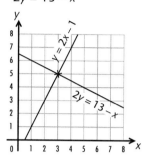

3 $y = -3x + 16$
$y = 2x - 4$

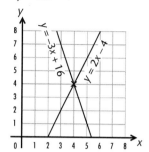

4 $y = \frac{1}{2}x + 3$
$y = 2x - 3$

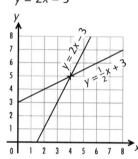

5 $3x + y = 9$
$x + y = 7$

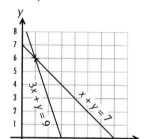

6 $x + y = 5$
$3y = x + 3$

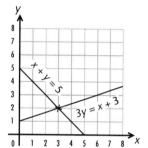

7 $3y = x + 6$
$y = x - 2$

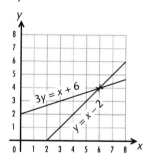

8 $x + 2y = 5$
$x + y = 1$

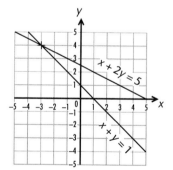

9 $x + y = -4$
$y = 2x + 2$

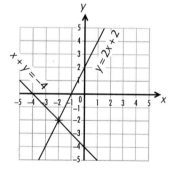

10 $x + y = 2$
$x + 4y = -4$

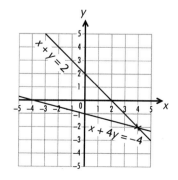

For each pair of equations:
(a) draw and label straight line graphs representing both equations on the same axes
(b) find the solution to the simultaneous equations.

11 $y = x + 1$
   $y = 4 - \frac{1}{2}x$

12 $y = 2x - 1$
   $y = 6 - 1\frac{1}{2}x$

13 $y = \frac{1}{2}x + 3$
   $y = x + 1$

14 $y = \frac{1}{2}x + 4$
   $y = x + 2$

15 $y = 2x - 1$
   $y = x + 2$

16 $y = x + 1$
   $y = 6 - x$

17 $y = \frac{1}{2}x + 4$
   $y = 2 - \frac{1}{2}x$

18 $y = 2x + 1$
   $y = x - 1$

19 $y = \frac{1}{2}x + 4$
   $y = 2x - 2$

20 $y = 2x + 3$
   $y = x + 1$

Exercise 43B

Write down the solution to the simultaneous equations, which are shown as straight line graphs.

1 $x + y = 8$
   $3y + x = 12$

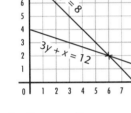

2 $y = x + 1$
   $x + y = 7$

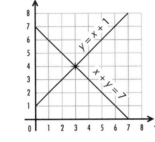

3 $x + y = 8$
   $2y + x = 9$

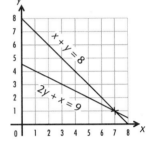

4 $2y = x + 5$
   $y = 2x - 5$

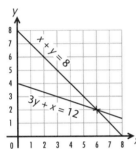

5 $x + y = 7$
   $y = x - 1$

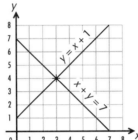

6 $y = \frac{1}{2}x + 2$
   $y = x - 1$

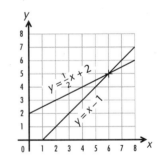

7 $y = x + 2$
   $y = 2x - 3$

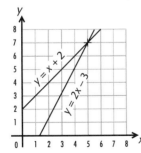

8 $y = 2x + 2$
   $y = x - 1$

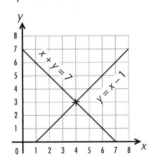

9 $y = x + 4$
   $x + y = 2$

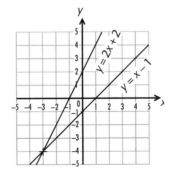

10 $2x + y = 1$
    $x + 2y = -4$

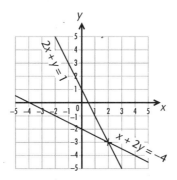

For each pair of equations (a) draw and label straight line graphs representing both equations on the same axes, (b) find the solution to the simultaneous equations.

11 $y = 3x - 1$
    $y = x + 3$

12 $y = 2x - 1$
    $y = \frac{1}{2}x + 2$

13 $y = 3 - x$
    $y = 5 - 4x$

14 $y = x + 3$
    $y = 2x + 1$

15 $y = x - 1$
    $y = 8 - x$

16 $y = x + \frac{1}{2}$
    $y = 2x - 1$

17 $y = 3x + 4$
    $y = x + 2$

18 $y = 5 - 2x$
    $y = x - 4$

19 $y = 1 - x$
    $y = 3 - 2x$

20 $y = x + 2\frac{1}{2}$
    $y = \frac{1}{2}x + 3$

EXAMPLE

▶ Solve the simultaneous equations $y + 1 = 3x$
            $y - 3 = x$

Using an algebraic method
Rearrange with the numbers on the right-hand side:
$$y - 3x = -1$$
$$y - x = 3 \qquad \text{Subtract.}$$
$$\overline{-3x + x = -1 - 3}$$
$$-2x = -4$$
$$x = 2$$

Substitute in the equation $y - x = 3$: $y - 2 = 3$
                    $y = 5$

Solution is $x = 2$, $y = 5$

Using a graphical method
Rearrange the equations with the ys on the left-hand side:
$$y = 3x - 1$$
$$y = x + 3$$

x	−1	0	1	2	3	4
$3x - 1$	−4	−1	2	5	8	11
$x + 3$	2	3	4	5	6	7

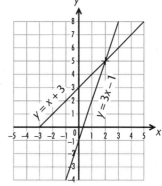

Graphs meet at (2, 5).
Solution is $x = 2$, $y = 5$.

If the equation is presented in the form $2y = x - 3$, then you will have to rearrange this equation before you can draw the graph. $2y = x - 3$ becomes $y = \frac{1}{2}x - 1\frac{1}{2}$ when you divide throughout by 2.

Exercise 43C

Solve these simultaneous equations by using either an algebraic method or a graphical method.

1 $y + 2x = 6$ **2** $y - 3 = 2x$ **3** $2y + 12 = 3x$ **4** $y - 4x = -6$
    $y + x = 2$ $y + 1 = x$ $2y + 4 = x$ $y - x = 3$

5 $2y = x + 8$ **6** $2y + x = 2$ **7** $y = 2x + 1$ **8** $2y = -4x + 5$
    $y = 3x - 1$ $y + x = -1$ $y = 7 - x$ $4y = -4x + 6$

9 $3x + 2y = 7$ **10** $4y - 2x = 10$ **11** $4x + 3y = 12$ **12** $x + y = 7$
    $3x - y = 1$ $3y - 4x = 5$ $y = 2x - 6$ $3x - 2y = 1$

13 $4x - 3y = 14$ **14** $2y = x + 7$ **15** $4y = x + 21$
    $3x + 2y = 19$ $y = 4x - 7$ $3y = 2x + 12$

Exercise 43D

Solve these simultaneous equations by using either an algebraic method or a graphical method.

1 $y + 4 = 2x$ **2** $y + x = 2$ **3** $2y = x + 8$ **4** $2y = 2x - 4$
    $y + 3 = x$ $y - \frac{1}{2}x = -1$ $4y = 8x - 2$ $2y = x + 2$

5 $y = x + 4$ **6** $2y = x - 2$ **7** $y = 3x - 4$ **8** $3y + 2x = 18$
    $y = 2x - 1$ $2y = 3x + 4$ $2y + x = 6$ $y + 3x = 6$

9 $5x - 3y = 1$ **10** $x + 4y = 16$ **11** $2x - y = 5$ **12** $3x - 2y = 13$
    $4x + 3y = 17$ $2x + y = 11$ $x + 2y = 5$ $3x + 7y = 22$

13 $2x - 3y = -19$ **14** $4x + 3y = 2$ **15** $2x + y = -7$
    $5x + 2y = 19$ $8x + 2y = 4$ $-3x + 2y = 7$

44/ INEQUALITIES

Inequalities can be represented on a number line.
An empty circle means the value circled is *not* included in the inequality.
A filled circle means the value circled *is* included in the inequality.
Common notation includes:

      < for 'less than'

      > for 'greater than'

      ≤ for 'less than or equal to'

      ≥ for 'greater than or equal to'

$2 < x < 5$ means x is between, but in this case does not include, 2 and 5.

> **EXAMPLE**
> ▶   Write down the inequality for (a)
>
> (b)   (c)
>
>   (a) $x \geq 4$ (b) $x < -1$ (c) $-2 \leq x < 4$

EXAMPLE

▶ Draw on a number line that part indicated by the inequality
(a) $x \le 1$ (b) $x > 3$ (c) $-4 < x \le 1$

(a)

(b)

(c)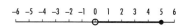

Exercise 44A

Write down the inequality shown on each of the following number lines.

1

2

3

4

5

6

7

8

9

10

11

12

13

14

15

For each question draw a number line from –6 to +6, and draw on the number line that part included in the inequality.

16 $x \le 4$	**17** $x > -1$	**18** $x \le 0$	**19** $x < 5$	**20** $x > 4$
21 $x \ge 2$	**22** $x \le -3$	**23** $x < -4$	**24** $x > -3$	**25** $x \ge -2$
26 $x \ge -5$	**27** $-1 < x \le 4$	**28** $-5 < x < -2$	**29** $0 \le x \le 3$	**30** $2 < x \le 5$

Exercise 44B

Write down the inequality shown on each of the following number lines.

1

2

3

4

5

6

7

8

9

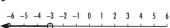

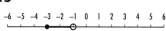

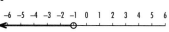

10

$-6\ -5\ -4\ -3\ -2\ -1\ \ 0\ \ 1\ \ 2\ \ 3\ \ 4\ \ 5\ \ 6$

11

$-6\ -5\ -4\ -3\ -2\ -1\ \ 0\ \ 1\ \ 2\ \ 3\ \ 4\ \ 5\ \ 6$

12

$-6\ -5\ -4\ -3\ -2\ -1\ \ 0\ \ 1\ \ 2\ \ 3\ \ 4\ \ 5\ \ 6$

13

$-6\ -5\ -4\ -3\ -2\ -1\ \ 0\ \ 1\ \ 2\ \ 3\ \ 4\ \ 5\ \ 6$

14

$-6\ -5\ -4\ -3\ -2\ -1\ \ 0\ \ 1\ \ 2\ \ 3\ \ 4\ \ 5\ \ 6$

15

$-6\ -5\ -4\ -3\ -2\ -1\ \ 0\ \ 1\ \ 2\ \ 3\ \ 4\ \ 5\ \ 6$

For each question draw a number line from –6 to +6, and draw on the number line that part included in the inequality.

16 $x > 1$	**17** $x \geq 0$	**18** $x \leq 3$	**19** $x > -4$	**20** $x \leq -1$
21 $x \geq -6$	**22** $x \leq 6$	**23** $x < 0$	**24** $x \geq 2$	**25** $x \leq -5$
26 $x > 3$	**27** $0 < x \leq 5$	**28** $1 \leq x < 3$	**29** $-2 \leq x \leq 0$	**30** $-5 < x < -1$

EXAMPLE

▶ Write down all the possible integer values of x if
(a) $-2 < x \leq 4$ (b) $1 \leq x < 6$.

(a) –1, 0, 1, 2, 3   Note: The –2 is not included.

(b) 1, 2, 3, 4, 5   Note: The 6 is not included.

Exercise 44C

Write down all possible *integer* values of x if

1 $-4 < x \leq 5$	**2** $-6 < x < 8$	**3** $0 \leq x < 7$	**4** $-5 \leq x \leq -1$
5 $-8 \leq x < 0$	**6** $4 < x < 9$	**7** $-1 < x \leq 7$	**8** $-3 \leq x < 2$

Write down all possible *even* values of x if

9 $-8 \leq x \leq 2$	**10** $-3 \leq x < 4$	**11** $-1 < x \leq 6$	**12** $-9 \leq x < -1$
13 $-7 < x < 3$	**14** $4 < x < 8$		

Write down all possible *odd* value of x if

15 $0 \leq x \leq 9$	**16** $-3 < x \leq 5$	**17** $-5 < x \leq 2$	**18** $-4 < x \leq 3$
19 $-8 \leq x \leq -1$	**20** $-2 < x < 7$		

Exercise 44D

Write down all possible *integer* values of x if

1 $-4 \leq x < 3$	**2** $-1 < x < 6$	**3** $0 \leq x < 5$	**4** $-2 < x < 5$
5 $-6 \leq x \leq -1$	**6** $-3 < x \leq 3$	**7** $-4 < x \leq 2$	**8** $-6 \leq x < -1$

Write down all possible *even* values of x if

9 $-4 \leq x < 5$	**10** $-3 \leq x < 7$	**11** $-7 < x \leq -1$	**12** $-5 \leq x \leq 3$
13 $-2 < x \leq 6$	**14** $-8 < x < -2$		

Write down all possible *odd* values of x if

15 $-4 < x \leq 5$	**16** $-1 \leq x \leq 7$	**17** $3 \leq x \leq 9$	**18** $-8 < x < 3$
19 $-3 \leq x \leq 6$	**20** $0 < x < 7$		

REVISION

Exercise D

1 Write down the coordinates of the points in the diagram.

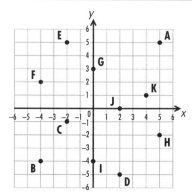

2 Draw axes from –6 to +6. Plot and label the following points.
A(3, 6), B(–4, 5), C(–4, –3), D(6, –3), E(4, 2), F(5, 0)
G(–3, 2), H(0, 2), I(–3, 0), J(–1, –5), K(2, –3)

3 (a) Copy and complete the table for the function shown.
(b) On graph or squared paper draw and label the graph of the function.

x	–2	–1	0	1	2	3	4
$y = 2x - 3$	–7					3	

4 (a) Copy and complete the table for the function shown.
(b) On graph or squared paper draw and label the graph of the function.

x	–6	–4	–2	0	2	4	6
$y = \frac{1}{2}x + 2$		0				4	

5 Solve the equations.
(a) $4x - 4 = 8$ (b) $2x + 3 = 13$ (c) $5x - 7 = 13$ (d) $8x + 5 = 17$
(e) $2(2x + 1) = 12$ (f) $4(3x - 4) = 8$ (g) $5(x + 3) = 50$ (h) $3(8x - 5) = 93$
(i) $4x + 2 = 7 + x$ (j) $3x + 7 = 25 - x$ (k) $5x + 2 = 20 + 3x$ (l) $6x - 7 = 2x + 6$

6 Solve these equations, to 2 decimal places, using the 'trial and improvement' process.
(a) $2x^2 = 100$ (b) $2x^2 + x = 25$ (c) $x^3 = 60$ (d) $x^3 - 3 = 20$
(e) $x(x - 2) = 300$ (f) $x^3 + 1 = 14$

7 Solve the simultaneous equations using algebraic methods.
(a) $3x + 4y = 19$ (b) $2x + 3y = 23$ (c) $3x + 2y = 7$ (d) $x + 2y = 16$
    $3x + 2y = 17$ $5x + 3y = 53$ $x + 4y = 9$ $2x + 3y = 29$
(e) $4x + 3y = 31$ (f) $3x + y = 14$ (g) $5x + 3y = 14$ (h) $2x + 3y = 25$
    $2x + 7y = 21$ $2x + 3y = 28$ $4x + y = 7$ $x + 4y = 25$

8 For each pair of equations
(i) draw and label straight line graphs representing both equations on the same axes
(ii) find the solution to the simultaneous equations.
(a) $y = 2x + 1$ (b) $y = x + 1$
    $y = 3x - 2$ $y = 2x + 2$

9 Write down all possible *integer* values of x for each inequality.
(a) $-3 < x \le 3$ (b) $-5 \le x < -1$ (c) $4 < x < 9$ (d) $-6 \le x < 3$

10 Write down all possible *even* values of x for each inequality.
(a) $-3 \le x \le 6$ (b) $-2 < x \le 6$ (c) $-6 \le x < -1$ (d) $-1 < x < 6$

Exercise DD

1 Write down an equation for each of the following problems, and solve it.

   (a) A number is multiplied by 2 and 3 is added. The result is 5.

   (b) A number has 6 taken away from it. The result is 3.

   (c) A number is multiplied by 3 and 1 is taken away. The result is 11.

   (d) A number is multiplied by 7 and 4 is added. The result is 25.

   (e) A number is multiplied by 8 and 3 is taken away. The result is 9.

   (f) Jomo is 4 years younger than his brother. The sum of their ages is 28 years. How old is Jomo?

   (g) Carl is 5 years older than Shirley. Their ages add up to 25 years. How old is Carl?

2 The perimeter of a rectangle is 22 cm. The width is x cm. The length is 3 cm longer than the width. Find x.

3 Write down an equation for each of the following diagrams, and use it to find the value of x.

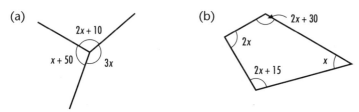

   For each problem write down a pair of simultaneous equations, and solve them to find the solution to the question.

4 Two rubbers and a pen cost 27p. A rubber and two pens cost 24p. Find the cost of (a) one rubber (b) one pen.

5 Four nuts and a bolt weigh 28 g. Two nuts and three bolts weigh 34 g. Find the cost of (a) one nut (b) one bolt.

6 Four buckets and three jars together contain 30 litres of water. Three buckets and six jars also have a total capacity of 30 litres. Find the capacity of (a) a bucket (b) a jar.

7 Five doll's plates and four doll's saucers laid end to end have a total length of 46 cm. Two plates laid end to end have the same length as when three saucers are laid end to end. Find the width of (a) a plate (b) a saucer.

8 Three tapes and two CDs cost £88. One tape and three CDs cost £76. Find the cost of (a) a tape (b) a CD.

Shape, space and measures

45/ FINDING UNKNOWN ANGLES ON PARALLEL LINES GIVING REASONS

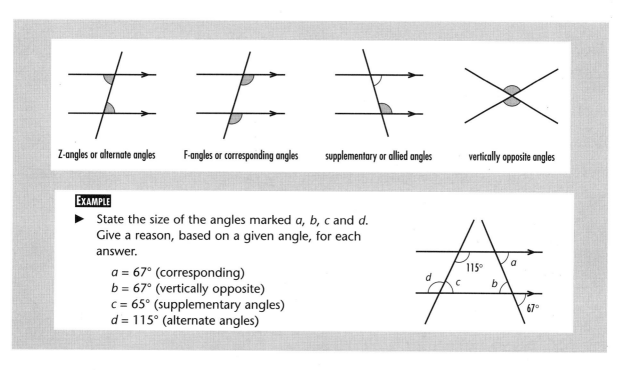

Z-angles or alternate angles   F-angles or corresponding angles   supplementary or allied angles   vertically opposite angles

EXAMPLE

▶ State the size of the angles marked *a*, *b*, *c* and *d*.
Give a reason, based on a given angle, for each answer.

 a = 67° (corresponding)
 b = 67° (vertically opposite)
 c = 65° (supplementary angles)
 d = 115° (alternate angles)

Exercise 45A

State the size of each of the angles marked with a letter and give reasons which refer to a **given** angle.
Diagrams are not accurate.

1

2

3

4

5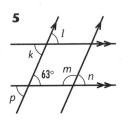

6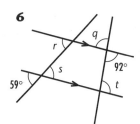

7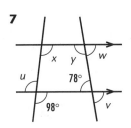

8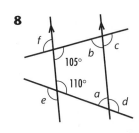

9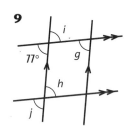

10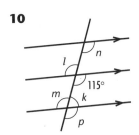

Exercise 45B

State the size of each of the angles marked with a letter and give reasons which refer to a **given** angle. Diagrams are not accurate.

1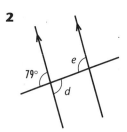

2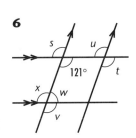

3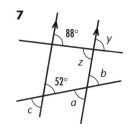

4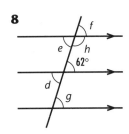

5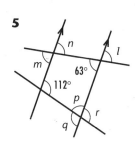

6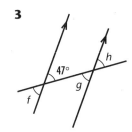

7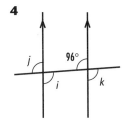

8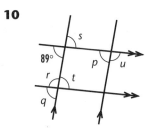

9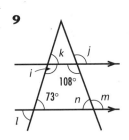

10

46/ FINDING UNKNOWN ANGLES IN VARIOUS SITUATIONS GIVING REASONS

You should know these facts:
   The base angles of an isosceles triangle are equal.
   The sum of the angles of a triangle = 180°
   The sum of the angles of any quadrilateral = 360°
   The sum of the angles on a straight line = 180°
   The sum of all the angles at a point = 360°
   The properties of angles on parallel lines (see section 45)

EXAMPLE

▶ State the size of each angle marked with a letter.
Give a reason for each answer.

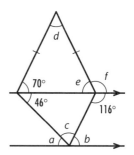

   a = 46° (alternate angles)
   b = 64° (supplementary angles)
   c = 70° (angles on a straight line)
   d = 40° (sum of angles in a triangle)
   e = 70° (base angles of an isosceles triangle)
   f = 110° (angles on a straight line)

Exercise 46A

State the size of each of the angles marked with a letter and *give reasons for your answers*. Diagrams are not accurate.

1

2

3

4

5

6

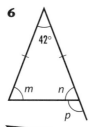

7

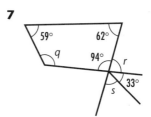

8

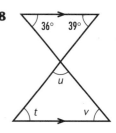

9

10

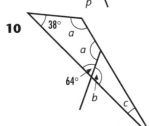

11

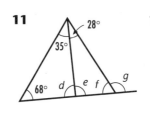

12

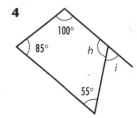

Exercise 46B

State the size of each of the angles marked with letters and *give reasons for your answers*. Diagrams are not accurate.

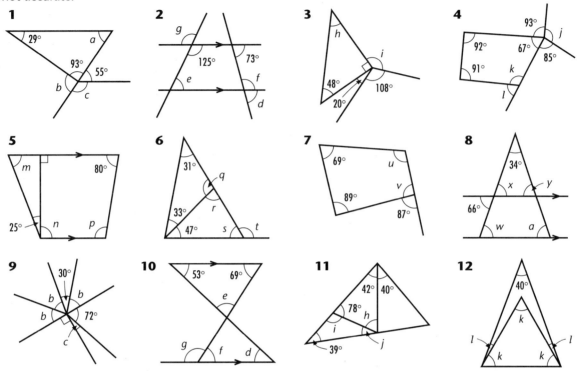

1

29° a
93° 55°
b c

2

g
125° 73°
e f
d

3

h
i
48° 108°
20°

4

93° j
92° 67°
91° 85°
k
l

5

m 80°
25° n p

6

31°
q
33° r
47° s t

7

69° u
v
89° 87°

8

34°
x y
66°
w a

9

30°
b b
b 72°
c

10

53° 69°
e
g f d

11

42° 40°
78° h
i
39° j

12

40°
k
l l
k k

47/ THE PROPERTIES OF QUADRILATERALS AND POLYGONS

The sum of the angles of a quadrilateral is 360°.
This fact can be used, together with the symmetries of certain quadrilaterals, to find unknown angles. Parallel lines can give us the opportunity to find unknown angles. The symmetries can be used to find some lengths.

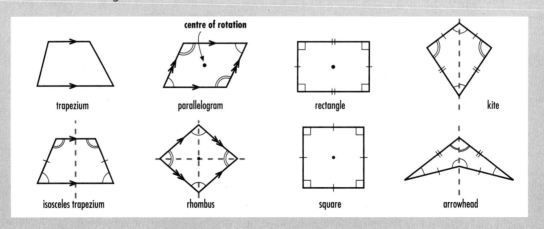

centre of rotation

trapezium parallelogram rectangle kite

isosceles trapezium rhombus square arrowhead

EXAMPLE

▶ Find the unknown angles marked *a*, *b* and *c* and the length marked *x* on the diagram.

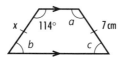

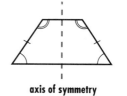

axis of symmetry

The shape is an isosceles trapezium and has an axis of reflective symmetry as shown.

This means that the length *x* is 7 cm and *a* = 114°.
Since the total of the angles is 360°, *b* = *c* = 66°

A **regular polygon** has all sides of the same length and all angles equal.

The **angles at the centre** and the **exterior angle** are $\frac{360°}{n}$ where *n* is the number of sides.

The **interior angle** can be found by using the angles on a straight line.

EXAMPLE

▶ Find the exterior and interior angles and the angle at the centre of a regular octagon.

Exterior angle = $\frac{360°}{8}$ = 45°
The angle at the centre will also be 45°.
Interior angle = 180° − 45° = 135°

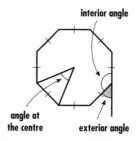

interior angle

angle at the centre   exterior angle

Exercise 47A

State the size of the angles and lengths marked with letters. Diagrams are not accurate.

1

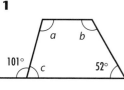

101° *a* *b* 52° *c*

trapezium

2

4 cm
e
8 cm
28°
f
d
41°
g

parallelogram

3

h *k* 31 mm
98° *j*
i
49° 56 mm

kite

4

l 35 cm
m *p*
n

regular pentagon

5

5 cm
112° *r*
t
s
q

isosceles trapezium

6

5 cm *x* *u*
25°
4 cm 150° *w*
v

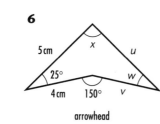

arrowhead

7

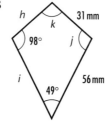

c 8 cm
d
b *a*

rhombus

8

g *e*
f
12 cm
32° *h*

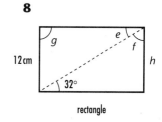

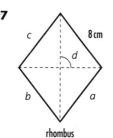

rectangle

In each of the following questions draw a careful diagram to show each situation.

9 One angle of a parallelogram is 48°. State the other three angles.

10 The exterior angle of a regular polygon is known to be between 50° and 55°. How many sides does the polygon have and what is its name?

11 One angle of an isosceles trapezium is 122°. State the other three angles.

12 Two of the angles of a kite are known to be 110° and 60°. Sketch *three* examples of what the kite might look like showing the positions of the two angles. Also show the size and position of the other two angles in each case.

13 The interior angle of a regular polygon is 120°. State (a) the exterior angle, (b) the angle at the centre and (c) the name of the polygon.

14 State *three* facts that you know about the diagonals of a rhombus.

15 For a decagon, state (a) the angle at the centre (b) the exterior angle and (c) the interior angle.

Exercise 47B

State the size of the angles and lengths marked with letters. Diagrams are not accurate.

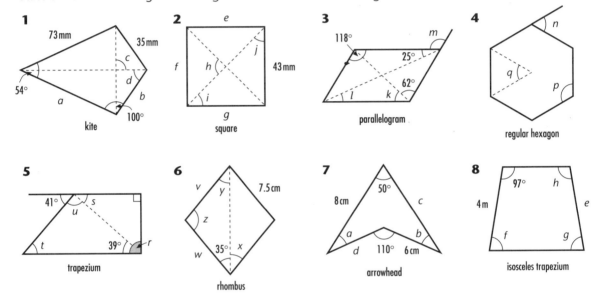

In each of the following questions draw a careful diagram to show each situation.

9 Two of the angles of a trapezium are known to be 120° and 50°. Sketch *two* examples of what the trapezium might look like showing the positions of the two angles. Also show the size and position of the other two angles in each case.

10 The exterior angle of a regular polygon is 45°. State (a) the interior angle (b) the angle at the centre and (c) the name of the polygon.

11 Does a diagonal of a parallelogram bisect (cut in half) the angles at each end? Draw a diagram to illustrate your answer.

12 The interior angle of a regular polygon is known to be between 100° and 110°. How many sides does the polygon have and what is its name?

13 Two internal angles of an arrowhead are 105° and 15°. Draw a sketch of the arrowhead showing the position of these two angles. Indicate the size and position of each of the other two angles.

14 State (a) the angle at the centre (b) the exterior angle and (c) the interior angle of a nonagon.

15 One of the angles of an isosceles trapezium is 79°. Draw a diagram showing the size and position of all four angles.

48/ SYMMETRY INCLUDING PROPERTIES OF QUADRILATERALS AND POLYGONS

EXAMPLE

▶

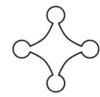 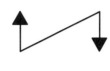

Show any axes of reflection or centres of rotation in each of the two shapes.

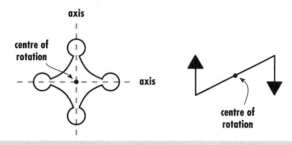

EXAMPLE

▶ (a) Complete the shape so that it has order 5 rotational
symmetry about the centre of enlargement.
(b) Draw in any axes of symmetry in the resulting shape.
(c) Name the shape.

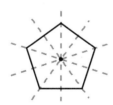

(c) The shape is a regular pentagon.

Exercise 48A

Copy each shape and draw in any axes of reflective symmetry and/or centre of rotational symmetry.

1   **2**   **3**   **4**

Copy each shape and complete it according to the symmetry indicated.

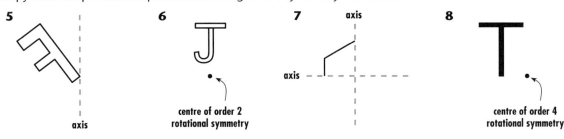

5 axis

6 centre of order 2 rotational symmetry

7 axis

8 centre of order 4 rotational symmetry

9 Copy the diagram and show the image of the letter P reflected in axis 1. Now reflect this image and the original object in axis 2.

axis 2

axis 1

(a) What order of symmetry does the complete drawing have?
(b) If the letter P is replaced by the letter T, what is the order of symmetry of the final diagram?

10 Draw a kite and show any axes and/or centre of symmetry.

11 Copy the shape and complete it by reflecting it in the axis.
Name the shape.

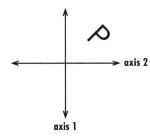

axis

12 Copy the shape and complete the quadrilateral so that it has order 2 rotational symmetry about the centre indicated. Name the shape.

centre

13 Draw a regular octagon and show any axes and/or centre of symmetry.
14 Give five examples of letters that have no symmetry, for example G.
15 Copy the following and show any symmetry:

H C Y Z A

Exercise 48B

Copy each shape and draw in any axes of reflective symmetry and/or centre of rotational symmetry.

1 　　**2** 　　**3** 　　**4**

Copy each shape and complete it according to the symmetry indicated.

5

centre of order 2
rotational symmetry

6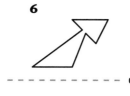

axis

7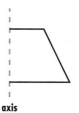

axis

8

centre of order 3
rotational symmetry

9　Draw an arrowhead and show any axes and/or centre of symmetry.

10　Draw a parallelogram and show any axes and/or centre of symmetry.

11　Draw a triangle that has order 3 rotational symmetry. Show any axes and/or centre of symmetry.

12　Show any symmetry in each of the following:

13　Give *three* examples of letters that have rotational symmetry but no axes of reflection.

14　Copy the shape and complete the quadrilateral so that it has order 4 rotational symmetry about the centre indicated. Name the shape.

centre

15　Copy the diagram and show the image of the letter Y reflected in axis 1. Now reflect this image and the original object in axis 2.

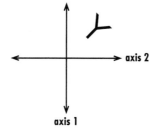

axis 2

axis 1

(a)　What order of symmetry does the complete drawing have?

(b)　What order of symmetry would the final diagram have if the letter were K rather than Y?

Note: Tracing paper can be useful for drawing reflections and rotations. Trace the object and then rotate the tracing paper to show the position of the image.

EXAMPLE

▶ Reflect the object accurately in the axis indicated.

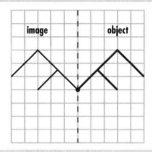

EXAMPLE

▶ Rotate the object through 90° clockwise about the centre of rotation.

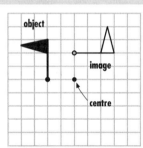

Exercise 48C

Copy the diagrams on squared paper and show the image of each object. If an axis is shown, you should reflect the object. If a centre, X, is shown, you should rotate the object through the angle indicated.

1

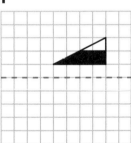

2

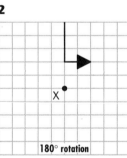

180° rotation

3

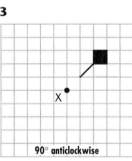

90° anticlockwise

4

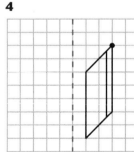

5

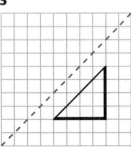

6

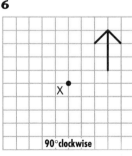

90° clockwise

7

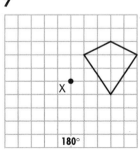

180°

8

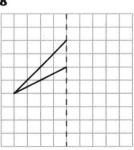

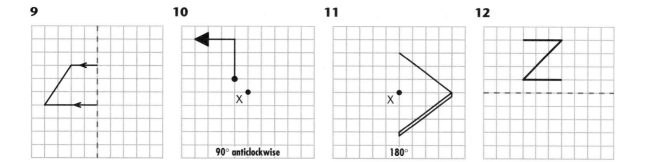

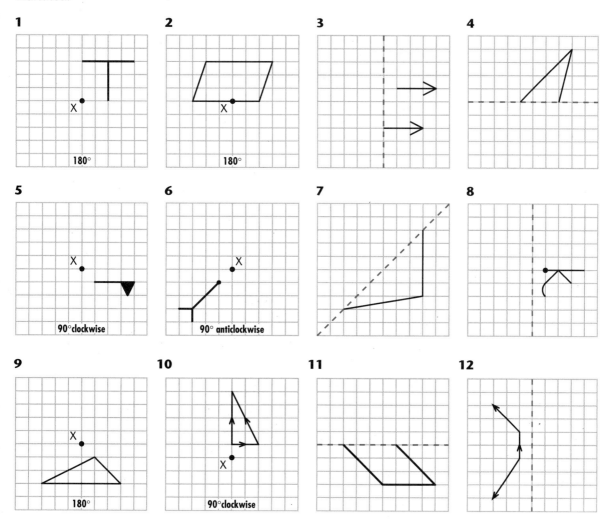

Exercise 48D

Copy the diagrams on squared paper and show the image of each object. If an axis is shown, you should reflect the object. If a centre, X, is shown, you should rotate the object through the angle indicated.

49/ SCALE: CONVERTING LENGTHS

1 cm ≡ 5 km and 1 : 500 000 are two different ways of writing the scale of a map that uses 1 cm on the map to represent 5 km in actual length.

Notice that we are using the sign '≡' rather than the sign '='.

The sign '≡' means **is equivalent to** or **represents**. This not the same as '=' which means **equals** or **is the same as**. 1 cm is *not* equal to 5 km.

1 : 500 000 is a ratio – there are 500 000 cm in 5 km so it means 1 cm : 5 km or 1 cm ≡ 5 km.

EXAMPLE

▶ What is the actual length which is represented by 2.4 cm on a scale drawing with scale of 1 cm ≡ 4 m?

1 cm ≡ 4 m. So 2.4 cm ≡ 4 × 2.4 = 9.60 m

EXAMPLE

▶ What is the actual length which is represented by 15 mm on a map which is drawn to the scale 1 : 200 000?

1 : 200 000 means that 1 mm represents 200 000 mm.
200 000 mm = 200 metres
So 15 mm represents 15 × 200 m = 3000 m = 3 km

Exercise 49A

Copy and complete the table.

Number	Length on map/drawing	Scale	Actual length
1	4 cm	1 cm ≡ 2 km	km
2	35 mm	1 cm ≡ 1 m	m
3	7 cm	1 cm ≡ 10 km	km
4	120 mm	1 cm ≡ 1 km	km
5	6 mm	1 mm ≡ 5 m	m
6	42 mm	1 : 1000	m
7	2 cm	1 : 200	m
8	25 mm	1 : 2000	m
9	15 cm	1 : 100 000	km
10	1.4 cm	1 : 200	m
11	mm	1 mm ≡ 2 km	14 km
12	cm	2 cm ≡ 5 m	20 m
13	cm	1 cm ≡ 5 km	30 km
14	cm	2 cm ≡ 1 km	4.5 km
15	mm	1 mm ≡ 2 m	30 m
16	cm	1 : 100	3 m
17	mm	1 : 2000	24 m
18	mm	1 : 10 000	250 m
19	mm	1 : 1 000 000	3 km

20	cm	1 : 100 000	4 km
21	2 cm	1 : 500	m
22	mm	1 : 2000	40 m
23	3.2 cm	1 cm ≡ 5 km	km
24	mm	5 mm ≡ 1 m	25 m
25	mm	1 : 1 000 000	9 km
26	3 cm	1 : 2 000 000	km
27	4.5 cm	1 mm ≡ 2 km	km
28	mm	1 cm ≡ 10 km	45 km
29	cm	1 : 500	10 m
30	1 cm	1 : 5 000 000	km

Exercise 49B

Copy and complete the table.

Number	Length on map/drawing	Scale	Actual length
1	4 cm	1 cm ≡ 1 km	km
2	20 mm	1 cm ≡ 2 m	m
3	6.5 cm	1 cm ≡ 2 km	km
4	18 mm	1 mm ≡ 10 m	m
5	9 cm	1 cm ≡ 5 km	km
6	5 cm	1 : 100	m
7	11 mm	1 : 1000	m
8	3 mm	1 : 1 000 000	km
9	3 cm	1 : 200 000	km
10	2 mm	1 : 5 000 000	km
11	mm	1 mm ≡ 2 m	6 m
12	cm	1 cm ≡5 km	10 km
13	mm	1 mm ≡ 2 km	30 km
14	cm	1 cm ≡ 10 m	70 m
15	mm	1 cm ≡ 10 km	12 km
16	mm	1 : 1000	55 m
17	mm	1 : 1 000 000	13 km
18	cm	1 : 100	7 m
19	mm	1 : 2000	24 m
20	cm	1 : 250	5 m
21	4 cm	1 cm ≡ 5 km	km
22	mm	5 mm ≡ 1 m	15 m
23	cm	1 : 200	34 m
24	2 mm	1 : 5000	m
25	12 mm	1 mm ≡ 2 km	km
26	mm	1 cm ≡ 4 m	10 m
27	mm	1 : 1 000 000	16 km
28	3.5 cm	1 : 200 000	km
29	15 mm	1 cm ≡ 100 km	km
30	cm	1 : 50 000	150 m

EXAMPLE

▶ The line is part of a scale drawing of scale 1 : 100 000. Measure and record the length of the line and calculate the actual distance that it represents.

—————————————

Length of line = 45 mm = 4.5 cm
1 : 100 000 = 1 cm : 100 000 cm
But 100 000 cm = 1000 m = 1 km
The line represents 4.5 km.

EXAMPLE

▶ Draw a line to represent 7 metres using a scale of 1 cm ≡ 2 m.

The required length = 7 ÷ 2 = 3.5 cm or 35 mm

—————————————

Exercise 50A

Measure and record the length of each line. Using the scale indicated for each, state the actual distance that each line represents.

1 ————————— 1 cm ≡ 2 km

2 ————————————— 1 cm ≡ 5 km

3 ———— 1 : 1 000 000

4 ———————————— 1 : 500

5 ——————————— 1 cm ≡ 1 km

6 ————————————————— 1 cm ≡ 2 m

7 —————————————— 1 : 1000

8 ——————————————— 1 : 200 000

9 ———————————— 1 cm ≡ 1 km

10 ————— 1 cm ≡ 2 km

Draw lines to represent each actual distance stated, using the scale indicated.

11	12 km; 1 cm ≡ 2 km		**12**	3 m; 1 : 100
13	25 m; 1 : 1000		**14**	50 km; 1 cm ≡ 20 km
15	15 m; 1 cm ≡ 2 m		**16**	22 cm; 1 : 20
17	140 km; 1 : 1 000 000		**18**	54 km; 1 mm ≡ 2 km
19	120 m; 1 cm ≡ 50 m		**20**	2 km; 1 : 200 000

Redraw each of the sketches accurately to the scale indicated. The lengths stated are the actual lengths.

21

1 cm ≡ 10 m

22

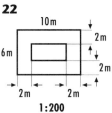

1 : 200

23

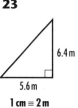

1 cm ≡ 2 m

24

1 : 100 000

25

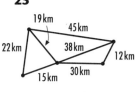

1 cm ≡ 10 km

Exercise 50B

Measure and record the length of each line. Using the scale indicated for each, state the actual distance that each line represents.

1 ──────────────────────────────── 1 cm ≡ 5 km

2 ──────────────────────────── 1 cm ≡ 2 km

3 ──────────── 1 : 1000

4 ──────────────── 1 : 200

5 ──────────── 1 cm ≡ 10 m

6 ────────── 1 cm ≡ 50 km

7 ──────────────────── 1 : 1 000 000

8 ──────── 1 : 5 000 000

9 ────── 1 mm ≡ 2 m

10 ──────────────────── 1 mm ≡ 5 km

Draw lines to represent each actual distance stated, using the scale indicated.

11 15 km; 1 cm ≡ 5 km   **12** 70 m; 1 : 1000
13 275 km; 1 mm ≡ 25 km   **14** 2.6 m; 1 : 200
15 180 m; 1 mm ≡ 5 m   **16** 17 km; 1 cm ≡ 2 km
17 550 km; 1 : 50 000 000   **18** 700 m; 1:10 000
19 6.5 km 1 cm ≡ 2 km   **20** 46 m; 1 : 2000

Redraw each of the sketches accurately to the scale indicated. The lengths stated are the actual lengths.

21

1 : 200

22

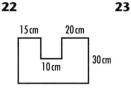

1 : 5

23

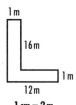

1 cm ≡ 2 m

24

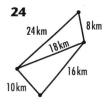

1 cm ≡ 2 km

25

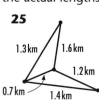

5 cm ≡ 1 km

51/ ENLARGEMENT: SCALE FACTOR AND CENTRE OF ENLARGEMENT

An **object** is enlarged to give an **image.**
Scale factor (S.F.): The ratio of corresponding lengths in the object and the image. (This means that a length in the object is multiplied by the scale factor to give the length in the image.)
Centre of enlargement: Lines from this point pass through corresponding points on the object and image.
From the centre of enlargement to corresponding points:

$$\frac{\text{distance to image}}{\text{distance to object}} = \text{scale factor}$$

EXAMPLE

▶ Show the centre of enlargement.
State the scale factor.

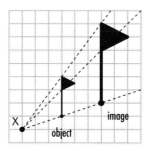

If you join corresponding points on the image and object and extend these lines, you find that they meet at the centre of enlargement, X.
All the lengths in the image are twice the lengths in the object. This means that the scale factor is 2.

EXAMPLE

▶ Show the centre of enlargement.
State the scale factor.

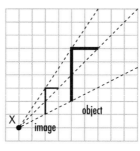

Note: The object and image are the opposite way around from the previous example.
The scale factor is $\frac{1}{2}$ because the image is only half the size of the object. The centre is found in the same way as before.

Exercise 51A

For each of the following copy the diagram on squared paper and show the centre of enlargement.
State the scale factor.

1

object   image

2

image

object

3

object

image

4

image

object

5

image

object

6

object

image

7

image

object

8

object

image

9

image

object

10

object

image

Exercise 51B

For each of the following copy the diagram on squared paper and show the centre of enlargement.
State the scale factor.

1

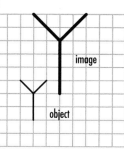

image

object

2

image

object

3

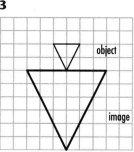

object

image

4

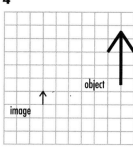

object

image

5

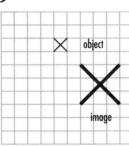

6

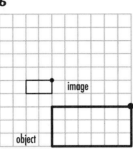

7

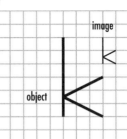

8

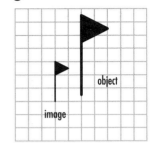

9

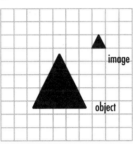

10

52/ DRAWING ENLARGEMENTS

A line drawn from the centre of enlargement through a point on the object will pass through the corresponding point on the image.

Distance to image : distance to object = scale factor : 1

EXAMPLE

▶ Enlarge the object by a scale factor of 3 about the centre of enlargement, X.

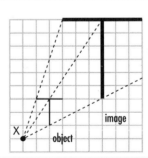

EXAMPLE

▶ Enlarge the object by a scale factor of $\frac{1}{2}$ about the centre of enlargement, X.

Notice that the lengths in the image are half the size of the lengths in the original object.

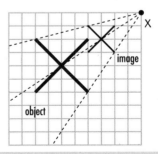

Exercise 52A

Copy and complete each diagram by drawing the image after enlargement by the stated scale factor (S.F.) from the centre of enlargement, X.

1

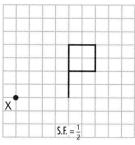

S.F. = $\frac{1}{2}$

2

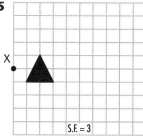

S.F. = 3

3

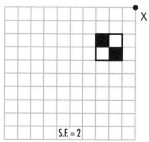

S.F. = 2

4

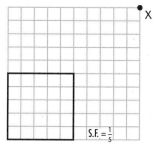

S.F. = $\frac{1}{4}$

5

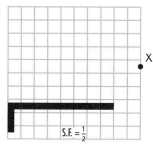

S.F. = 3

6

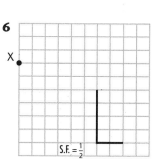

S.F. = $\frac{1}{2}$

7

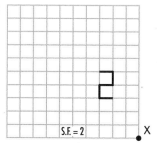

S.F. = $\frac{1}{5}$

8

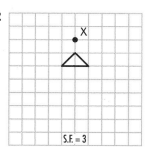

S.F. = $\frac{1}{2}$

9

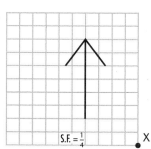

S.F. = 3

10

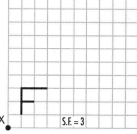

S.F. = 2

Exercise 52B

Copy and complete each diagram by drawing the image after enlargement by the stated scale factor (S.F.) from the centre of enlargement, X.

1
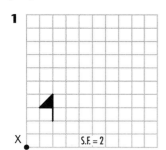
S.F. = 2

2
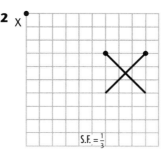
S.F. = $\frac{1}{3}$

3
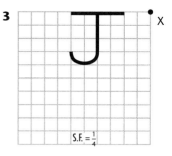
S.F. = $\frac{1}{4}$

4
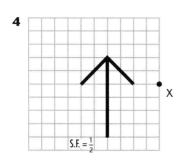
S.F. = $\frac{1}{2}$

5
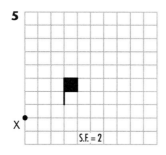
S.F. = 2

6
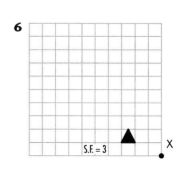
S.F. = 3

7
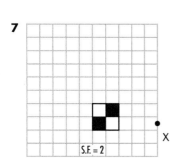
S.F. = 2

8
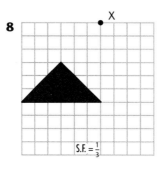
S.F. = $\frac{1}{3}$

9
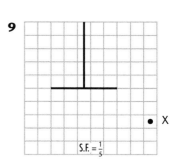
S.F. = $\frac{1}{5}$

10
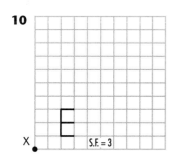
S.F. = 3

53/ THE LOCUS OF A POINT

The **locus** of a point is the path that the point traces out when it moves according to a given rule.

Note: The plural of locus is **loci**.

Here are some examples of common loci:

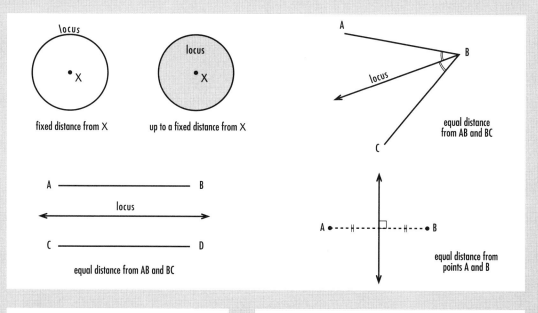

EXAMPLE
▶ Sketch the locus of a point that moves so as to be always 5 metres from a fixed point.

EXAMPLE
▶ A goat has a 3 metre lead. The end of the lead is allowed to slide along a 10 metre rail. Sketch the area of grass that the goat can eat.

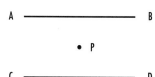

Exercise 53A

In this exercise your drawings should be of good quality and to scale where necessary.

1 Sketch the locus of a point that moves so as to be 4 cm or more from the point O.

2 The point P is equidistant from the lines AB and CD.
  (a) Copy the diagram and draw in two lines that show the distance from P to AB and to CD.
  (b) Draw the locus of the point that moves so as to be equidistant from AB and CD.

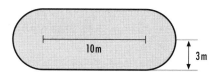

3 Draw a sketch of the locus of a point that is always 3 cm away from a straight line. The line is very long so you can only show a part of it.

4 The point P is equidistant from the points A and B.

(a) Copy the diagram and draw in the distances from P to A and B.

(b) Draw the locus of the point that moves so as to be equidistant from A and B.

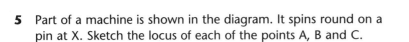

5 Part of a machine is shown in the diagram. It spins round on a pin at X. Sketch the locus of each of the points A, B and C.

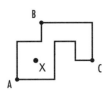

6 Mark a point on the rim of a coin. Use the coin to find the locus of this point as the coin is rolled along a straight line on a flat surface.

7 Sketch the locus of a person's nose as they climb a flight of stairs.

8 Sketch the locus of point P, which moves so that the angle APB is always 90°.

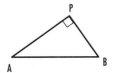

9 A goat is tied to a rope fixed at the point X on the wall of a 10 m × 5 m shed. Draw diagrams to show the area of grass that can be eaten by the goat when the rope has a length of

(a) 4 m
(b) 5 m
(c) 8 m
(d) 10 m

10 Draw an accurate drawing of the triangle ABC where AB = 5 cm, BC = 6 cm and AC = 8 cm.

(a) Draw the locus of the point that is equidistant from the lines AB and BC

(b) Repeat this for the lines AB and AC and also for the lines BC and AC.

(c) If you have completed (a) and (b) correctly, all three loci should meet at a point, X. With centre at X, draw a circle that just *touches* each of the sides of the triangle.

Exercise 53B

In this exercise your drawings should be of good quality and to scale where necessary.

1 Sketch the path of the pencil point of the pair of damaged compasses shown in the diagram as a person attempts to use them to draw a circle.

2 Sketch the locus of the point that is equidistant from all three points A, B and C.

• A

B •   • C

3 Mark a point on the centre of a coin. Use the coin to find the locus of this point as the coin is rolled along a straight line on a flat surface.

4 The point Q in the diagram is equidistant from the lines ST and TU. Copy the diagram and show the distances that Q is from ST and TU. Show the locus of a point that moves so as to be equidistant from ST and TU.

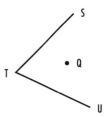

5 A cyclist rides in a straight line on a flat surface. Draw a sketch that shows the path of a point on the rim of one wheel of the cycle.

6 Copy the line AB and sketch the locus of a point that moves so as to be 3 cm from the line.

A ——————— B

7 A certain painter is well known for having accidents! The diagram shows his ladder resting on an icy surface and leaning against a smooth wall. When the painter reaches the point P, the foot of the ladder, A, slips away in the direction shown. Draw a sketch of the paths of the points A, B and P.

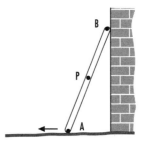

8 Give the name of the shape created by a point that moves in three dimensions so as to be a fixed distance from a point.

9 A goat is tied to the corner of a shed in the middle of a field. The shed measures 10 m × 5 m. Draw diagrams to show the area of grass that can be eaten by the goat when the rope has a length of
  (a) 4 m
  (b) 5 m
  (c) 10 m
  (d) 12 m.

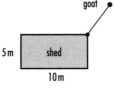

10 Draw the triangle PQR accurately given that PQ = 52 mm, PR = 59 mm and QR = 62 mm.
  (a) Draw the locus of the point that is equidistant from the points P and Q.
  (b) Draw the locus of the point that is equidistant from the points P and R.
  (c) Draw the locus of the point that is equidistant from the points Q and R.

If you have completed (a), (b) and (c) correctly, the three loci should pass through a single point; label this X. With centre X and radius of length XP, draw a circle that passes through the points P, Q and R.

54/ COMPOUND MEASURE

Examples of compound units are:

Density: normally measured in g/cm^3 or grams per cubic centimetre.
For example, the density of iron is 7.9 g/cm^3. This means that 1 cm^3 of iron weighs 7.9 grams.

Consumption: measured in compound units such as litres per mile (l/mile) or litres per kilometre (l/km) etc.
For example, a certain car is said to have a fuel consumption of 0.09 l/km. This means that it uses 0.09 l for each kilometre travelled.

Economy: measured in units such as miles per gallon (m.p.g. or miles/gallon) or kilometres per litre (km/l or km l^{-1}) etc.
For example, a car with an economy of 30 m.p.g. will be able to travel 30 miles for each gallon of fuel used.

Speed: measured in units that combine distance and time such as kilometres per hour (km/h or km h^{-1}) or metres per second (m/s or m s^{-1}) or miles per hour (m.p.h.) etc.
For example, a motorcycle travelling at a speed of 110 km/h will cover 110 km in 1 hour at this rate.

EXAMPLE

▶ The density of lead is 11.4 g/cm^3. What is the weight of 2.5 cm^3 of lead?

1 cm^3 of lead weighs 11.4 g
So 2.5 cm^3 of lead weigh 11.4 × 2.5 = 28.5 g.

EXAMPLE

▶ A car is said to be able to travel 350 miles on a full tank of 9.2 gallons of petrol. Calculate the economy of the car in m.p.g. (miles per gallon).

The car travels 350 miles using 9.2 gallons.
It will travel 350 ÷ 9.2 miles on 1 gallon = 38 m.p.g.
(to the nearest one m.p.g.).

Exercise 54A

1 The density of iron is 7.9 g/cm^3. What is the weight of 4.7 cm^3 of iron?

2 Alex drives at a speed that allows her to travel 500 km in 8 hours. Calculate the speed.

3 A particle travelling at a steady speed moves 85 m in 0.5 second. Calculate the speed of the particle in m s^{-1}

4 How far can Stephen travel in $2\frac{1}{2}$ hours at 56 m.p.h.?

5 The rate of fuel consumption of a car is 45.3 m.p.g. (miles per gallon). How many miles can be travelled using 3 gallons of petrol?

6 The density of gold is 13.3 g/cm^3. What is the weight (in kg) of a bar of gold measuring 3 cm by 5 cm by 20 cm?

7 Toni drives at a speed that allows her to travel 300 miles in $2\frac{1}{2}$ hours. Calculate the speed.

8 15 cm^3 of sulphur weighs 31.05 g. What is the density of sulphur?

9 The rate of fuel consumption of a car is 0.12 litres/mile. How many miles can be travelled using 30 litres of petrol?

10 A car travels 400 miles on 7 gallons of fuel. Calculate the fuel economy of the car in m.p.g.

11 The density of mercury is 14.2 g/cm^3. What is the volume of 20 g of mercury?

12 98 cm^3 of zinc weighs 695.8 g. What is the density of zinc?

13 Sharon drives at a speed that allows her to travel 140 miles in 4 hours. Calculate the speed.

14 How long does it take to travel 135 miles at 45 m.p.h.?

15 How far can Jason travel in 4 hours at 85 km/h?

16 Water flows into a tank which can hold 260 litres at the rate of 6.5 litre/min. How long will it take to fill the tank from empty?

17 Cathy walks 2 km in 40 min. Assuming that she walks at a constant speed, calculate this speed in km/h.

18 Paul's car gets 48 m.p.g. (miles per gallon) at 30 m.p.h. but only gets 38 m.p.g. at 70 m.p.h. How many more miles can Paul travel on 5 gallons at 30 m.p.h. than at 70 m.p.h.?

19 A car travels 345 km on a tank of 29 litres of fuel. Calculate the fuel economy of the car in km/litre.

20 The density of water is 1.00 g/cm^3 but this density changes to 0.92 gm/cm^3 when the water changes to ice. Calculate the change in volume when 250 g of water freezes.

Exercise 54B

1 The density of silver is 10.5 g/cm^3. What is the weight of 2.5 cm^3 of silver?

2 Neil drives at a speed that would allow him to travel 250 miles in $3\frac{1}{2}$ hours. Calculate his speed.

3 Roy can run 100 metres in 11.5 seconds. Assuming that his speed is the same throughout, calculate Roy's speed in m s^{-1}.

4 The density of a piece of brass is 8.5 g/cm^3. What is the weight of 7.8 cm^3 of the brass?

5 How long does it take to travel 200 km at a speed of 60 km/h? Answer to the nearest minute.

6 How long does it take to travel 164 miles at 60 m.p.h.? Answer to the nearest minute.

7 How far can Adam travel in 15 minutes at 120 km/h?

8 Shareen travels 212 miles using $4\frac{1}{2}$ gallons of petrol. Calculate the fuel economy of her car in m.p.g. (miles per gallon).

9 A particle travelling at a steady speed moves 12 m in 0.025 second. Calculate the speed of the particle in m s^{-1}.

10 The density of a piece of steel is 7.8 g/cm^3. What is the volume of 39 g of the steel?

11 Oil flows into a 60 litre tank at the rate of 1.2 l/min. How long will it take to fill the tank from empty?

12 A car has a fuel economy of 12.2 km/l. How far can it travel (to the nearest 10 km) on 24 litres of petrol?

13 A car travels 136 km on a tank of 15 litres of fuel. Calculate the fuel economy of the car in km/l.

14 12 cm^3 of iron weighs 94.8 g. What is the density of iron?

15 How far can Jenny travel in $3\frac{1}{2}$ hours at 110 km/h?

16 The rate of fuel consumption of a car is 0.18 litres/mile. How many miles can be travelled using 45 litres of petrol?

17 25 cm^3 of gold weighs 482.5 g. What is the density of gold?

18 Mary's car gets 62 m.p.g. (miles per gallon) at 30 m.p.h. but only gets 55 m.p.g. at 56 m.p.h. How many more miles can Mary travel on 3 gallons at 30 m.p.h. than at 56 m.p.h.?

19 A car travels 210 miles on a tank of $3\frac{1}{2}$ gallons of fuel. Calculate the fuel economy of the car in m.p.g.

20 The density of ice is 0.92 g/cm^3 but when it melts the water has a density of 1.0 g/cm^3. Calculate the increase in volume when 400 g of ice melts.

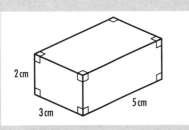

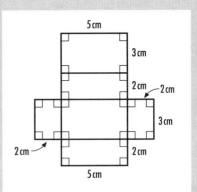

This cuboid has a **net**.

The net is a drawing which can be cut out and folded to make the cuboid.

This is the net of the cuboid:

These are two other common nets:

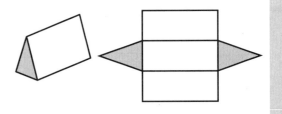

Exercise 55A

Draw nets for each of the following cuboids. Your drawings should be of good quality although they do not have to be exactly to scale. Write the lengths of the lines on each of the diagrams.

1
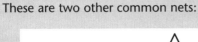
4 cm
3 cm 5 cm

2
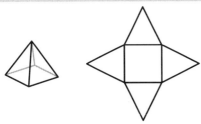
4 cm
2 cm 6 cm

3
4 cm
4 cm 4 cm

4
6 cm
4 cm 4 cm

5
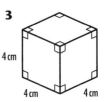
3 cm
3 cm 6 cm

Draw nets for each of these 3-dimensional shapes.

6
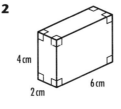
5 cm
3 cm 3 cm

7
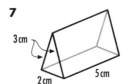
3 cm
2 cm 5 cm

8
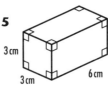
4 cm 4 cm
4 cm 4 cm

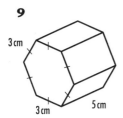

9

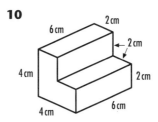

10

Exercise 55B

Draw nets for each of the following cuboids. Your drawings should be of good quality although they do not have to be exactly to scale. Write the lengths of the lines on each of the diagrams.

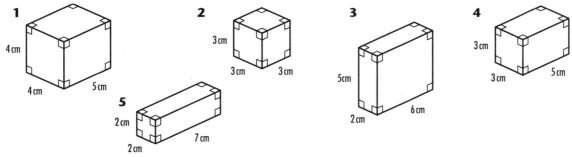

1 4 cm, 4 cm, 5 cm

2 3 cm, 3 cm, 3 cm

3 5 cm, 2 cm, 6 cm

4 3 cm, 3 cm, 5 cm

5 2 cm, 2 cm, 7 cm

Draw nets for each of these 3-dimensional shapes.

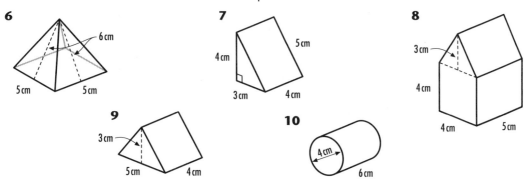

6 6 cm, 5 cm, 5 cm

7 5 cm, 4 cm, 3 cm, 4 cm

8 3 cm, 4 cm, 4 cm, 5 cm

9 3 cm, 5 cm, 4 cm

10 4 cm, 6 cm

Exercise 55C

Each net has a letter. Each diagram of a solid has a number. Match each lettered net with a numbered solid.

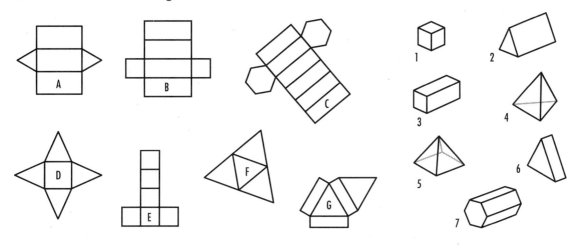

Exercise 55D

Each net has a letter. Each diagram of a solid has a number. Match each lettered net with a numbered solid.

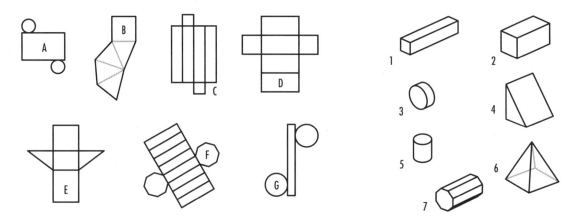

56/ DRAWING SECTIONS THROUGH 3D SHAPES IN A GIVEN PLANE

It is very difficult to calculate lengths and angles in a 3D shape. You can make the task less difficult by drawing 2D (flat) diagrams showing a part of the 3D shape. At this stage you will not be doing the calculations but practising how to make these simpler 2D drawings.

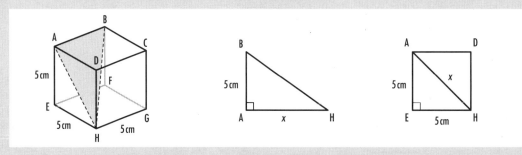

Suppose you need to find the length of BH in the cube ABCDEFGH, which has edges of length 5 cm. This is shown in the diagram

Take a section containing BH, through the cube. This is the plane shown in the diagram. Draw the triangle ABH which contains BH. Remember that angle BAH is a right angle although it does not look like one in the 3D drawing.

You know that AB = 5 cm but you do not know the length of AH. This can be found by considering another section through ADHE as shown

▶ The diagram shows a **right square-based pyramid**, PABCD, which has a base ABCD and a vertex P. It is called 'right' because P is directly above the centre, X, of ABCD. PC = 5 cm and CD = 6 cm.

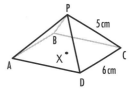

Draw sketches that show clearly any known lengths or angles and indicate the approximate shape of the following:
(a) PBA   (b) ACB   (c) BPD   (d) PXB

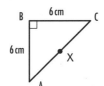
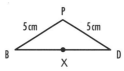

Exercise 56A

Your sketches should show the correct shape and any known angles or lengths.

1 PQRSTUVW is a cube of edge 4 cm.
Draw sketches of the following:
(a) SRVW   (b) QSWU
(c) QUT   (d) QUW.

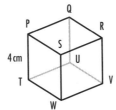

2 The triangular prism ACBDEF has angle ACB = 90°.
Draw sketches of the following:
(a) ADFC   (b) ADEB
(c) CFEB   (d) DFB.

3 In the cuboid ABCDWXYZ, AD = 6 cm, AW = 5 cm and CD = 8 cm.
Draw sketches of the following:
(a) DZYC   (b) BXYC
(c) WZD   (d) WZC.

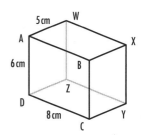

4 PLMNO is a right square-based pyramid. The point X is at the centre of the base LMNO. All edges are of length 40 mm.
Draw sketches of the following:
(a) MPL   (b) MNOL
(c) MPO   (d) PXN.

5 In the pentagonal prism ABCDEFGHIJ, ABCDE and FGHIJ are the regular pentagon-shaped ends. DE = 35 mm and CH = 60 mm. Draw sketches of the following:

(a) BGHC   (b) FGHIJ

(c) EBG   (d) AFHC.

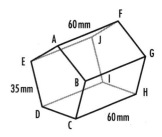

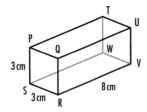

6 In the square prism PQRSTUVW, SR = 3 cm and RV = 8 cm. Draw sketches of the following:

(a) TUVW   (b) PTVR

(c) PTU   (d) UTW.

Exercise 56B

Your sketches should show the correct shape and any known angles or lengths.

1 The a cube ABCDEFGH has edges of length 5 cm. Draw sketches of the following:

(a) BFGC   (b) ADH

(c) DCG   (d) AFG.

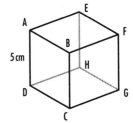

2 PSTU is a triangular pyramid (tetrahedron) where all edges are of length 6 cm. X is the centre of the base STU and Y is the midpoint of SU. Draw sketches of the following:

(a) PTU   (b) SXY

(c) PXS   (d) SXT.

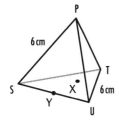

3 In the cuboid ABCDEFGH, AD = 4 cm, AE = 5 cm and CD = 6 cm. Draw sketches of the following:

(a) AEHD   (b) EHG

(c) FBG   (d) BEH.

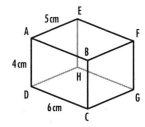

4 In the triangular prism OPQRST, OPQ is an equilateral triangle of side 28 mm and QT = 45 mm. X is the midpoint of OQ and Y is the midpoint of RT. Draw sketches of the following:

(a) PSTQ   (b) PTQ

(c) PSYX   (d) RSY.

5 ABCDEFGH is a prism, where ABCD is a square with sides of
length 35 mm. The length CG = 55 mm.
Draw sketches of the following:
  (a) AEHD   (b) AEGC
  (c) CDG   (d) AFC.

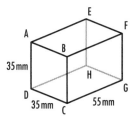

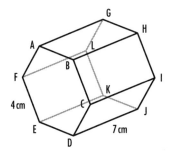

6 In the hexagonal prism ABCDEFGHIJKL, ABCDEF and GHIJKL
are regular hexagons with sides of length 4 cm.
The length DJ = 7 cm.
Draw sketches of the following:
  (a) GHIJKL   (b) AGLF
  (c) CIJ   (d) BHKE.

REVISION

Exercise E

1 State the size of each of the angles marked with letters. Diagrams are not accurate.

(a)

(b)

(c)

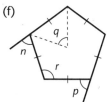

(d)

(e)

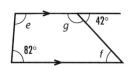

(f)

2 Give the best name for each of these shapes.

(a)

(b)

(c)

(d)

(e)

(f)

(g)

3 Copy each shape and draw in any axes of reflective symmetry and/or centre of rotational symmetry.

4 State the length the following would need to be drawn using the scale stated.
(a) 12.4 km; scale: 1 cm ≡ 2 km
(b) 8 m; scale: 1 : 2000
(c) 5 km; scale: 1 : 100 000
(d) 17.5 m; scale: 1 cm ≡ 5 m

5 State the actual length that the following lengths on a drawing or map would represent using the stated scale.
(a) 105 mm; scale: 1 mm ≡ 5 m
(b) 8.5 cm; scale: 1 : 200 000
(c) 25 mm; scale: 1 cm ≡ 10 km
(d) 15.4 cm; scale: 1 : 1 000 000

6 For each of the following copy the diagram on squared paper and show the centre of enlargement. State the scale factor.
(a)

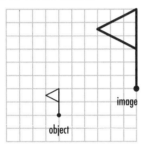

(b)

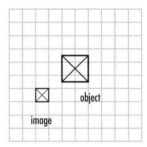

7 Sketch the locus of a point that moves so as to be 23 mm or less from a point X.

8 A car travels at a speed that would allow it to travel 250 miles in 4 hours. Calculate the speed of the car.

9 A piece of lead has a volume of 124 cm³ and a mass of 1414 g. Calculate the density of lead.

10 Match the correct net (1, 2, 3 or 4) with its 3D shape (A, B, C or D).

11 ABCDEFG is a triangular prism. The triangle ABC is isosceles and the length AB = AC = 42 mm, BC = 67 mm. X is the midpoint of BC and Y is the midpoint of EF. The length BE = 61 mm. Sketch the following, showing any lengths and angles that can be identified.
(a) ADYX
(b) ADEB
(c) DYE
(d) DYC

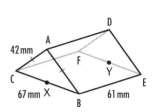

Exercise EE

1 State the size of each of the angles marked with letters, giving reasons for your answers. Diagrams are not accurate.

(a)
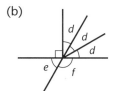

(b)
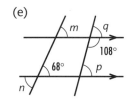

(c)
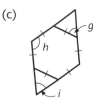

(d)
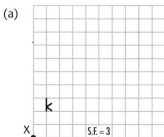

(e)
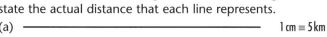

(f)
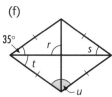

2 Two of the angles of a kite are known to be 120° and 50°. Sketch *three* examples of what the kite might look like showing the positions of the two angles. Also show the size and position of the other two angles in each case.

3 Draw a rhombus and show any axes and/or centre of symmetry.

4 Copy the shape and complete it by reflecting it in the axis. Name the shape. Show any further axes of reflection and the position of its centre of rotation and state the order of any rotational symmetry.

5 Measure and record the length of each line. Using the scale indicated for each, state the actual distance that each line represents.

(a) ──────────────────────────── $1\,cm \equiv 5\,km$

(b) ──────────────── $1 : 100\,000$

6 Draw lines to represent each actual distance stated using the scale indicated.
(a) 15 km;   scale: $1\,cm \equiv 2\,km$ (b) 6.5 m;   scale: $1 : 500$

7 Copy and complete each diagram by drawing the image after enlargement by the stated scale factor from the centre of enlargement, X.

(a)
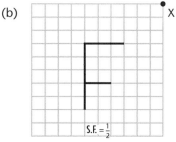

(b)

8 Draw the triangle ABC accurately where AB = 56 mm, AC = 45 mm and BC = 43 mm.
(a) Draw the locus of the point that is equidistant from the points A and C.
(b) Draw the locus of the point that is equidistant from the points A and B.
(c) Draw the locus of the point that is equidistant from the points B and C.
The three loci should all intersect at a single point; label this point X. With centre at X and with radius XA, draw a circle to pass through A, B and C.

9 The density of water is 1.00 g/cm³ but this density changes to 0.92 g/cm³ when the water changes to ice. Calculate the change in volume when 1 litre of water freezes.

10 The diagram shows a cube, ABCDEFGH, of edge 4 cm.
Draw the following *accurately* to size

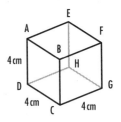

    (a) AEFB   (b) EBCH

    (c) BFG   (d) BGH.

57/ PYTHAGORAS' THEOREM: FINDING THE HYPOTENUSE

In a right-angled triangle, Pythagoras' theorem states:

$$h^2 = a^2 + b^2$$

where h is the hypotenuse of the triangle.
The hypotenuse is the longest side and is found opposite the right angle.
This formula can be written:

$$h = \sqrt{a^2 + b^2}$$

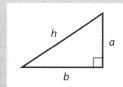

EXAMPLE

▶ In the right-angled triangle PQR, PQ = 3 cm and QR = 5 cm.
Calculate the length of PR to 3 significant figures.

$$h^2 = a^2 + b^2$$
$$= 3^2 + 5^2$$
$$= 9 + 25$$
$$= 34$$

So $h = \sqrt{34} = 5.83$ to 3 s.f.
PR = 5.83 cm

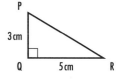

Exercise 57A

The diagram shows the positions of a, b and h.

Use Pythagoras' theorem to calculate the length of the hypotenuse, h, in each case.

Give your answers to 3 significant figures if necessary.

1 $a = 5$ cm, $b = 12$ cm	**2** $a = 3$ cm, $b = 4$ cm	**3** $a = 4$ m, $b = 4$ m
4 $a = 30$ mm, $b = 45$ mm	**5** $a = 25$ mm, $b = 15$ mm	**6** $a = 6$ cm, $b = 8$ cm
7 $a = 13$ cm, $b = 12$ cm	**8** $a = 1.2$ m, $b = 1.6$ m	**9** $a = 5$ m, $b = 3$ m
10 $a = 85$ mm, $b = 64$ mm	**11** $a = 7.2$ cm, $b = 4.8$ cm	**12** $a = 14.4$ m, $b = 10.5$ m
13 $a = 25$ m, $b = 75$ m	**14** $a = 6.9$ cm, $b = 4.2$ cm	**15** $a = 10$ cm, $b = 10$ cm
16 $a = 88$ mm, $b = 7.2$ cm	**17** $a = 17$ cm, $b = 19$ cm	**18** $a = 3.2$ m, $b = 2.4$ m.
19 $a = 95$ cm, $b = 1.15$ m	**20** $a = 34$ mm, $b = 25$ mm	

Exercise 57B

The diagram shows the positions of a, b and h.

Use Pythagoras' theorem to calculate the length of the hypotenuse, h, in each case.
Give your answers to 3 significant figures if necessary.

1 $a = 7\,\text{cm}$, $b = 24\,\text{cm}$	**2** $a = 6\,\text{cm}$, $b = 8\,\text{cm}$	**3** $a = 12\,\text{m}$, $b = 12\,\text{m}$
4 $a = 4\,\text{m}$, $b = 6\,\text{m}$	**5** $a = 32\,\text{mm}$, $b = 27\,\text{mm}$	**6** $a = 16\,\text{m}$, $b = 12\,\text{m}$
7 $a = 10\,\text{cm}$, $b = 20\,\text{cm}$	**8** $a = 15\,\text{m}$, $b = 25\,\text{m}$	**9** $a = 4.8\,\text{m}$, $b = 6.4\,\text{m}$
10 $a = 0.85\,\text{m}$, $b = 0.75\,\text{m}$	**11** $a = 78\,\text{cm}$, $b = 63\,\text{cm}$	**12** $a = 42\,\text{cm}$, $b = 36\,\text{cm}$
13 $a = 11.4\,\text{m}$, $b = 12.5\,\text{m}$	**14** $a = 1.75\,\text{m}$, $b = 1.75\,\text{m}$	**15** $a = 2.35\,\text{m}$, $b = 1.98\,\text{m}$
16 $a = 2\,\text{m}$, $b = 200\,\text{cm}$	**17** $a = 16\,\text{cm}$, $b = 8\,\text{cm}$	**18** $a = 2.5\,\text{cm}$, $b = 35\,\text{mm}$
19 $a = 1.02\,\text{m}$, $b = 1.42\,\text{m}$	**20** $a = 3.75\,\text{m}$, $b = 3.75\,\text{m}$	

58/ PYTHAGORAS' THEOREM: FINDING A LENGTH GIVEN THE HYPOTENUSE

The hypotenuse of a right-angled triangle is the longest side.
If the length of the hypotenuse is given, any other side of the triangle must be smaller.

The formula for finding one of the other sides is:

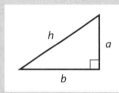

$$a^2 = h^2 - b^2 \qquad \text{or} \qquad b^2 = h^2 - a^2$$
$$\text{So} \qquad a = \sqrt{h^2 - b^2} \qquad \text{or} \qquad b = \sqrt{h^2 - a^2}$$

Notice the *minus sign*, not a plus sign, after h^2.

> **EXAMPLE**
>
> ▶ Calculate the length of PR in the triangle PQR.
>
> By Pythagoras' theorem: $a^2 = h^2 - b^2$
> $$PR^2 = 15^2 - 7^2$$
> $$= 225 - 49$$
> $$= 176$$
> $$PR = \sqrt{176} = 13.3\,\text{cm}$$

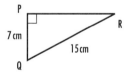

Exercise 58A

Given the length of the hypotenuse and the length of one of the other sides of these triangles, use Pythagoras' theorem to calculate the length of the remaining side. Give your answers to 3 significant figures if necessary.

1 Hypotenuse = 15 cm, other side = 12 cm	**2** Hypotenuse = 25 m, other side = 7 m
3 Hypotenuse = 13 cm, other side = 6 cm	**4** Hypotenuse = 10 cm, other side = 7 cm
5 Hypotenuse = 35 mm, other side = 28 mm	**6** Hypotenuse = 32 cm, other side = 12 cm
7 Hypotenuse = 1.5 m, other side = 1.2 m	**8** Hypotenuse = 2 m, other side = 1.3 m
9 Hypotenuse = 45 mm, other side = 40 mm	**10** Hypotenuse = 12 cm, other side = 9 cm

11 Hypotenuse = 30 m, other side = 18 m	**12** Hypotenuse = 50 mm, other side = 40 mm
13 Hypotenuse = 1.8 m, other side = 1.6 m	**14** Hypotenuse = 9 cm, other side = 3 cm
15 Hypotenuse = 100 mm, other side = 6 cm	**16** Hypotenuse = 92 mm, other side = 45 mm
17 Hypotenuse = 7.5 cm, other side = 3.6 cm	**18** Hypotenuse = 5.5 m, other side = 2.8 m
19 Hypotenuse = 6 m, other side = 105 cm	**20** Hypotenuse = 3.4 m, other side = 2.2 m

Exercise 58B

Given the length of the hypotenuse and the length of one of the other sides of these triangles, use Pythagoras' theorem to calculate the length of the remaining side. Give your answers to 3 significant figures if necessary.

1 Hypotenuse = 13 m, other side = 5 m	**2** Hypotenuse = 20 cm, other side = 12 cm
3 Hypotenuse = 4.6 m, other side = 2.6 m	**4** Hypotenuse = 54 mm, other side = 17 mm
5 Hypotenuse = 75 mm, other side = 60 mm	**6** Hypotenuse = 2.4 m, other side = 1.6 m
7 Hypotenuse = 110 m, other side = 70 m	**8** Hypotenuse = 14 cm, other side = 9 cm
9 Hypotenuse = 3.6 cm, other side = 3.1 cm	**10** Hypotenuse = 12.5 cm, other side = 7.5 cm
11 Hypotenuse = 62 mm, other side = 30 mm	**12** Hypotenuse = 11.5 cm, other side = 5.4 cm
13 Hypotenuse = 0.9 m, other side = 0.4 m	**14** Hypotenuse = 16 cm, other side = 90 mm
15 Hypotenuse = 3.7 m, other side = 2.3 m	**16** Hypotenuse = 17 cm, other side = 6 cm
17 Hypotenuse = 7.8 cm, other side = 4.5 cm	**18** Hypotenuse = 12.5 m, other side = 6.5 m
19 Hypotenuse = 48 mm, other side = 2.4 cm	**20** Hypotenuse = 125 mm, other side = 61 mm

59/ FINDING LENGTHS USING PYTHAGORAS' THEOREM

EXAMPLE

▶ In the right-angled triangle, $a = 13$ cm and $b = 7$ cm. Find the length h.

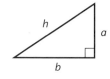

$$h^2 = a^2 + b^2$$
$$= 13^2 + 7^2$$
$$= 169 + 49$$
$$= 218$$
$$\text{So } h = \sqrt{218}$$
$$= 14.8 \text{ cm (to 3 s.f.)}$$

Note: You are *calculating the hypotenuse* so you *add* the squares.

EXAMPLE

▶ In the right-angled triangle PQR, PR = 17 m and PQ = 15 m. Calculate the length of QR.

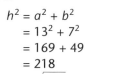

$$QR^2 = PR^2 - PQ^2$$
$$= 17^2 - 15^2$$
$$= 289 - 225 = 64$$
$$\text{So } QR = \sqrt{64} = 8 \text{ m}$$

Note: You *know the hypotenuse* so you *subtract* the squares: of course, PR^2 is larger than PQ^2 so it is placed first.

Exercise 59A

Answer all questions to 3 significant figures.

In the table below h is the hypotenuse and a and b are the other two sides of a right-angled triangle. Two of the lengths are given. Calculate the missing length in each case.

	a	b	h
1	12 cm	16 cm	?
2	30 cm	?	34 cm
3	52 mm	25 mm	?
4	32 m	?	50 m
5	110 m	70 m	?

	a	b	h
6	?	5 cm	13 cm
7	0.8 m	?	120 cm
8	112 mm	94 mm	?
9	?	3.5 cm	45 mm
10	4 m	4 m	?

Calculate the length marked x in each of the following.

11

12

13

14

15

16

17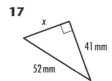

18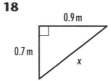

19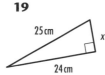

20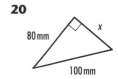

The following questions refer to the triangle ABC as shown in the diagram.

21 Calculate AB given that AC = 7 cm and BC = 3 cm.
22 Calculate AC given that AB = 27 mm and BC = 15 mm.
23 Calculate AC given that AB = 15 cm and BC = 7 cm.
24 Calculate BC given that AC = 2.1 m and AB = 3.2 m.
25 Calculate AB given that AC = 28 mm and BC = 21 mm.
26 Calculate AB given that AC = 64 mm and BC = 32 mm.
27 Calculate BC given that AB = 8.5 m and AC = 650 cm.
28 Calculate AC given that AB = 10 cm and BC = 9.5 cm.
29 Calculate AB given that AC = 2.8 m and BC = 1.9 m.
30 Calculate AC given that BC = 7.5 cm and AB = 12.5 cm.

Exercise 59B

Answer all questions to 3 significant figures.

In the table below h is the hypotenuse and a and b are the other two sides of a right-angled triangle. Two of the lengths are given. Calculate the missing length in each case.

	a	b	h
1	15 cm	20 cm	?
2	?	48 mm	50 mm
3	95 mm	45 mm	?
4	4.7 m	?	6.8 m
5	?	30 cm	34 cm

	a	b	h
6	11 cm	12 cm	?
7	10 cm	10 cm	?
8	2.1 m	?	3.5 m
9	?	1.25 m	200 cm
10	75 mm	12 cm	?

Calculate the length marked *x* in each of the following:

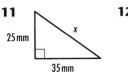

11
25 mm
x
35 mm

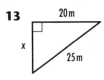

12
13 cm
12 cm
x
x

13
20 m
x
25 m

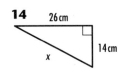

14
26 cm
14 cm
x

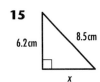

15
8.5 cm
6.2 cm
x

16
9 m
6 m
x

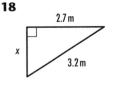

17
75 mm
6 cm
x

18
2.7 m
x
3.2 m

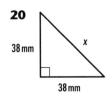

19
75 m
x
65 m

20
38 mm
x
38 mm

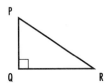

The following questions refer to the triangle PQR shown in the diagram.

P

Q   R

21 Calculate PR given that PQ = 5 cm and QR = 2 cm.
22 Calculate QR given that PQ = 13 cm and PR = 20 cm.
23 Calculate QR given that PQ = 1.5 m and PR = 2.2 m.
24 Calculate PR given that PQ = 5 cm and QR = 5 cm.
25 Calculate PR given that QR = 65 mm and PQ = 75 mm.
26 Calculate PQ given that PR = 170 mm and QR = 15 cm.
27 Calculate QR given that PQ = 0.8 m and PR = 1.0 m.
28 Calculate PR given that PQ = 24 cm and QR = 5 cm.
29 Calculate PQ given that QR = 112 mm and PR = 185 mm.
30 Calculate PR given that PQ = 6.5 m and QR = 4.2 m.

60/ PROBLEMS INVOLVING PYTHAGORAS' THEOREM

Exercise 60A

Draw a diagram of the situation in each question showing clearly the position of any right angle.
Answer all questions to 3 significant figures where necessary.

1 One side of a rectangle has a length of 60 mm. The length of each diagonal is 100 mm. Find the length of the other side.

2 A TV screen measures 36 cm by 49 cm. Calculate the length of the diagonal.

3 A circular can has a diameter of 9 cm and a height of 12 cm. Calculate the longest length for a stick that will fit inside the can.

4 Calculate the height, *h*, of the isosceles triangle ABC in the diagram.

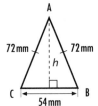

A
72 mm   72 mm
h
C   B
54 mm

5 The diagonal of a square is 13 cm. Find the length of each side.

6 A room measures 3.5 m by 4.2 m. Calculate the length of the diagonal of the room.

7 If the distance between the points (1, 1) and (1, 2) is 1 unit and the distance between (1, 1) and (2, 1) is also 1 unit, calculate the distance between the points (1, 1) and (5, 5).

8 Calculate the length of the diagonal of a rectangle which has sides of length 60 mm and 75 mm.

9 A boat sails 3 km due south and then 2 km due east. How far is the ship from its starting point?

10 Calculate the length of *d* in this trapezium.

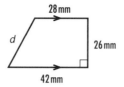

11 A flag pole of length 7.8 m is positioned vertically in flat horizontal ground so that 1.5 m of the pole is buried beneath the ground. A rope is fixed to the top of the pole and to a point on the ground 5 m away from the foot of the post (at ground level). Calculate the minimum length of this rope if 0.5 m is allowed at each end for fixing.

12 Mr Green has a vegetable plot measuring 5.5 m by 22 m. Calculate the length of string required to stretch from one corner to the corner opposite.

13 Calculate the lengths AX and CX as shown on the diagram of the kite ABCD if the diagonal DB has a length of 5 cm.

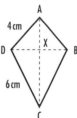

14

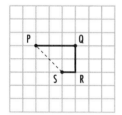

The line PQ in the diagram has a length of 3 units.
Calculate the length of PS.

15 Calculate the length *d* in the diagram, which shows a regular octagon of side 2 cm.

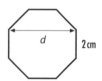

Exercise 60B

Draw a diagram of the situation in each question showing clearly the position of any right angle. Answer all questions to 3 significant figures where necessary.

1 Calculate the diagonal of a square of side 8 cm.

2 One side of a rectangle has a length of 12 cm. The length of each diagonal is 18 cm. Find the length of the other side.

3 A ladder of length 7 m is placed on horizontal ground 3 m away from the foot of a vertical wall. Calculate the distance that the ladder will reach up the wall.

4 The diagram shows the net of a cube of edge length 5 cm. Calculate the length shown with a dotted line.

5

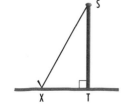

The diagram shows a vertical mast, ST, of height 12 m. A wire of length 12.5 m is fixed to the top of the mast and to a point X on the horizontal ground. Calculate the distance XT.

6 Calculate the length of the diagonals of a rectangle measuring 10 cm by 15 cm.

7 A shed of width 2 m has heights 2.1 m and 2.3 m as shown in the diagram. Calculate the width of the roof if the builder includes overhangs of 10 cm and 15 cm to stop the rain pouring down the walls.

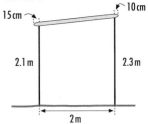

8 The diagonal of a square is 14.1 cm. Find the length of each side.

9 Calculate the diagonal of a rectangular piece of paper measuring 200 mm by 297 mm

10 A right-angled triangle has an hypotenuse of length 17 cm and one side of length 15 cm. Calculate the length of the other side.

11 The line AB in the diagram has a length of 5 units. Calculate the lengths of CD and AE.

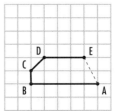

12

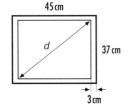

A picture frame is made from strips of wood of width 3 cm. The outside dimensions of the frame are 45 cm by 37 cm. Calculate the diagonal, *d*, of the picture area as shown in the diagram.

13 Calculate *x* and *y* in the diagram.

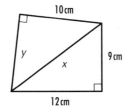

14 Calculate the length of the chord PQ, as shown in the diagram. The centre of the circle is X and the length of the diameter is 10 cm.

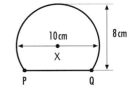

15 The diagonals of a rhombus measure 8 cm and 12 cm. Calculate the length of each side.

61/ AREA: QUADRILATERALS AND TRIANGLES

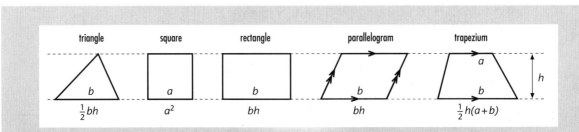

triangle	square	rectangle	parallelogram	trapezium
$\frac{1}{2}bh$	a^2	bh	bh	$\frac{1}{2}h(a+b)$

Remember: The height **must be perpendicular** (at right angles) to the base.

▶ Calculate the area of the trapezium ABCD.

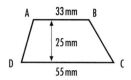

Method 1

Area $= \frac{1}{2}h(a + b)$

$\qquad = \frac{1}{2} \times 25 \times (33 + 55)$

$\qquad = \frac{1}{2} \times 25 \times 88$

$\qquad = 1100\,\text{mm}^2$

Method 2

Divide the trapezium up into two triangles.

Triangle 1: Area $= \frac{1}{2}bh = \frac{1}{2} \times 33 \times 25$ Triangle 2: Area $= \frac{1}{2}bh = \frac{1}{2} \times 55 \times 25$

$\qquad\qquad\qquad = 412.5\,\text{mm}^2$ $\qquad\qquad\qquad = 687.5\,\text{mm}^2$

Total area $= 412.5 + 687.5 = 1100\,\text{mm}^2$

▶ Calculate the area of a rhombus with diagonals of length
8 cm and 6 cm.

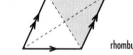

The diagonals of a rhombus bisect (cut in half)
each other at right angles.

The rhombus can be divided into two triangles of equal area.

The shaded area $= \frac{1}{2}bh = \frac{1}{2} \times 4 \times 6 = 12\,\text{cm}^2$

Total area $= 2 \times 12 = 24\,\text{cm}^2$

▶ A triangle has an area of 132 cm². If the length of its base is 22 cm, find its height.

$\qquad$ Area $= \frac{1}{2}bh = \frac{1}{2} \times 22 \times h = 132\,\text{cm}^2$

So $11h = 132$

$\qquad h = 12\,\text{cm}$

Exercise 61A

Calculate the area of each of the following shapes to 3 significant figures when necessary.

1   Triangle: base = 14 cm, height = 8 cm
2   Rectangle: base = 12 cm, height = 108 mm
3   Trapezium: parallel sides 8 cm and 12 cm, distance between parallel sides = 6 cm
4   Parallelogram: base = 4.5 cm, height = 3.5 cm
5   Square: side length = 2.5 m
6   Trapezium: parallel sides 15 cm and 19 cm, distance between parallel sides = 11 cm
7   Triangle: base = 1.7 m, height = 0.8 m
8   Rectangle: base = 250 cm, height = 3.5 m
9   Triangle: base = 36 mm, height = 3 cm
10   Parallelogram: base = 48 mm, height = 28 mm

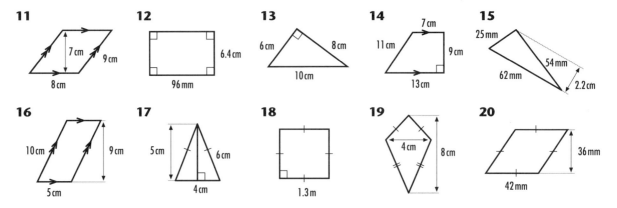

In questions 21–30, find lengths to 3 significant figures when necessary.

21 The area of a triangle is 64 cm². If the height is 8 cm, find the base.

22 The area of a parallelogram is 75 cm². If the height is 11.5 cm, find the base.

23 The area of a square is 225 m². Find the length of its sides.

24 The area of a rectangle is 1.08 m². If one of its sides has a length of 60 cm, find the length of the other side.

25 The area of a trapezium is 1200 mm². If the two parallel sides have lengths of 45 mm and 37 mm, find the distance between these two sides.

26 The area of a parallelogram is 60 cm². If the height is 120 mm, find the base.

27 The area of a triangle is 72 cm². If the height is 9 cm, find the base.

28 The area of a square is 85 cm². Find the length of its sides.

29 The area of a trapezium is 86 cm². If one of the two parallel sides has a length of 9 cm and the distance between the parallel sides is 8 cm, find the length of the other parallel side.

30 The area of a rectangle is 45 cm². If one of its sides has a length of 120 mm, find the length of the other side.

Exercise 61B

Calculate the area of each of the following shapes to 3 significant figures when necessary.

1 Rectangle: base = 15 cm, height = 8 cm

2 Triangle: base = 72 mm, height = 45 mm

3 Trapezium: parallel sides 116 mm and 94 mm, distance between parallel sides = 85 mm

4 Square: side length = 7.2 cm

5 Triangle: base = 1.25 cm, height = 1.4 cm

6 Parallelogram: base = 13.5 cm, height = 110 mm

7 Trapezium; parallel sides 7 cm and 13 cm, distance between parallel sides = 6.5 cm

8 Triangle: base = 110 mm, height = 9 cm

9 Parallelogram: base = 6 cm, height = 80 mm

10 Triangle: base = 7.2 cm, height = 84 mm

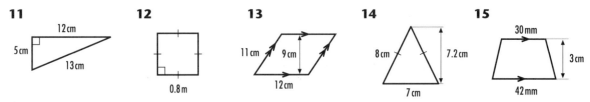

16
1.1 m
1.9 m

17
5 cm
9 cm
4 cm

18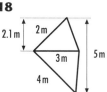
2.1 m 2 m
3 m
4 m
5 m

19
21 mm
18 mm

20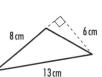
8 cm
6 cm
13 cm

In questions 21–30 find lengths to 3 significant figures when necessary.

21 The area of a square is 150 cm². Find the length of its sides.

22 The area of a triangle is 5.4 cm². If the height is 45 mm, find the base.

23 The area of a rectangle is 1200 mm². If one of its sides has a length of 4 cm, find the length of the other side.

24 The area of a trapezium is 56 cm². If the two parallel sides have lengths of 11 cm and 21 cm, find the distance between these two sides.

25 The area of a square is 1.96 m². Find the length of its sides.

26 The area of a triangle is 7.5 cm². If the height is 50 mm, find the base.

27 The area of a parallelogram is 124 cm². If the height is 155 mm, find the base.

28 The area of a rectangle is 3600 mm². If one of its sides has a length of 4.5 cm, find the length of the other side.

29 The area of a parallelogram is 2.16 m². If the height is 81 cm, find the base.

30 The area of a trapezium is 7.0 cm². If one of the two parallel sides has a length of 3 cm and the distance between the parallel sides is 4 cm, find the length of the other parallel side.

62/ CIRCUMFERENCE OF A CIRCLE

The formula for the **circumference** of a circle is $C = \pi d$, where d is the diameter. If the radius is known, just double the radius to find the diameter.

π has the value 3.142 159 265... . This number goes on for ever! It cannot be written exactly. Use the values 3.14, 3.142, etc. or the π button on a calculator.

There is another formula, $C = 2\pi r$, where r is the radius. However, the formula $C = \pi d$ is all you need to remember really.

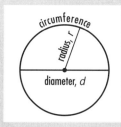
circumference
radius, r
diameter, d

EXAMPLE

▶ Calculate the circumference of a circle of radius 125 mm.

$r = 125$ mm and so $d = 250$ mm

$C = \pi d = \pi \times 250$ or 250π

    $= 785.398...$

    $= 785$ mm (to 3 s.f.)

Exercise 62A

Calculate the circumference of each circle correct to 3 significant figures.

1 Radius = 6 cm
2 Diameter = 42 mm
3 Radius = 0.8 m
4 Diameter = 32 cm
5 Diameter = 44 mm
6 Radius = 13 cm
7 Radius = 1.3 m
8 Diameter = 11 cm
9 Radius = 65 mm

10	Diameter = 28 cm	**11**	Radius = 7.5 cm	**12**	Diameter = 7.5 cm
13	Radius = 48 mm	**14**	Radius = 0.6 m	**15**	Diameter = 26 cm
16	Diameter = 108 mm	**17**	Radius = 27 mm	**18**	Diameter = 1.4 m
19	Radius = 4.5 cm	**20**	Radius = 11.7 cm		

Calculate the circumference of each circle shown in questions 21–24.

21   56 mm

22   1.5 m

23   4.5 cm

24   3.2 m

25 A circular cup has a diameter of 8 cm. Calculate the distance around the rim of the cup.

26 A circular cake measures 21 cm across. What is the minimum length of decoration needed to go around the edge?

27 A wheel has a radius of 25 cm. Calculate the distance around the edge of the wheel.

28 The distance across a coin is measured as 13 mm. How far does it travel if it rolls through 10 complete revolutions?

29 A circular lawn has a diameter of 13 metres. Lawn edging is sold in packs of 10 metres. How many packets will need to be purchased in order to put edging around the whole lawn?

30 The minute hand of a large clock measures 1.25 m from the centre of the clock to the tip of the hand. Calculate the distance travelled by the tip in one hour.

Exercise 62B

Calculate the circumference of each circle correct to 3 significant figures.

1	Radius = 5 cm	**2**	Diameter = 6 cm	**3**	Diameter = 28 mm
4	Radius = 6.6 m	**5**	Radius = 3 cm	**6**	Radius = 3.5 cm
7	Diameter = 1.8 m	**8**	Radius = 31 mm	**9**	Diameter = 95 mm
10	Diameter = 14 cm	**11**	Radius = 8 cm	**12**	Diameter = 1.3 m
13	Radius = 66 mm	**14**	Radius = 2.8 cm	**15**	Diameter = 10.5 cm
16	Radius = 2.1 m	**17**	Radius = 54 mm	**18**	Diameter = 78 mm
19	Diameter = 16 cm	**20**	Radius = 3.6 m		

Calculate the circumference of each circle shown in questions 21–24.

21   8 cm

22   5.4 m

23   17 cm

24   9.5 cm

25 A circular plate measures 32 cm across. Calculate the distance around the edge of the plate.

26 A circular pond has a radius of 3.1 metres. Calculate the distance around the outside of the pond.

27 Line is wound onto the spool of a fishing reel. The spool has a circular cross-section of diameter 45 mm. How much line is there on one turn around the spool?

28 A coin measuring 10 mm across is rolled down a slight slope. Through what distance will it roll in 12 complete revolutions?

29 A wire hoop is formed into a circle of radius 10 cm. What length of wire is required to the nearest cm?

30 Julia runs one lap around the edge of a circular running track of diameter 32 metres. Her friend runs with her but 2 metres further out from the centre of the circle. How much further than Julia did her friend run?

63/ AREA OF A CIRCLE

The formula for the area of a circle of radius r is $A = \pi r^2$.
If the diameter is given rather than the radius, then just divide the diameter by 2 to find the radius.

> **EXAMPLE**
>
> ▶ Calculate the area of a circle of diameter 13 cm.
>
> The diameter is 13 cm so $r = 6.5$ cm.
> $$A = \pi r^2 = \pi \times 6.5 \times 6.5$$
> $$= 132.732... = 133 \text{ cm (to 3 s.f.)}$$

Exercise 63A

1–24

Calculate the area (to 3 significant figures) of each of the circles in the first 24 questions of Exercise 62A.

25 Calculate the area of ovenproof paper needed to cover the bottom of a circular dish of diameter 20 cm.

26 The circular dial of a clock measures 15 cm across. Calculate the area of the dial.

27 Calculate the area of a circular flower bed of diameter 6 metres.

28 Calculate the area of the circular base of a plastic water tank which has a radius of 35 cm.

29 A straight edge of a semicircular rug measures 2.4 metres. Calculate the area of the rug.

30 The inside area of a track of radius 16 metres needs to be seeded with grass seed at the rate of 100 g per square metre. Calculate the quantity of seed required.

Exercise 63B

1–24

Calculate the area (to 3 significant figures) of each of the circles in the first 24 questions of Exercise 62B

25 What is the area of a circular disc of diameter 18 cm?

26 A restaurant has a dance floor which is in the form of a circle of diameter 9.5 metres. Calculate the area of the dance floor.

27 Mr Hill wants to know the area of his circular lawn so that he can apply fertiliser. Calculate the area if the diameter of the lawn is 17 metres.

28 A circular rug measures 120 cm across. Calculate the area of the rug in square metres.

29 A garden sprinkler can water a circle of radius 12.5 metres. Calculate the area of garden it can water.

30 A circular medal of diameter 41 mm needs to be gold-plated on both sides (you may ignore the edge). Calculate the area to be plated.

The length, width and height of a cube are all the same.

The volume of a cube is l^3 where l is the length of an edge.

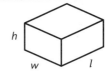

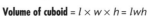

Volume of cuboid $= l \times w \times h = lwh$ **Volume of cube** $= l^3$

EXAMPLE

▶ Calculate the volume of the cube in the diagram.

$V = l^3 = 7.5 \times 7.5 \times 7.5$
$= 421.875 = 422\,\text{cm}^3$ (to 3 s.f.)

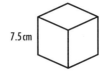

7.5 cm

EXAMPLE

▶ Calculate the volume of a cuboid of length 4.4 cm, width 24 mm and height 3.2 cm.

$V = l \times w \times h = 4.4\,\text{cm} \times 2.4\,\text{cm} \times 3.2\,\text{cm}$
$= 33.792 = 33.8\,\text{cm}^3$ (to 3 s.f.)

Exercise 64A

Calculate the volume of each of the following, to 3 significant figures where necessary.

1 Cube of edge length 5 cm
2 Cuboid of height 8 mm, width 6 mm and length 9 mm
3 Cuboid of height 3 cm, length 7 cm and width 2 cm
4 Cube of edge length 6 cm
5 Cuboid of width 32 mm, length 12 mm and height 20 mm
6 Cuboid of length 0.5 m, height 0.6 m and width 0.8 m
7 Cube of edge length 45 mm
8 Cuboid of height 7 cm, width 4 cm and length 11 cm
9 Cuboid of width 3.2 cm, length 3.2 cm and height 2.4 cm
10 Cube of edge length 0.9 m
11 Cuboid of length 75 mm, height 40 mm and width 32 mm
12 Cuboid of width 2.4 cm, length 3.6 cm and height 3.2 cm
13 Cuboid of height 26 cm, length 28 cm and width 30 cm
14 Cuboid of width 1.3 m, length 1.1 m and height 0.8 m

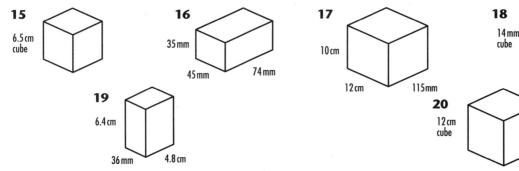

15 6.5 cm cube
16 35 mm 45 mm 74 mm
17 10 cm 12 cm 115 mm
18 14 mm cube
19 6.4 cm 36 mm 4.8 cm
20 12 cm cube

Exercise 64B

Calculate the volume of each of the following, to 3 significant figures where necessary.

1 Cuboid of width 4 cm, length 5 cm and height 8 cm
2 Cube of edge length 6 cm
3 Cuboid of length 12 mm, width 15 mm and height 18 mm
4 Cuboid of height 0.8 m, length 0.6 m and width 0.9 m
5 Cube of edge length 7.5 cm
6 Cuboid of width 2 cm, height 3.5 cm and length 3.5 cm
7 Cuboid of height 4.2 m, length 2.1 m and width 5.5 m
8 Cuboid of width 28 mm, height 30 mm and length 32 mm
9 Cube of edge length 0.5 m
10 Cuboid of length 32 cm, width 25 cm and height 25 cm
11 Cuboid of height 1.8 cm, length 2.4 cm and width 1.5 cm
12 Cube of edge length 15 mm
13 Cuboid of width 3.6 cm, height 7.2 cm and length 6.5 cm
14 Cuboid of length 0.4 m, width 0.4 m and height 0.5 m

15
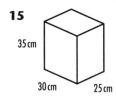
35 cm
30 cm   25 cm

16
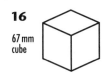
67 mm cube

17
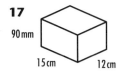
90 mm
15 cm   12 cm

18

550 cm
4.5 m   2.3 m

19

2.8 cm cube

20
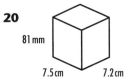
81 mm
7.5 cm   7.2 cm

EXAMPLE

▶ If the volume of this cuboid is 5400 cm³, calculate the length.

Volume of a cuboid $= l \times h \times w$
So $l \times 12 \times 25 = 5400$
$300 \times l = 5400$
$3 \times l = 54$
$l = 18$ cm

12 cm
25 cm l

EXAMPLE

▶ Calculate the volume of a cube of edge length 1.25 m in (a) m³ (b) cm³ and (c) litres.

(a) Volume $= l^3 = 1.25 \times 1.25 \times 1.25$
$= 1.953\,125$ m³ $= 1.95$ m³ (to 3 s.f.)

(b) 1 m³ $= 100$ cm $\times$ 100 cm $\times$ 100 cm
$= 1\,000\,000$ cm³ (There really *are* 1 million cm³ in 1m³!)
So 1.953 125 m³ $= 1.953\,125 \times 1\,000\,000$
$= 1\,953\,125$ cm³ or 1 950 000 cm³ (to 3 s.f.)

(c) 1 litre $= 1000$ ml or 1000 cm³
Volume in litres $= 1\,953\,125 \div 1000$
$= 1953.125\,l$ or $1950\,l$ (to 3 s.f.)

▶ A cube has a volume of 1728 cm³. Calculate the length of each edge.

$$V = l^3 = 1728$$
$$l = \sqrt[3]{1728} = 12 \text{ cm}$$

Exercise 64C

The volume and two of the lengths are given in each of the following. Calculate the third length.

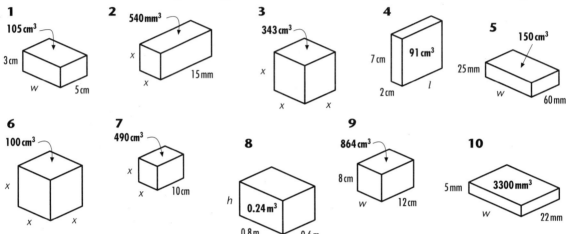

1 105 cm³, 3 cm, w, 5 cm

2 540 mm³, x, x, 15 mm

3 343 cm³, x, x, x

4 7 cm, 91 cm³, 2 cm, l

5 150 cm³, 25 mm, w, 60 mm

6 100 cm³, x, x, x

7 490 cm³, x, x, 10 cm

8 h, 0.24 m³, 0.8 m, 0.6 m

9 864 cm³, 8 cm, w, 12 cm

10 5 mm, 3300 mm³, w, 22 mm

11 The volume of a cube is 8 m³. Calculate the length of its edges.

12 The volume of a cuboid is 315 cm³. If the length is 7 cm and the width is 9 cm, calculate the height.

13 Calculate the volume of a cuboid of height 2.0 cm, width 25 mm and length 3.6 cm in (a) cm³ (b) mm³.

14 The volume of a cube is 27 000 cm³. Calculate the length of its edges.

15 The volume of a cuboid is 1120 cm³. If the width is 14 cm and the length is 10 cm, calculate the height.

16 Calculate the volume of a cube of edge length 1.5 m in (a) m³ (b) cm³ (c) litres.

17 The volume of a cube is 15.625 m³. Calculate the length of its edges.

18 Calculate the volume of a cuboid measuring 1.5 m by 2.2 m by 1.8 m in (a) m³ (b) cm³ (c) litres.

19 The volume of a cuboid is 141 750 cm³. If the length and height are both 45 cm, calculate the width.

20 The volume of a cube is 6859 cm. Calculate the length of its edges.

Exercise 64D

The volume and two of the lengths are given in each of the following. Calculate the third length.

1 600 cm³, x, 12 cm, x

2 252 cm³, 6 cm, 6 cm, l

3 3840 mm³, 12 mm, w, 10 mm

4 0.48 m³, 1.5 m, w, 0.8 m

5 255 cm³, h, 8.5 cm, 6 cm

6

784 cm³

7 cm

w   14 cm

7

4.5 m³

h

2 m   3 m

8

3375 cm³

x

x   x

9

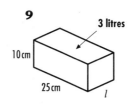

10 cm

25 cm

3 litres

l

10

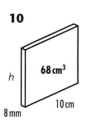

h   68 cm³

8 mm   10 cm

11 The volume of a cuboid is 48.75 cm³. If the width is 25 mm and the length is 6.5 cm, calculate the height.

12 Calculate the volume of a cuboid measuring 120 mm by 6.8 cm by 100 mm in (a) cm³ (b) mm³.

13 The volume of a cube is 1000 cm³. Calculate the length of its edges.

14 Calculate the volume of a cube of edge length 62 cm in (a) cm³ (b) mm³ (c) litres.

15 The volume of a cube is 2000 cm³. Calculate the length of its edges.

16 The volume of a cuboid is 2.52 m³. If the length is 1.5 m and the width is 1.4 m, calculate the height.

17 The volume of a cube is 3375 cm³. Calculate the length of its edges.

18 Calculate the volume of a cube of edge length 1.6 m in (a) m³ (b) cm³ (c) litres.

19 The volume of a cuboid is 97 200 mm³. If the width is 3 cm and the height is 72 mm, calculate the length.

20 Calculate the volume of a cuboid measuring 1.2 m by 95 cm by 0.7 m in (a) cm³ (b) m³ (c) litres.

65/ VOLUME OF A PRISM USING AREA OF CROSS-SECTION

A prism is a 3D shape that has the same cross-section throughout its length. That means that if you 'slice' the shape up, every slice will look the same.

The volume of a prism is given by the formula:

$V = Al$

where A is the area of the cross-section and l is the length (or height).

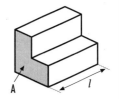

A   l

EXAMPLE

▶ The area, A, of the cross-section of a prism is 44.5 cm² and the length is 80 mm. Calculate the volume of the prism.

$V = Al = 44.5 \times 8 = 356$ cm³

Note: The length 80 mm must be changed to 8 cm so that it matches the cm² of the area, A.

Exercise 65A

Calculate the volume of each of these prisms.

1 Area of cross-section = 45 cm², length = 5 cm

2 Area of cross-section = 32 cm², length = 6 cm

3 Area of cross-section = 17 cm², length = 3 cm

4 Area of cross-section = 1.25 m², length = 0.8 m

5 Area of cross-section = 145 mm², length = 25 mm

6 Area of cross-section = 5.4 cm^2, length = 2.1 cm

7 Area of cross-section = 1.3 m^2, length = 110 cm

8 Area of cross-section = 75 cm^2, length = 9.5 cm

9 Area of cross-section = 34 cm^2, length = 124 mm

10 Area of cross-section = 1600 mm^2, length = 45 mm

11 Area of cross-section = 63 cm^2, length = 45 mm

12 Area of cross-section = 1.45 m^2, length = 0.5 m

13

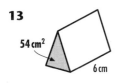

54 cm^2 6 cm

14

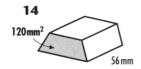

120mm^2 56 mm

15

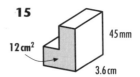

12 cm^2 45 mm 3.6 cm

16

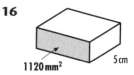

1120 mm^2 5 cm

17

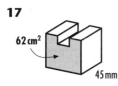

62 cm^2 45 mm

18

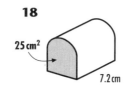

25 cm^2 7.2 cm

19

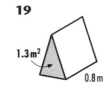

1.3 m^2 0.8 m

20

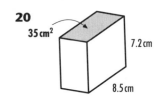

35 cm^2 7.2 cm 8.5 cm

Exercise 65B

Calculate the volume of each of these prisms.

1 Area of cross-section = 15 cm^2, length = 4 cm

2 Area of cross-section = 72 cm^2, length = 7 cm

3 Area of cross-section = 145 mm^2, length = 24 mm

4 Area of cross-section = 66 cm^2, length = 11 cm

5 Area of cross-section = 2.1 m^2, length = 1.1 m

6 Area of cross-section = 0.75 m^2, length = 0.06 m

7 Area of cross-section = 69 cm^2, length = 21 cm

8 Area of cross-section = 200 mm^2, length = 7.2 cm

9 Area of cross-section = 11.2 cm^2, length = 6.5 cm

10 Area of cross-section = 0.95 m^2, length = 80 cm

11 Area of cross-section = 24.7 cm^2, length = 40 mm

12 Area of cross-section = 1150 mm^2, length = 66 mm

13

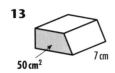

50 cm^2 7 cm

14

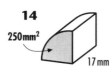

250mm^2 17 mm

15

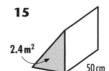

2.4 m^2 50 cm

16

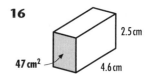

2.5 cm 47 cm^2 4.6 cm

17

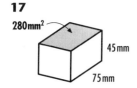

280mm^2 45 mm 75 mm

18

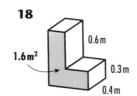

0.6 m 1.6 m^2 0.3 m 0.4 m

19

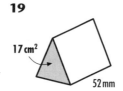

17 cm^2 52 mm

20

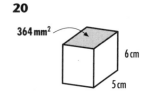

364 mm^2 6 cm 5 cm

EXAMPLE

▶ The volume of a prism is 576 cm³. If the height of the prism is 16 cm, calculate the area of the cross-section.

$V = Al$ or Ah
So $576 = A \times 16$
So $A = 576 \div 16 = 36$ cm²

EXAMPLE

▶ The volume of a prism is 600 cm³ and the area of the cross-section is 132 cm². Calculate the length of the prism.

$V = Al$
So $600 = 132 \times l$
So $l = 600 \div 132$
$= 4.5454... = 4.55$ cm (to 3 s.f.)

Exercise 65C

Fill in the missing values in the table.

	Volume of prism	Area of cross-section	Length of prism
1	340 cm³	17 cm²	cm
2	2.2 m³	m²	20 m
3	75 cm³	cm²	3 cm
4	560 mm³	35 mm²	mm
5	400 cm³	cm²	8 cm
6	1.05 m³	3 m²	m
7	36 cm³	4.5 cm²	cm
8	1200 mm³	mm²	15 mm
9	70 cm³	cm²	4 cm
10	2.5 m³	m²	1.25 m

11 The volume of a prism is 18 cm³ and its area of cross-section is 12 cm²; find the length of the prism.

12 The length of a prism is 20 mm and its volume is 5000 mm³; find the area of the cross-section of the prism.

13 The volume of a prism is 99 cm³ and length of the prism is 2.75 cm; find the area of the cross-section of the prism.

14 The volume of a prism is 44 cm³ and its area of cross-section is 5.5 cm²; find the length of the prism.

15 The area of cross-section of a prism is 3.2 m² and the volume is 0.8 m³; find the length of the prism.

16 The length of a prism is 1.25 m and the volume is 5.5 m³; find the area of the cross-section of the prism.

17 The volume of a prism is 125 cm³ and its area of cross-section is 100 cm²; find the length of the prism.

18 The volume of a prism is 480 mm³ and its area of cross-section is 80 mm²; find the length of the prism.

19 The area of cross-section of a prism is 1.5 mm² and the volume is 600 mm³; find the length of the prism.

20 The volume of a prism is 3.2 m³ and the length of the prism is 25 m; find the area of the cross-section of the prism.

Exercise 65D

Fill in the missing values in the table.

	Volume of prism	Area of cross-section	Length of prism
1	$84 \, cm^3$	cm^2	$4 \, cm$
2	$56 \, cm^3$	$32 \, cm^2$	cm
3	$540 \, mm^3$	$600 \, mm^2$	mm
4	$1.6 \, m^3$	m^2	$0.5 \, m$
5	$27 \, cm^3$	cm^2	$1.5 \, cm$
6	$4500 \, mm^3$	$500 \, mm^2$	mm
7	$72 \, cm^3$	cm^2	$80 \, cm$
8	$3.2 \, m^3$	$0.02 \, m^2$	m
9	$46 \, cm^3$	cm^2	$4 \, cm$
10	$78 \, cm^3$	$13 \, cm^2$	cm

11 The volume of a prism is $3000 \, mm^3$ and its area of cross-section is $200 \, mm^2$; find the length of the prism.

12 The length of a prism is $1.5 \, m$ and the volume is $1.8 \, m^3$; find the area of the cross-section of the prism.

13 The volume of a prism is $54 \, cm^3$ and the length of the prism is $4.5 \, cm$; find the area of the cross-section of the prism.

14 The volume of a prism is $310 \, cm^3$ and its area of cross-section is $62 \, cm^2$; find the length of the prism.

15 The area of the cross-section of a prism is $6 \, cm^2$ and the volume is $15 \, cm^3$; find the length of the prism.

16 The length of a prism is $16 \, mm$ and the volume is $320 \, mm^3$; find the area of the cross-section of the prism.

17 The volume of a prism is $175 \, mm^3$ and its area of cross-section is $2.5 \, mm^2$; find the length of the prism.

18 The area of the cross-section of a prism is $5.2 \, m^2$ and the volume is $11 \, m^3$; find the length of the prism.

19 The volume of a prism is $0.54 \, m^3$ and the length of the prism is $0.675 \, m$; find the area of the cross-section of the prism.

20 The length of a prism is $32 \, mm$ and its volume is $1600 \, mm^3$; find the area of the cross-section of the prism.

66/ VOLUME OF A PRISM, INCLUDING THE CYLINDER

The volume of a prism is given by the formula:

$V = Al$

where l is the length (or height) and A is the area of the cross-section of the prism.
If A is not given, then you will need to calculate it using the appropriate formula for the shape of the cross-section.

EXAMPLE

▶ Calculate the volume of the triangular prism in the diagram.

Area of cross-section, $A = \frac{1}{2}bh$

$= \frac{1}{2} \times 4 \times 5 = 10 \, cm^2$

$V = Al$

$= 10 \times 7 = 70 \, cm^3$

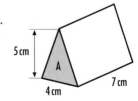

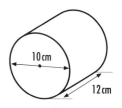
Exercise 66A

Calculate the volume of each of the prisms. Answer to 3 significant figures where necessary.

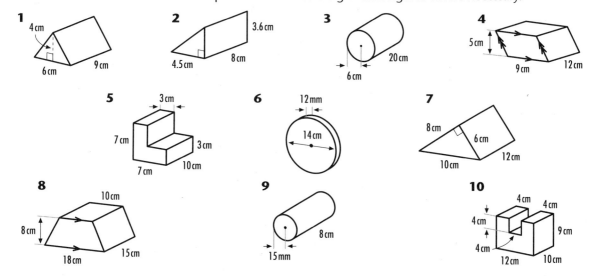

1 4 cm, 6 cm, 9 cm

2 3.6 cm, 4.5 cm, 8 cm

3 20 cm, 6 cm

4 5 cm, 9 cm, 12 cm

5 3 cm, 7 cm, 3 cm, 7 cm, 10 cm

6 12 mm, 14 cm

7 8 cm, 6 cm, 10 cm, 12 cm

8 10 cm, 8 cm, 18 cm, 15 cm

9 8 cm, 15 mm

10 4 cm, 4 cm, 4 cm, 4 cm, 12 cm, 10 cm, 9 cm

11 A prism of length 5 cm has a triangular cross-section of height 3 cm and base 4 cm. Calculate its volume.

12 Calculate the volume of a cylinder of radius 6.3 cm and height 12.5 cm.

13 Calculate the volume of a prism of length 15 cm if the cross-section is a rhombus with diagonals of length 8 cm and 6 cm.

14 Calculate the volume of a cylinder of diameter 8.6 cm and height 10 cm.

15 The cross-section of a prism is a trapezium with parallel sides of length 5 cm and 9 cm; the distance between these parallel lines is 6 cm. Calculate the volume of the prism if its length is 8 cm.

16 Calculate the volume of a cylinder of radius 125 mm and height 102 mm. Answer in cm^3.

17 The volume of a cylinder, of radius 5 cm, is 864 cm^3. Calculate the length of the cylinder.

18 A prism has a volume of 252 cm^3. The cross-section is a parallelogram of height 4 cm. If the length of the prism is 9 cm, calculate the length of the base of the parallelogram.

19 Calculate the volume of a cylinder of diameter 4.8 cm and length 9.5 cm.

20 The cross-section of a prism is a right-angled triangle with sides of length 6 cm, 8 cm and 10 cm. The length of the prism is 12 cm. Calculate (a) the area of the cross-section (b) the volume of the prism.

Exercise 66B

Calculate the volume of each of the prisms. Answer to 3 significant figures where necessary.

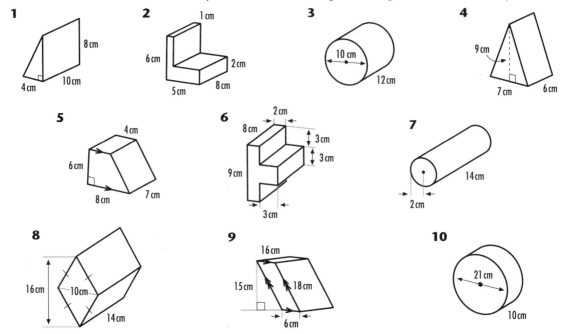

11 Calculate the volume of a prism of length 8 cm if the cross-section is a triangle of height 6 cm and base 9 cm.

12 Calculate the volume of a cylinder of radius 4 cm and height 10 cm.

13 Calculate the volume of a prism of height 14 cm if the cross-section is a kite with diagonals of length 8 cm and 11 cm.

14 Calculate the volume of a cylinder of diameter 2.4 cm and height 3.5 cm.

15 The volume of a prism is 21 cm^3 and the cross-section has an area of 300 mm^2. Calculate the length of the prism.

16 A prism of length 21 cm has a cross-section which is a parallelogram. If the base of the parallelogram is of length 7 cm and of height 6 cm, calculate the volume of the prism.

17 Calculate the volume of a cylinder of diameter 62 mm and height 98 mm. Answer in cm^3.

18 The volume of a cylinder is 1197 cm^3. If the radius is 6.3 cm, calculate the length of the cylinder to the nearest mm.

19 Calculate the volume of a cylinder of radius 0.5 m and height 1.2 m.

20 The cross-section of a prism is a trapezium with parallel sides of length 124 mm and 102 mm. The distance between these parallel sides is 62 mm. If the prism has a height of 3.6 cm, calculate its volume (a) in mm^3 (b) in cm^3.

When calculating the surface area of a shape, it is often helpful to draw a net of the shape.

EXAMPLE

▶ Calculate the surface area of the cuboid in the diagram.

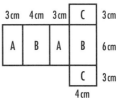

You can see that there are two of each of the rectangles A, B and C.

A = 3 × 6 = 18 cm²   B = 4 × 6 = 24 cm²
C = 3 × 4 = 12 cm²
A + B + C = 54 cm² so total area = 54 × 2 = 108 cm²

Or, you can say that there are two C areas and a large rectangle which measures 14 cm × 6 cm.

EXAMPLE

▶ Calculate the surface area of the triangular prism shown in the diagram.

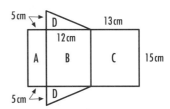

The hypotenuse of the triangle is given by $h^2 = 5^2 + 12^2$
$h^2 = 25 + 144 = 169$
So $h = 13$ cm, which is the width of rectangle C.

The net shows that the prism has five areas that make up the total surface area.
A + B + C = (5 + 12 + 13) × 15 = 30 × 15 = 450 cm²
D = $\frac{1}{2}$ × 5 × 12 = 30 cm² (Remember: there are two of area D.)
Total surface area = 450 + 30 + 30 = 510 cm²

Exercise 67A

Find the total surface area of each of the shapes. Answer to 3 significant figures where necessary.

1

5 cm   5 cm   5 cm

2

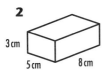

3 cm   5 cm   8 cm

3

8 cm   1.5 cm   12 cm

4

4 cm   5 cm   6 cm   9 cm

5

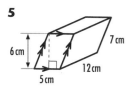

6 cm   7 cm   12 cm   5 cm

6

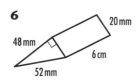

20 mm   48 mm   6 cm   52 mm

7

3 cm   5 cm   4 cm   6 cm   7 cm

8

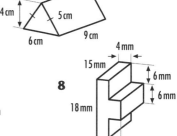

4 mm   15 mm   6 mm   6 mm   18 mm   4 mm

9

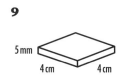

5 mm
4 cm   4 cm

10

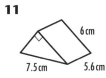

2.04 m
1.8 m
2.2 m
2.0 m   2.8 m

11

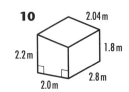

6 cm
7.5 cm   5.6 cm

12

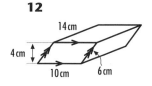

14 cm
4 cm
10 cm   6 cm

Exercise 67B

Find the total surface area of each of the shapes. Answer to 3 significant figures where necessary.

1

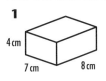

4 cm
7 cm   8 cm

2

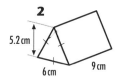

5.2 cm
6 cm   9 cm

3

4.5 cm

4

7 cm
2 cm   5 cm

5

2 cm
10 cm   4 cm
8 cm
6 cm

6

7 cm
3 cm   7 cm

7

8 cm
42 mm

8

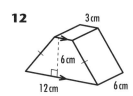

4 cm   4 cm
4 cm
12 cm   8 cm
12 cm

9

32 mm
75 mm
24 mm

10

8 cm
10 cm   15 cm

11

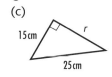

3.5 m
3.0 m
4.2 m
1.2 m

12

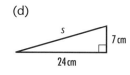

3 cm
6 cm
12 cm   6 cm

REVISION

Exercise F

1 Calculate the unknown lengths marked in the diagrams.

(a)

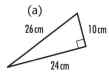

6 cm
8 cm
p

(b)

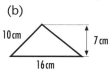

12 cm   13 cm
q

(c)

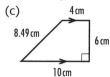

15 cm   r
25 cm

(d)

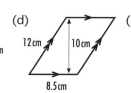

s   7 cm
24 cm

2 Calculate the area of each of the shapes in the diagrams.

(a)

26 cm   10 cm
24 cm

(b)

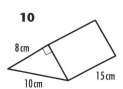

10 cm   7 cm
16 cm

(c)

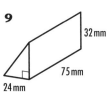

4 cm
8.49 cm   6 cm
10 cm

(d)

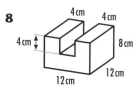

12 cm   10 cm
8.5 cm

(e)

32 mm

3 Give your answer to 3 significant figures in each of the following.
  (a) Calculate the circumference of a circle of diameter 12 cm.
  (b) Calculate the area of a circle of radius 7 cm.
  (c) Calculate the area of a circle of diameter 10 m.
  (d) Calculate the circumference of a circle of radius 15 mm.

4 Calculate the volume of each of the following:
  (a) a cube of edge length 5 cm   (b) a cuboid measuring 2.5 cm × 4 cm × 6 cm.

5 Calculate the volume and the total surface area of the following.

(a)
2 cm
50 mm   6 cm

(b)
10.8 cm²
5 cm   7 cm

(c)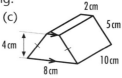
2 cm
5 cm
4 cm
8 cm
10 cm

6 Calculate the volume of a cylinder of height 8 cm and diameter 6 cm.

Exercise FF

1 The cuboid ABCDEFGH shown in the diagram has edge lengths AD = 5 cm, DC = 6 cm and CG = 8 cm. Calculate (a) DG (b) AG.

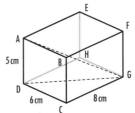
E
A   F
H
5 cm
B
G
D
6 cm   8 cm
C

B
0
X
A

2 X is the midpoint of the chord AB shown in the diagram. The distance OX is 35 mm and the radius of the circle is 55 mm. Find the length of the chord AB.

3 A rope is used to hold the vertical pole of a tent in place. It is fixed to a point on the pole 2.4 metres above the ground. The other end of the rope is fixed to a point on the ground 1.7 metres from the base of the pole.
(a) Calculate the length of the rope when it is taut.
(b) If the fixing point on the ground was moved 50 cm nearer the base of the pole, how much would the rope need to be shortened in order to keep it taut?

4 A triangle has an area of 23.5 cm² and a base length of 5 cm. Calculate the height.

5 A circle of diameter 30 cm is cut out of a rectangle measuring 40 cm by 45 cm.
(a) Calculate the area of the rectangle that remains.
(b) Express this area as a percentage of the original rectangle.

6 A wheel is required to move 2 metres along the ground when rotated once. Calculate the diameter of the wheel.

7 A rectangular tank (cuboid) has a base which measures 60 cm by 52 cm. If the water in the tank is 35 cm deep, calculate the following.
(a) the volume of the water in cm³   (b) the volume of the water in m³
(c) the quantity of water in litres.

8 Calculate the volume of each of the prisms shown.

(a)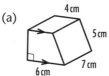
4 cm
5 cm
6 cm   7 cm

(b)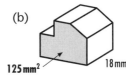
125 mm²   18 mm

9 The whole of a rectangular shaped room is to be painted except the floor (that is, ignoring windows and doors, etc.). If the room measures 5.5 metres by 3.4 metres and is 2.4 metres high, calculate the area to be painted.

10 A triangular prism has a length of 12 cm. The triangle is right-angled and the lengths of two of its sides are known to be 5 cm and 13 cm.
(a) If one of these two lengths was the hypotenuse, which of the two lengths would it be?
(b) Draw two sketches of the triangle, one sketch with the hypotenuse known and one sketch with the hypotenuse unknown.
(c) Calculate the area of each of the two possible triangles.
(d) Calculate the volume of each the two prisms possible.
(e) Calculate the total surface area of the prism in each case.

Handling data

68/ CONTINUOUS DATA: CREATING FREQUENCY TABLES AND FREQUENCY DIAGRAMS

Discrete data is information that can only be measured in definite steps (normally whole numbers).
Examples of discrete data are:
The number of children in a family – '2.4 children', for example, has no meaning.
The size of a shoe – these increase in steps: 7, $7\frac{1}{2}$, 8, etc. but 8.2, 8.25, 8.27 … have no meaning.

Continuous data includes all types of data derived from *measurement* (for example 6.1 m, 4.5 kg, 9.55 seconds).
Continuous data can be grouped together in frequency tables so that the information is easier to understand.

EXAMPLE

▶ Group this continuous data in a frequency table. The data represents masses (*M*) in kilograms.

545	408	401	585	320	158	300	254	500	480
67	420	315	476	705	645	710	267	562	125
463	695	700	525	275	538	644	436	756	532
429	636	349	683	632	320	450	588	365	466

Mass M (kg)	Tally	Frequency
$0 \le M < 100$	I	1
$100 \le M < 200$	II	2
$200 \le M < 300$	III	3
$300 \le M < 400$	⫴⫴ I	6
$400 \le M < 500$	⫴⫴ ⫴⫴	10
$500 \le M < 600$	⫴⫴ III	8
$600 \le M < 700$	⫴⫴ I	6
$700 \le M < 800$	IIII	4
	Total	40

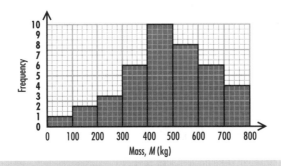

The group $100 \leq M < 200$ (mass includes 100 kg, and up to *but not including,* 200 kg) is a **class interval**. The table is called a **frequency table**.

The frequency table can be shown as a bar chart, which can also be called a **frequency diagram**.

Note: The horizontal axis should show a continuous scale.

Exercise 68A

For each set of continuous data (a) draw and complete a frequency table (b) draw a frequency diagram.

1 The ages of the people staying in a hostel for the homeless are recorded *to the nearest year.*

18	34	21	23	48	24	62	24	47	22
57	19	53	46	27	18	70	73	17	19
51	39	35	19	24	18	32	28	62	36
23	25	32	43						

Use class intervals $10 \leq A < 20$ years, etc.

2 The speeds of cars passing through a country village are recorded to the nearest mile per hour.

37	33	29	19	34	28	33	32	50	39
28	41	37	31	52	19	35	43	28	32
34	29	57	32	41	67	44	37	34	42
41	35	28	42	35	38	32	27	32	29

Use class intervals $10 \leq S < 20$ m.p.h. etc.

3 A pochard is a small attractive duck which is in danger of disappearing from south-east England. As part of a survey the lengths of a number of these birds are measured and recorded to the nearest centimetre.

39	38	29	47	31	45	34	40	46	41
41	43	53	32	48	43	33	46	44	42
44	37	40	50	35	47	48	37	49	38
52	42								

Use class intervals $25 \leq L < 30$ cm etc.

4 The amounts left at the bottom of glasses of drink in a café are measured and recorded to the nearest millilitre.

33	35	12	10	38	5	9	19	21	10
43	4	5	17	8	4	27	1	51	15
15	17	12	44	26	11	8	20	4	24
12	8	24	45	36	13	24	15	51	25

Use class intervals $0 \leq v < 10$ ml, etc.

5 The distances (in metres) achieved by athletes throwing the discus are recorded.

54.38	51.45	57.69	44.55	36.24	49.54	53.23	54.37	48.78	58.37
47.62	54.40	43.70	59.61	58.25	59.95	55.67	42.37	57.05	61.16
44.75	46.09	57.45	47.60	56.27	48.00	39.76	56.78	55.45	61.09
57.96	50.05	52.37	48.95	59.24					

Use class intervals $35 \leq d < 40$ m, etc.

6 The heights of a group of 3-year-old trees are measured and recorded in metres.

0.75	2.07	2.12	1.23	1.64	0.67	1.85	1.27	2.45	2.33
2.30	2.01	0.98	2.10	2.39	2.00	2.15	2.27	2.09	1.45
2.12	2.25	2.34	1.36	2.34	2.19	2.49	2.10	1.02	2.38
2.45									

Use class intervals $0.50 \leq h < 1.00$ m, etc.

7 A machine weighs out 40 grams of a chemical to be put into packets. Samples from the machine are reweighed accurately to 0.01 g. The results are listed below.

39.93	39.82	39.96	40.02	40.05	39.96	39.80	40.11	40.29	39.85
40.14	39.80	40.19	40.14	39.75	40.12	40.01	40.12	40.37	40.09
40.02	40.13	39.65	40.06	40.02	40.01	39.95	40.04	39.85	40.21
39.93	40.07	39.98	39.75	40.03	39.99				

Use class intervals $39.6 \leq m < 39.7$ g, etc.

8 The area of carpet (square metres) sold to each customer in a morning is noted.

6.4	13.6	7.1	9.8	7.5	10.2	9.0	5.6	8.2	10.4
26.7	3.4	20.2	8.6	10.6	3.1	7.0	6.4	2.7	14.4
7.6	25.3	7.8	18.0	7.4	6.7	18.9	4.3	12.1	8.9
4.1	14.8	21.4	4.2	12.0	10.1	8.9	9.6	5.2	12.4
15.6	6.3	8.6	11.3	5.7	3.2	15.6	6.2	9.7	7.2

Use class intervals $0 \leq a < 5\,\text{m}^2$, etc.

9 The heights of 40 small children are noted to the nearest centimetre.

58	60	63	74	82	56	72	59	67	73
80	59	67	82	76	68	71	70	69	59
66	59	64	62	73	78	76	58	60	74
68	67	72	77	80	69				

Choose your own class intervals.

10 The time spent on homework is surveyed. A group of students are asked how many minutes they had spent the previous evening.

25	35	65	75	45	30	25	10	75	65
75	45	35	30	90	5	50	45	60	75
90	80	50	45	35	15	20	35	40	85
75	95	5							

Choose your own class intervals.

Exercise 68B

For each set of continuous data (a) draw and complete a frequency table (b) draw a frequency diagram.

1 A tropical fish breeder measures the lengths of one-year-old flag tetras to the nearest millimetre.

42	50	44	51	45	56	52	47	45	35
45	49	55	48	49	36	58	45	46	47
43	54	63	52	54	48	49	45	46	41
47	45	40	38	49	42	39	50	46	51

Use class intervals $35 \leq L < 40$ mm, etc.

2 As part of a scientific experiment the mass of randomly selected tomatoes is recorded to the nearest gram.

62	53	41	50	63	72	116	69	81	63
90	59	74	115	49	81	65	90	54	100
63	76	69	54	72	67	108	69	94	47
55	70	83	57	64					

Use class intervals of $40 \leq m < 50$ g, etc.

3 An amateur weather forecaster records the rainfall for each month over a period of 3 years. He records these values to the nearest millimetre.

67	11	64	45	12	40	50	31	34	29
101	23	105	51	25	15	43	83	44	6
80	55	18	54	72	24	75	27	47	37
96	20	59	35	64	18				

Use class intervals of $0 \leq R < 20$ mm, etc.

4   Pupils carry out a survey of the heights of the members of their class. These are measured to the nearest centimetre.

153	133	164	136	160	156	177	166	152	177
146	150	169	143	148	152	163	183	166	162
171	161	140	181	143	165	150	162	152	165
158	167								

Use class intervals of $130 \leq H < 140\,\text{cm}$, etc.

5   The average yield per square metre of various randomly selected areas of several fields are calculated to the nearest 0.1 kg.

1.7	2.8	3.2	1.5	1.1	2.4	1.8	2.5	2.6	3.8
3.2	2.0	3.1	2.3	3.4	2.1	1.0	3.7	3.3	4.4
3.1	2.0	1.2	2.1	3.7	3.9	2.5	2.9	2.6	4.4
2.5	3.9	3.3	4.8	3.1	2.5	3.6	3.9	2.6	4.3

Use class intervals of $1.0 \leq Y < 1.5\,\text{kg}$, etc.

6   As part of a survey the handspan of each pupil in a class is measured in centimetres (to the nearest millimetre).

14.2	17.7	18.1	12.0	16.6	16.7	17.2	19.6	15.2	18.9
22.0	14.3	17.7	19.2	17.4	13.5	14.0	17.4	21.1	19.7
16.8	20.0	21.5	16.9	12.9	17.3	15.7	16.6	16.0	18.4
23.4	19.5	17.8							

Use class intervals of $12 \leq S < 14\,\text{cm}$, etc.

7   The times for the athletes in the heats of the 100 m event are recorded to the nearest 0.01 s.

10.64	10.90	11.48	10.51	10.79	10.60	10.86	10.72	11.09	10.86
10.70	10.78	10.75	11.36	10.73	10.87	10.53	11.15	10.75	10.73
10.70	10.61	10.87	10.94	10.78	11.26	10.72	10.81	10.73	10.80
10.62	10.61								

Use class intervals of $10.5 \leq t < 10.6\,\text{s}$, etc.

8   The midday temperature (to the nearest °C) at a resort is noted every day for two months.

29	28	30	30	31	29	28	27	27	26
28	25	22	20	19	19	18	18	19	24
25	28	28	29	30	30	31	32	35	35
36	37	35	35	31	30	28	27	27	26
27	25	25	28	30	31	32	30	24	25
26	26	29	30	33	34	36	32	30	24
24	23								

Use class intervals of $15 \leq T < 20°\text{C}$, etc.

9   A machine is designed to deliver 25 ml of a chemical into bottles. As part of a quality control exercise samples are taken and measured to the nearest 0.1 ml.

25.2	25.6	24.8	25.2	25.0	25.1	24.9	23.9	24.2	25.9
25.8	24.2	24.5	24.6	25.0	25.5	24.0	26.0	24.2	25.3
25.7	24.8	26.1	25.2	24.3	23.8	26.5	24.9	25.1	25.5
24.6	24.4	25.6	24.8	25.0					

Use class intervals that you feel are appropriate.

10 The number of miles travelled by each car in a company fleet during a particular week is noted to the nearest mile.

98	254	535	898	149	100	237	749	205	581
320	298	749	512	265	393	505	632	517	636
208	554	162	206	390	215	482	122	75	857
603	589	480	600	395	108	168	435	382	317
125	283	552	628	322	470	209	113		

Use class intervals that you feel are appropriate.

69/ CONTINUOUS DATA: INTERPRETING FREQUENCY DIAGRAMS

In order to draw frequency diagrams for continuous data, it is necessary to group the data together within **class intervals**.

The heights of people could be grouped together as 150 cm $\leq h <$ 160 cm, 160 cm $\leq h <$ 170 cm, 170 cm $\leq h <$ 180 cm, etc. (where h stands for heights).

The class interval 150 cm $\leq h <$ 160 cm includes $h =$ 150 cm and all values of h up to, *but not including,* 160 cm.

EXAMPLE

▶ Paul draws a graph of the rainfall per day (in mm) over the period of time that he has been keeping records. Use the graph to answer the following questions.

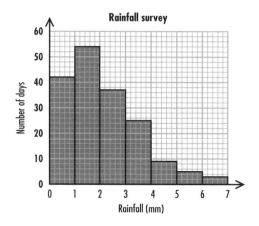

(a) How long has Paul been keeping records?
(b) During this period there were 23 days without rain. How many other days were there with less than 1 mm of rain?
(c) On how many days was there 3 mm or more of rain?
(d) What percentage of days have less than 2 mm of rain?

(a) 42 + 54 + 37 + 25 + 9 + 5 + 3 = 175 days
(b) 42 − 23 = 19 days
(c) 25 + 9 + 5 + 3 = 42 days
(d) Number of days with less than 2 mm of rain = 96
   Percentage = $\frac{96}{175} \times 100 = 54.9\%$

Exercise 69A

1 The quantity of petrol (litres) sold per hour by a small garage is noted over a period of 14 days. A frequency diagram is drawn to show these results (class intervals $0 \leq p < 500$ litres per hour, etc.). Use the frequency diagram to answer the following.

(a) The garage stays open for the same amount of time each day. How many hours is it open each day?

(b) The manager of the garage calculates that it makes a profit if the sales are 1000 litres or more per hour. During how many hours does the garage not make a profit?

(c) Calculate the percentage of hours when sales are 2000 litres or more.

(d) During how many hours are sales less than 25 litres per minute?

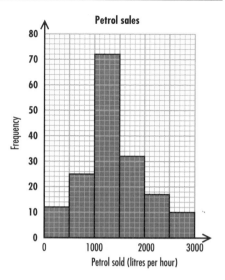

2 The weights of students are surveyed as part of a 'Health Week'. Use the frequency diagram (class intervals $40 \leq w < 45$ kg, etc.) to answer the following.

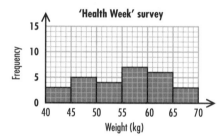

(a) How many students are there in the group?

(b) What is the range of each class interval?

(c) How many of the students weigh 55 kg or more?

(d) What percentage of the group weigh less than 50 kg?

3 The time for each competitor in the heats of the 100 m race is recorded and the results are plotted as a frequency diagram (class intervals $10.8 \leq t < 10.9$ s, etc.).
Use the frequency diagram to answer the following.

(a) How many competitors are there?

(b) The competitor who was second in one of the heats was timed at 10.87 s. In how many of the other heats was the winner's time less than 10.9 s?

(c) How many competitors failed to run the race in less than 11.3 s?

(d) What percentage of the competitors had times of less than 11.0 s?

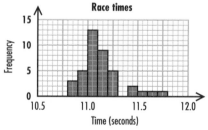

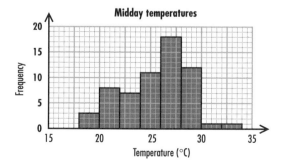

4 The midday temperatures are noted over a period of two calendar months at a holiday resort. Use the frequency diagram of the results (class intervals $18 \leq T < 20°C$, etc.) to answer the following.

(a) One of the months is July. What is the other one, June or August? Give a reason for your answer.

(b) What is the range of each class interval?

(c) On how many days is the midday temperature less than 24°C?

(d) Calculate what percentage of the days had a midday temperature of 30°C or more.

5 A machine is designed to weigh out 100 g of salt but a survey of randomly chosen samples shows that it is not very accurate. The results of the survey are shown as a frequency diagram (class intervals $85 \le w < 90$ g, etc.); use this to answer the following.

(a) How many samples are there?

(b) How many of the samples weigh less than 100 g?

(c) If 11 of the samples appear to weigh exactly 100 g, how many samples are there with weights between 100 and 110 g?

(d) What percentage of the samples weigh less than 100 g?

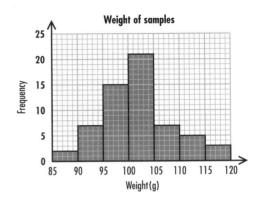

6 The ages of a group of people occupying the ground floor flats on an estate are noted and the information used to draw the frequency diagram (class intervals $0 \le y < 10$ years ,etc.). Use this to answer the following.

(a) How many people are there in the group?

(b) How many of the group are 60 years old or older?

(c) Two of the group have their 30th birthdays on the day of the survey. How many other people are 30 years old or more but less than 40?

(d) What percentage of the group are less than 20 years old?

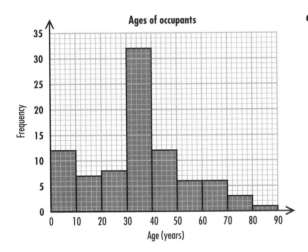

Exercise 69B

1 The distances thrown by competitors in a discus throwing event are listed and recorded in the form of a frequency diagram (class intervals $25 \le d < 30$ metres, etc.).
Use this to answer the following.

(a) How many throws are there?

(b) Three of the throws appeared to measure exactly 45 metres. How many throws are there *between* 45 and 50 metres?

(c) How many of the throws are less than 40 metres?

(d) What percentage of the throws are 50 metres or more?

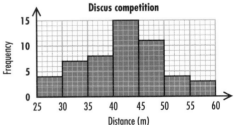

2 Michael keeps records of the weather over a period of 72 days. He draws a frequency diagram to show the frequency of the number of hours of sunshine per day (class intervals $0 \le h < 2$ hours, etc.). He accidentally misses out one class interval.

(a) How many days have less than 2 hours sunshine?

(b) The highest value is 11.7 hours. Which class interval has Michael missed out of the frequency diagram?

(c) How many days are there within this missing class interval?

(d) What fraction of the days have less than 6 hours sunshine?

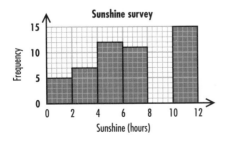

3 A machine is designed to fill sacks with 50 kg of fertiliser. As part of a quality control exercise a random sample of sacks is taken and each is reweighed. These weights (kg) are noted and a frequency diagram is drawn (class intervals $44 \leq w < 46$ kg, etc.). Use this to answer the following.

(a) How many sacks are reweighed?
(b) What is the range of each class interval?
(c) Five sacks appear to weigh exactly 52 kg. How many sacks weighed more than 52 kg?
(d) What percentage of the sample weigh less than 50 kg?

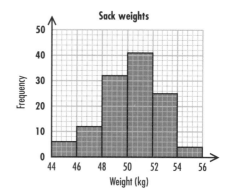

4 A scientist is trying to develop a tall variety of a plant. As part of her work she measures the height (cm) of each plant in a group of the plants. The results of this work are plotted (class intervals $45 \leq p < 50$ cm, etc.). Use this frequency diagram to answer the following.

(a) How many plants are measured?
(b) The scientist wants plants to be 70 cm tall or more. How many of the plants reach this standard?
(c) Seven of the plants appear to measure 50 cm exactly. How many other plants are in this class interval?
(d) What fraction of the plants are less than 60 cm tall?

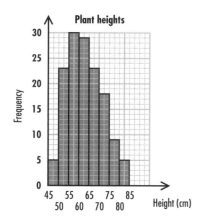

5 The times for a cross-country event are noted and are used to produce the frequency diagram shown (class intervals $30 \leq T < 40$ min, etc.). Answer the following by using the frequency diagram.

(a) How many runners took part in the cross-country?
(b) If one runner was timed at exactly 80 minutes, how many took more than 80 minutes?
(c) How many runners took one hour or more to complete the course?
(d) What percentage of the runners completed the course in less than an hour?

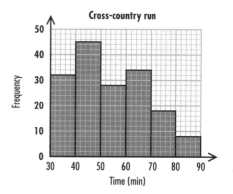

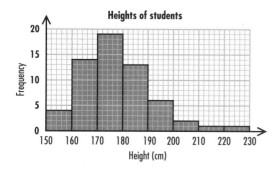

6 The height of each of a group of students is measured and recorded. This information is shown as a frequency diagram (class intervals $150 \leq h < 160$ cm, etc.). Use this to answer the following.

(a) How many students are there in the group?
(b) What is the range of each class interval?
(c) How many students are less than 1.700 m tall?
(d) What percentage of the students have heights of 180 cm or more?

A **frequency** polygon can be constructed by plotting the midpoint of the top of each column of a bar graph or frequency diagram. The points are then joined with straight lines. It is necessary to *close* the polygon; the two points that do this are shown with an asterisk (*) on Graph A. They are on the midpoints of empty columns.

When the scale on the horizontal axis is in the middle of each column, it is easier to plot the frequency polygon as in Graph B.

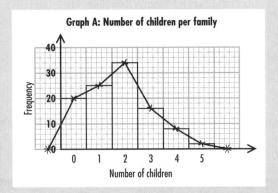

Graph A: Number of children per family

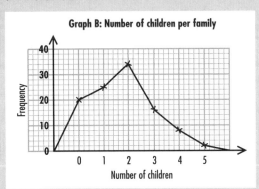

Graph B: Number of children per family

Note: It is not necessary to draw the frequency diagram first; this just helps you to understand the idea behind a frequency polygon.

EXAMPLE

▶ Paul records the rainfall per day (in mm) over a period of time. He creates a frequency table to show this data.

Rainfall (mm)	$0 \leq r < 1$	$1 \leq r < 2$	$2 \leq r < 3$	$3 \leq r < 4$	$4 \leq r < 5$	$5 \leq r < 6$	$6 \leq r < 7$
Frequency	42	54	37	25	9	5	3

Show this information as a frequency polygon.

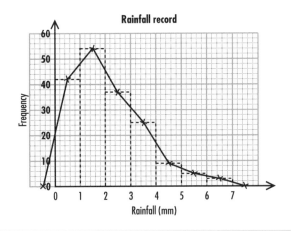

Exercise 70A

In each question draw the frequency polygon to show the data in the frequency table provided.

1 A poor quality dice is thrown 100 times and the score noted.

Score on dice	1	2	3	4	5	6
Frequency	12	18	17	25	19	9

Use 2 cm to represent each score on the dice and 2 cm to represent 10 on the vertical axis.

2 Five coins are thrown and the number of heads obtained is noted.

Number of heads	0	1	2	3	4	5
Frequency	6	23	45	42	24	5

Use 1 cm to represent each horizontal unit and 2 cm to represent 10 on the vertical axis.

3 The length of each word in a paragraph of a book is recorded.

Word length (number of letters)	1	2	3	4	5	6	7	8	9	10
Frequency	8	10	28	21	14	12	7	8	0	4

Use 1 cm to represent each horizontal unit and 2 cm to represent 10 on the vertical axis.

4 The marks in a test are:

Mark	1	2	3	4	5	6	7	8	9	10
Frequency	2	4	10	8	10	7	4	3	1	2

Use 1 cm to represent one mark and 2 cm to represent 5 on the vertical axis.

5 The times of runners in a Fun Half Marathon are noted in minutes to the nearest minute.

Time, T (min)	$80 \leq T < 100$	$100 \leq T < 120$	$120 \leq T < 140$	$140 \leq T < 160$	$160 \leq T < 180$	$180 \leq T < 200$
Frequency	12	63	56	45	21	11

Use 1 cm to represent 10 minutes and 1 cm to represent 10 on the vertical axis.

6 The ages of passengers on a day trip are noted.

Age, A (years)	$0 \leq A < 5$	$5 \leq A < 10$	$10 \leq A < 15$	$15 \leq A < 20$	$20 \leq A < 25$	$25 \leq A < 30$	$30 \leq A < 35$
Frequency	3	5	8	8	6	4	1

Use 2 cm to represent 10 years and 2 cm to represent 2 on the vertical axis.

7 Ria keeps records of the rainfall per week over a period of three years.

Rainfall, w per week (mm)	$0 \leq w < 10$	$10 \leq w < 20$	$20 \leq w < 30$	$30 \leq w < 40$	$40 \leq w < 50$	$50 \leq w < 60$	$60 \leq w < 70$
Frequency	20	4	41	25	8	5	3

Use 2 cm to represent 20 mm of rainfall and 2 cm to represent 10 on the vertical axis.

Exercise 70B

In each question draw the frequency polygon to show the data in the frequency table provided.

1 The number of rainy days in each month is noted over the period of a year.

Month	Jan.	Feb.	Mar.	Apr.	May	Jun.	Jul.	Aug.	Sep.	Oct.	Nov.	Dec.
Days	23	18	13	21	9	4	7	14	5	21	13	14

Use 1 cm to represent each month and 2 cm to represent 10 on the vertical axis.

2 A bowler notes the number of runs scored off each over that he bowls over a season.

Number of runs	0	1	2	3	4	5	6	7	8	9
Frequency	45	54	30	15	20	12	5	6	2	2

Use 1 cm to represent one run and 1 cm to represent 10 on the vertical axis.

3 Two dice are rolled and the total score noted each time.

Total score	2	3	4	5	6	7	8	9	10	11	12
Frequency	4	7	10	13	13	18	11	10	7	4	3

Use 1 cm to represent each score and 2 cm to represent 10 on the vertical axis.

4 Six coins are tossed and the number of tails noted.

Number of tails	0	1	2	3	4	5	6
Frequency	2	13	27	36	24	15	3

Use 2 cm to represent each tail and 2 cm to represent 10 on the vertical axis.

5 The distances thrown by competitors in the discus event are noted.

Distance, d (m)	$25 \leq d < 30$	$30 \leq d < 35$	$35 \leq d < 40$	$40 \leq d < 45$	$45 \leq d < 50$	$50 \leq d < 55$	$55 \leq d < 60$
Frequency	5	8	17	10	9	5	2

Use 2 cm to represent 5 m distance and 2 cm to represent 5 on the vertical axis.

6 The weight of each of a group of pupils is recorded as part of a survey.

Weight, W (kg)	$40 \leq W < 45$	$45 \leq W < 50$	$50 \leq W < 55$	$55 \leq W < 60$	$60 \leq W < 65$	$65 \leq W < 70$
Frequency	2	6	8	9	3	2

Use 2 cm to represent 5 kg and 2 cm to represent 2 on the vertical axis.

7 As part of a survey students are asked how much time they had each spent on their assignment.

Time, T (min)	$60 \leq T < 80$	$80 \leq T < 100$	$100 \leq T < 120$	$120 \leq T < 140$	$140 \leq T < 160$	$160 \leq T < 180$
Frequency	12	25	21	17	14	5

Use 2 cm to represent 20 minutes and 2 cm to represent 10 on the vertical axis.

71/ INTERPRETING AND COMPARING FREQUENCY POLYGONS

▶ The graph shows the performances of a set of students in Assignment 1 and 2

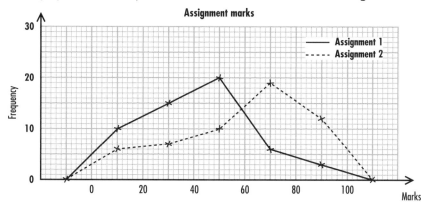

State whether the following statements about the two frequency polygons are *true* or *false*. If you think that a statement is false, state your reason for thinking that it is false.

(a) Five students scored 0 marks in Assignment 1.

(b) The total number of students taking each assignment is the same.

(c) Seven students had scores (S) in the class interval $20 \leq S < 40$ marks for Assignment 2.

(d) Students performed better in Assignment 1 than in Assignment 2.

   (a) False – only the marked points are significant. The lines merely join these points. We know that 10 students scored $0 \leq S < 10$ but we have no other details.

   (b) True

   (c) True

   (d) False – there are more students scoring the high marks in Assignment 2.

Exercise 71A

In each of the following questions study the frequency polygons and say whether the statements about them are *true* or *false*. If you think that a statement is false, state your reason for thinking that it is false.

1 Sam tosses five coins 64 times. He notes the number of tails he gets each time. He plots his results on the same graph as the theoretical results, using the rules of probability.

(a) The theoretical results are symmetrical.

(b) In theory 1 tail is just as likely as 4 tails.

(c) Sam's coins are biased towards tails.

(d) Sam's coins have landed with 3 heads more often than they should in theory.

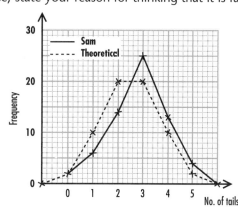

2 The numbers of letters in each of the words in two texts (A and B) are counted.

(a) Text A contains a higher number of short words.

(b) There are more words in Text A.

(c) Text B contains more words with exactly 8 letters.

(d) Text B is probably more difficult to read than Text A.

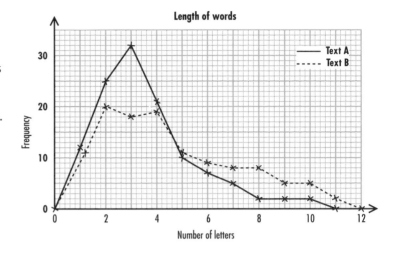

3 The frequency polygons show the progress of two batches of plants which are grown in identical conditions. The heights are measured and then the results are put into class intervals 50 ≤ height < 55 cm, etc.

(a) There are the same number of plants in each batch.

(b) Batch 2 has no plants less than 50 cm in height.

(c) There are more than 10 plants in Batch 2 with heights of 85 cm or more.

(d) Plants in Batch 1 have not grown as tall as those in Batch 2 in general.

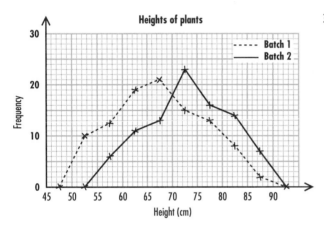

4 The frequency polygons show the distribution of ages in two towns, one in the UK and one in Kenya. The ages are put into class intervals of 0 ≤ age < 10 years, etc.

(a) The total populations of the two towns are approximately the same.

(b) The Kenyan town has a lower percentage in the 10–20 years age group than the UK town.

(c) Most people live far longer in the UK town.

(d) There are approximately 10 000 people aged 40 years in the UK town.

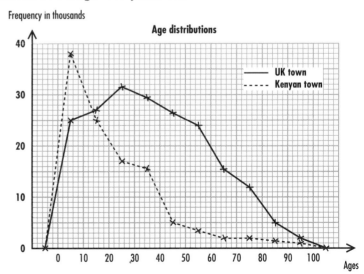

5 Two different groups of people are given the same IQ (intelligence) test. The frequency polygons show the performances of the two groups (A and B) where the results have been placed into classes 70 ≤ IQ < 80, etc.

(a) There are 100 people in each group.
(b) The second test is harder.
(c) Twenty people in group B score 100.
(d) Less people in group A have high scores.

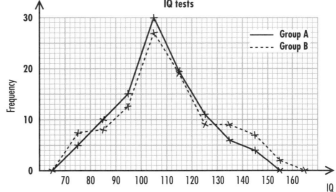

6 Two brands (A and B) of fishing line both claim to have a breaking strain of 0.91 kg. The staff of a magazine decide to test the two brands. They take samples of the line and apply force until each breaks. They note the actual breaking strain in each case and put the results into class intervals 0.87 ≤ breaking strain < 0.88 kg, etc.

(a) The same number of each brand are tested.
(b) More samples of brand A reach the required breaking strain.
(c) Brand B is more predictable.
(d) Twenty-eight samples of brand B broke at 0.895 kg.

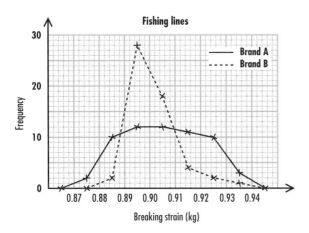

Exercise 71B

In each of the following questions study the frequency polygons and say whether the statements about them are *true* or *false*. If you think that a statement is false, state your reason for thinking that it is false.

1 Two dice (A and B) are rolled and the score on each noted and recorded.

(a) Each of the dice is thrown the same number of times.
(b) A score of 2 was achieved 12 times with dice A.
(c) Dice B appears to be fairer than dice A.
(d) A score of less than 3 was achieved 14 times with dice B.

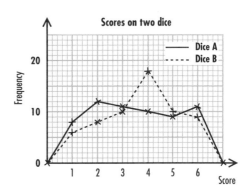

2 The average monthly temperature is recorded in London and Moscow for a period of one year.

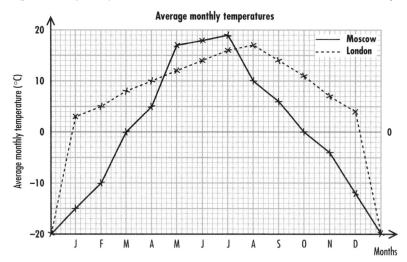

(a) The average monthly temperature in Moscow is higher than the average monthly temperature in London during three months of the year.
(b) The average monthly temperature in Moscow during November is –6°C.
(c) The average monthly temperature in London falls below 0°C for two months in the year.
(d) The greatest difference in average monthly temperature between London and Moscow occurred during May.

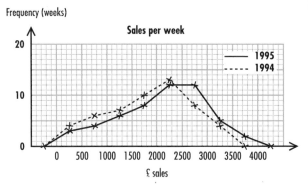

3 The sales per week at a small shop are recorded during 1994 and 1995 and put into class intervals of £0 ≤ sales < £500, etc. per week.

(a) Sales in the early months of both years start badly but both improve in the summer.
(b) The total sales in 1994 are greater than the total sales in 1995.
(c) The lowest amount of sales in a week is £250.
(d) There are 7 weeks in 1995 with sales of £3000 or more per week.

4 Two salespersons, Mrs Lee and Mr How, need to drive considerable distances to reach customers each day. Their distances per day are put into class intervals of 0 ≤ distance < 50 km, etc. and are plotted as frequency polygons.

(a) Since they each work 5 days per week, the graph shows a period of approximately 6 months for Mr How.
(b) Mrs Lee drives for 5 more days during this period than Mr How.
(c) The graph shows that they both drive 275 miles on a particular day.
(d) Mrs Lee has more days than Mr How in which she drives 300 miles or more.

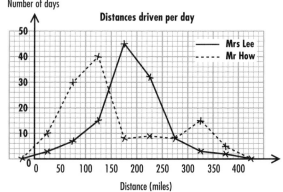

5 The total score for each set of three darts is recorded for two darts players (Bob and Sue) during a tournament. These scores are grouped into class intervals of 0 ≤ score < 20, etc. and plotted as frequency polygons.

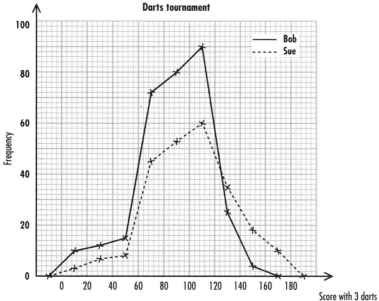

(a) Bob threw more times than Sue.
(b) Sue scored 100 or more a greater number of times than Bob.
(c) The graph shows that Sue scored 180 at least four times.
(d) Approximately 40% of Bob's scores were 100 or more.

6 Two machines (A and B) measure out 25 gram of sugar into packets. Samples from each machine are reweighed and the results placed in groups (21 ≤ weight < 22 g, etc.) and are plotted as frequency polygons.

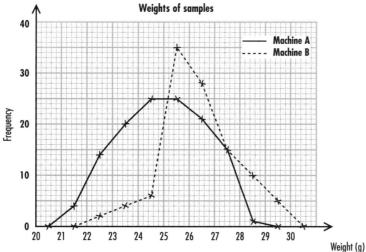

(a) There are the same number of samples from machine B as there are from machine A.
(b) The graph shows that there are an equal number of samples from each machine that weigh 27.5 g.
(c) The graph indicates that about 20% of machine A's packets cannot be sold. Note: Packets containing less than 24 g of sugar cannot be sold.
(d) The graph indicates that over 90% of packets from machine B can be sold.

EXAMPLE

▶ Construct a pie chart to show the number of phone calls made. Use the following values: free calls 12; local calls 135; calls over 10 units 54; calls over 20 units 32.

Total number of calls = 12 + 135 + 54 + 32 = 233

Type of call	Frequency	Angle of sector
Free	12	$\frac{12}{233} \times 360 = 18.54° \approx 18.5°$
Local	135	$\frac{135}{233} \times 360 = 208.58° \approx 208.6°$
Over 10 units	54	$\frac{54}{233} \times 360 = 83.43° \approx 83.4°$
Over 20 units	32	$\frac{32}{233} \times 360 = 49.44° \approx 49.4°$
Total	233	359.9°

You can see that the total of the angles is not exactly 360°. This is due to rounding errors. Angles are normally drawn to the nearest degree.

Although the angles have been written on the pie chart in this example, this is as part of the explanation to the reader. You should not include these values on your pie chart as a usual practice.

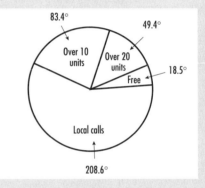

Exercise 72A

In each question create a frequency table which contains an extra column showing the calculated angle (to nearest 0.1° if necessary) for each sector. Use the values in the frequency table to draw the pie chart. Do not forget to give each pie chart a title and to *label* each sector.

1 One hundred and eighty people were asked, 'What is your favourite type of TV programme?'. Each chose from a list of types of programme.
   Soaps 53   Sport 17   Films 40   Comedy 18   Music 26   Drama 26

2 A pizza delivery firm notes the number and type (by distance) of deliveries made on a particular day.
   1–2 km 43   2–5 km 21   5–7 km 17   over 7 km 6   under 1 km 7

3 A snack bar in a parking area beside a busy main road sells the following in a particular hour.
   Beefburger 25   Vegetarian 15   Fish 7   Sausage 13   Roll 10

4 The personnel manager of a large firm lists the method by which employees claim to travel to work each day.
   Walk 92   Cycle 75   Car 145   Train 20   Coach or bus 38   Motorbike 16

5 According to a survey the three main areas for tropical forests in the world accounted for the following percentages of tropical forests. [*Courtesy of WWF, 1992*]
   Asia 16%   Africa 35%   Latin America 49%

6 Energy Consumption 1987

USA	24%	Japan	5%
USSR	17.5%	Africa	2.5%
W. Europe	17%	Rest of world	25%
China	9%		

7 Calcutta has a considerable amount of rain each year. The average rainfall is more than 1600 mm per year but this tends to be concentrated into certain times of the year.

Jan. – Mar. 74 mm   Apr. – June 481 mm   July – Sept 910 mm   Oct. – Dec. 139 mm

8 According to the World Wild Fund for Nature (1992) the percentage of literacy for women in the world falls far behind the percentage of literacy for men. Draw *two* pie charts, one to show literacy for women and one to show literacy for men

Literacy – Women		**Literacy – Men**	
Can read	54%	Can read	70%
Cannot read	46%	Cannot read	30%

Exercise 72B

In each question create a frequency table which contains an extra column showing the calculated angle (to nearest 0.1° if necessary) for each sector. Use the values in the frequency table to draw the pie chart. Do not forget to give each pie chart a title and to *label* each sector.

1 A survey by a travel agent about what customers considered to be their best holiday revealed the following information.

Ski 13   Winter Sun 35   Summer Sun 92   Touring 17   UK 23

2 Over one hundred chefs were asked about the type of preparation they liked best.

Main meal 32   Starters 12   Desserts 24   Specials 42

3 Members of an athletics group were asked about which event they liked best.

Long distance 15   Middle distance 37   Hurdles 8   Sprint 28

4 The way in which dangerous waste was managed in the UK has been analysed and the results are as follows.

Dumping at sea 8%   Treatment 8%   Burning 2%   Landfill 82%

[*Courtesy of WWF UK's Atlas of the Environment, 1990*]

5 World consumption of energy

Natural gas	24%	Nuclear	7%
Coal	32%	Hydroelectric, etc.	2%
Oil	35%		

6 Literacy in 1990 was not spread evenly around the populations of the world. The percentage of the adult population who cannot read was as follows in various areas of the world.

Developing countries 98%   Developed countries 2%   Africa 54%   Asia 33%
Latin America 17%

[*Courtesy of WWF UK's Atlas of the Environment, 1990*]

7 Tokyo has more than 1500 mm of rain each year but this is not uniform throughout the year. Winter is drier.

Mar. – May 367 mm   June – Aug. 475 mm   Sept. – Nov. 538 mm
Dec. – Feb. 182 mm

8 Jon analyses the results of his favourite team in 1994 and 1995. He finds a considerable difference between the two years. Draw *two* pie charts, one for each year.

	1994	**1995**
Win	12	7
Draw	7	8
Lose	1	5

EXAMPLE

▶ The lengths of the words on a page are noted and the results are shown in the frequency table.

Number of letters	Number of words
1	8
2	10
3	23
4	27
5	42
6	39
7	15
8	5
9	3

(a) Calculate the mean, mode, median and range of the data.

(b) Comment on which type of average is most suitable for the data.

(a) You must calculate **frequency × number of letters** for each value.

Number of letters	Number of words	Freq. × No. of letters
1	8	8
2	10	20
3	23	69
4	27	108
5	42	210
6	39	234
7	15	105
8	5	40
9	3	27

The total number of letters is 821 (add values in third column).

The total number of words is 172 (add values in second column).

Mean = $\frac{821}{172}$ = 4.77 (to 3 s.f.)

Modal class = 5 letters

There are 172 letters, so the median is found between the 86th and 87th values.

8 + 20 + 69 = 97, so the median will be 3 letters.

Range = 9 − 1 = 8 letters.

(b) The most suitable value is the mode since it tells you which size of word occurs most frequently.

▶ The length of each of 100 one-year-old fish from a batch at a fish farm is measured and the results are grouped to give the following table.

Length (cm)	Frequency
$7 \leq L < 8$	5
$8 \leq L < 9$	7
$9 \leq L < 10$	10
$10 \leq L < 11$	15
$11 \leq L < 12$	32
$12 \leq L < 13$	18
$13 \leq L < 14$	9
$14 \leq L < 15$	2

(a) Calculate an estimated value for the mean, median and range.

(b) State the modal class.

(c) Comment on which of the averages would be most useful in comparing this year's with last year's results.

(a)

Length (cm)	Frequency, f	Mid-interval, m	$f \times m$
$7 \leq L < 8$	5	7.5	37.5
$8 \leq L < 9$	7	8.5	59.5
$9 \leq L < 10$	10	9.5	95
$10 \leq L < 11$	15	10.5	157.5
$11 \leq L < 12$	32	11.5	368
$12 \leq L < 13$	18	12.5	225
$13 \leq L < 14$	9	13.5	121.5
$14 \leq L < 15$	2	14.5	29

Sum of $f \times m = 1093$

Mean $= \dfrac{1093}{100} = 10.9$ cm (to 3 s.f.)

Median is the 50th to 51st fish. $5 + 7 + 10 + 15 = 37$

Next group has 32 fish; so the middle ranked fish will be in this group.

Median is in the $11 \leq L < 12$ cm group.

The range is estimated as $15 - 7 = 8$ cm at maximum.

(b) Modal class is $11 \leq L < 12$ cm

(c) The mean is probably the most useful way of comparing the two years because it takes all lengths into account and gives a single value answer that can be used for simple comparison.

Exercise 73A

1 Jonathan is taking part in a sponsored silence and has persuaded friends to pledge money in units of £1.

Pledges (£)	Frequency
1	39
2	15
3	5
4	3
5	8
6	1

Calculate (a) mean (b) median (c) mode and (d) range of the data.

2 An experiment in probability involves tossing five coins and counting the number of heads. This is repeated many times and the results are put into a frequency table.

No. of heads	Frequency
0	2
1	12
2	20
3	24
4	11
5	2

Calculate (a) mean (b) median (c) mode and (d) range of the data.

3 The mass of each package and parcel is noted at a small office one day.

Mass (kg)	Frequency
$0 \leq M < 1$	2
$1 \leq M < 2$	9
$2 \leq M < 3$	11
$3 \leq M < 4$	24
$4 \leq M < 5$	4

Calculate an estimated value of (a) the mean and (b) the median. State (c) the modal class (d) the maximum range of the data.

4 A shopkeeper sells bags of mixed long nails. He is curious to find out about the contents, so he opens a bag and quickly measures each nail.

Length (cm)	Frequency
$7 \leq L < 8$	35
$8 \leq L < 9$	23
$9 \leq L < 10$	11
$10 \leq L < 11$	20
$11 \leq L < 12$	5
$12 \leq L < 13$	6

Calculate an estimated value of (a) the total length of the nails in the bag (b) the mean length. State (c) the modal class (d) the maximum range of the data.

5 Glenda works for a firm that sells car spares. She needs to list the distances from one garage to another. She decides to list them in a grouped frequency table.

Miles	Frequency
$10 \leq M < 20$	1
$20 \leq M < 30$	2
$30 \leq M < 40$	7
$40 \leq M < 50$	45
$50 \leq M < 60$	22
$60 \leq M < 70$	2

Calculate an estimated value of (a) the mean and (b) the median. State (c) the modal class (d) the maximum range of the data.

6 An evening class, 'Pottery for Beginners', is set the task of making vases to hold about half a litre. They try their best but not too many were very close to the required capacity.

Capacity (ml)	Frequency
$400 \leq C < 450$	3
$450 \leq C < 500$	3
$500 \leq C < 550$	13
$550 \leq C < 600$	5
$600 \leq C < 650$	6
$650 \leq C < 700$	3

Calculate an estimated value of (a) the mean and (b) the median. State (c) the modal class (d) the maximum range of the data.

7 The weight of each sack from a sample of sacks taken from a machine that is meant to deliver 50 kg is measured.

Weight (kg)	Frequency
$30 \leq w < 40$	5
$40 \leq w < 50$	7
$50 \leq w < 60$	58
$60 \leq w < 70$	6
$70 \leq w < 80$	3
$80 \leq w < 90$	1

Calculate an estimated value of (a) the mean and (b) the median. State (c) the modal class (d) the maximum range of the data.

8 The speed of each vehicle passing through a village is measured and the results are grouped as follows.

Speed (m.p.h.)	Frequency
$0 \leq S < 10$	3
$10 \leq S < 20$	4
$20 \leq S < 30$	6
$30 \leq S < 40$	12
$40 \leq S < 50$	9
$50 \leq S < 60$	6

Calculate an estimated value of (a) the mean and (b) the median. (c) State the modal class. (d) State the maximum range of the data.

Exercise 73B

1 A group of 25-year-olds are questioned about their motor insurance. Each one is asked, 'How many years no claims bonus do you have?' The responses are shown as a frequency table.

Years	Frequency
0	20
1	55
2	32
3	16
4	9

Calculate (a) mean (b) median (c) mode and (d) range of the data.

2 As part of an experiment in probability a dice is thrown many times and each score is noted. The results are shown in the frequency table.

Score	Frequency
1	15
2	38
3	14
4	15
5	5
6	13

Calculate (a) mean (b) median (c) mode and (d) range of the data.

3 The mass of the load on each lorry that passes through a weigh-bridge is noted and the data are grouped as shown:

Mass (t)	Frequency
$0 \leq M < 2$	66
$2 \leq M < 4$	8
$4 \leq M < 6$	4
$6 \leq M < 8$	12
$8 \leq M < 10$	7

Calculate an estimated value of (a) the mean and
(b) the median.
(c) State the modal class.
(d) State the maximum range.

4 The distribution of the ages of the members of a group of people are shown:

Ages (years)	Frequency
$15 \leq y < 20$	10
$20 \leq y < 25$	8
$25 \leq y < 30$	6
$30 \leq y < 35$	7
$35 \leq y < 40$	4
$40 \leq y < 45$	5

Calculate an estimated value of (a) the mean and
(b) the median.
State (c) the modal class (d) the maximum range of the data.

5 Contestants in a strength competition have to hold a heavy weight at arm's length. The times for the contestants are grouped and are shown below:

Time (s)	Frequency
$0 \leq T < 5$	1
$5 \leq T < 10$	10
$10 \leq T < 15$	17
$15 \leq T < 20$	11
$20 \leq T < 25$	6
$25 \leq T < 30$	4
$30 \leq T < 35$	2

Calculate an estimated value of (a) the mean and
(b) the median.
(c) State the modal class.
(d) State the maximum range.

6 Denise measures the distance between each of the houses on her paper round by pacing them out as she delivers the papers. She groups the distances and puts the information in the form of a table.

Distance (paces)	Frequency
$30 \leq d < 40$	3
$40 \leq d < 50$	5
$50 \leq d < 60$	17
$60 \leq d < 70$	9
$70 \leq d < 80$	4
$80 \leq d < 90$	3
$90 \leq d < 100$	2

Calculate an estimated value of (a) the mean and
(b) the median.
State (c) the modal class (d) the maximum range of the data.

7 The soil in a particular district is very variable and so the yields, measured in tonnes per hectare, also vary considerably. The yields from over sixty fields are noted and grouped to give the table.

Yields (t)	Frequency
$0 \leq y < 2$	3
$2 \leq y < 4$	9
$4 \leq y < 6$	18
$6 \leq y < 8$	10
$8 \leq y < 10$	13
$10 \leq y < 12$	11

Calculate an estimated value of (a) the mean and
(b) the median.
(c) State the modal class.
(d) State the maximum range.

8 The heights of the pupils in a class are grouped and listed.

Height (cm)	Frequency
$140 \leq h < 150$	4
$150 \leq h < 160$	13
$160 \leq h < 170$	7
$170 \leq h < 180$	4
$180 \leq h < 190$	2
$190 \leq h < 200$	1

Calculate an estimated value of (a) the mean and
(b) the median.
State (c) the modal class (d) the maximum range
of the data.

REVISION

Exercise G

1 Brenda's journey to work should take about 20 minutes but, since it involves travelling on a busy
motorway, the time can vary greatly. She notes the journey times to the nearest minute.

18	22	23	25	19	20	35	22	24	28
19	43	23	29	31	30	27	23	24	42
31	32	25	27	23	22	20	24	29	30
38	47	36	41	39	31	28	28	21	20

Copy and complete the grouped frequency table for these times.

Time, T (min)	Tally	Frequency
$15 \leq T < 20$		
$20 \leq T < 25$		
etc.		

2 In a laboratory the length of time taken for 75 seeds to
germinate (start to show signs of sprouting) is measured
to the nearest day. The results are shown as a grouped
frequency diagram – class intervals $0 \leq d < 5$ days, etc.
Use this to answer the following.
  (a) How many seeds take less than 15 days to germinate?
  (b) How many seeds fail to germinate?
  (c) What fraction of the seeds that germinate take
     20 days or more?
  (d) What percentage of all the seeds in the test take
     20 days or more to germinate?

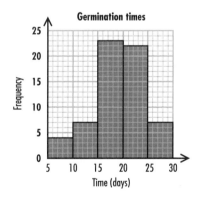

3 Draw a frequency polygon to show the number of children per household on a particular estate.

Number of children	0	1	2	3	4	5	6
Number of households	3	5	23	16	8	3	2

4 The information in question 3 is to be shown as a pie chart.
  (a) Copy the frequency table and complete it by adding the angle required for each sector of the
     pie chart.
  (b) Draw the pie chart.

5 Use the *actual* times (not the grouped frequency table) listed in question 1 to answer the following.
Calculate (a) the mean (b) the median (c) the range.
  (d) State the modal class using the grouped frequency table.

Exercise GG

1 The actual weights of packed meat in a supermarket are surveyed by a trading standards officer. The packs are claimed to be 2 kg. She lists the actual weights (to the nearest gram).

1.995	1.982	2.001	1.984	1.992	1.972	2.005	1.987	2.003	1.995
2.006	1.990	2.007	2.003	2.020	1.991	1.988	2.015	1.990	2.005
1.990	1.995	1.982	2.002	1.984	2.016	1.978	1.999	2.010	1.982
2.007	2.021	1.999	2.000	2.005	2.002				

(a) Create a grouped frequency table for this data. Use class intervals of $1.970 \leq$ weight < 1.980 kg, etc.

(b) Draw a grouped frequency diagram to show this information.

2 The grouped frequency diagram shows the floor areas that need to be cleaned by a small cleaning company (class intervals $0 \leq$ area < 100 m²). Use this to answer the following:

(a) How many of the floor areas are 300 m² or more?

(b) What is the frequency of the modal class?

(c) How many floors does the company clean?

(d) What percentage of the floors are less than 100 m²?

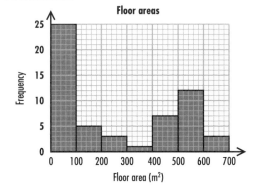

3 Two new varieties (A and B) of tomatoes are tested. The total crop for each of 100 plants of each variety is weighed and the results are shown as two frequency polygons. The class intervals are $9 \leq$ weight < 10 kg, etc. Use these frequency polygons to answer the following.

(a) How many plants in total have yields of 14 kg or more?

(b) State the modal class for each of the varieties.

(c) State the minimum possible yield that could have been obtained from each of the varieties in these tests.

(d) Write two short sentences comparing the yields for the two varieties.

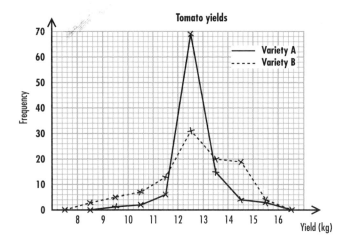

4 A faulty paper printing machine keeps breaking down on a particular shift. The printout on the machine's logbook is analysed as follows:

Distance (m)	Frequency
$0 \leq d < 25$	3
$25 \leq d < 50$	5
$50 \leq d < 75$	8
$75 \leq d < 100$	7
$100 \leq d < 125$	9
$125 \leq d < 150$	17
$150 \leq d < 175$	32

(a) Copy the frequency table and add an extra column which contains the results of your calculations about the angle needed for each class on a pie chart.

(b) Draw a pie chart to show the information in the frequency diagram.

5 (a) Calculate the mean and median for the *actual* weights of the packs listed in question 1.
   (b) Use the frequency table requested in question 1 and recalculate the mean and median values.
   (c) Comment on the accuracy of the grouped frequency estimations for the mean and median as compared with the values obtained using the actual values.
   (d) State the modal class for this distribution.
   (e) State (i) the maximum range for the grouped data and (ii) the range of the listed times.
   (iii) Explain the difference between these results.

74/ SCATTER DIAGRAMS: DRAWING FROM GIVEN DATA

A **scatter graph** (or **scatter diagram**) is created by plotting one quantity on the horizontal axis against another quantity on the vertical axis. The result is a number of points.

EXAMPLE

▶ A small group of students take a NVR (non-verbal reasoning) test and also a mathematics examination. The results are listed for each of the students.

Student	Colin	Dean	Julie	Harry	Bill	Alec	Norah	Anne	Neil	Ahmed
NVR	125	113	98	82	118	138	120	131	92	100
Maths (%)	83	75	43	34	67	98	77	89	39	56

   (a) Plot a scatter diagram to show these results.
   (b) Label the points that show Alec's and Julie's results.

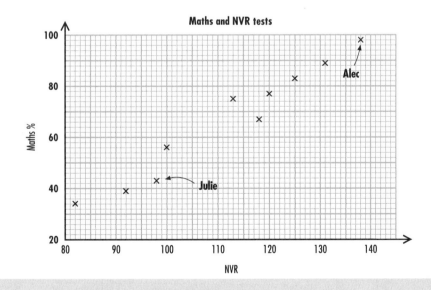

Exercise 74A

Draw a scatter graph for each of the questions and label the required points.

Note: Keep your scatter diagrams – they will be useful for Exercises 75A and 76C.

1 Seven athletes take part in 100 m and 200 m races. They record their times to 0.1 of a second.

Names	Bob	Carol	Fiona	Cilla	Roger	Ali	Ruth
Time, 100 m (s)	12.5	14.6	12.7	13.9	12.1	13.1	14.9
Time, 200 m (s)	22.6	25.3	23.4	24.5	22.1	23.1	26.2

Use the horizontal axis for the times of the 100 m race: 12–15 s; 2 cm to represent 1 s.
Use the vertical axis for the times of the 200 m race: 22–27 s; 2 cm to represent 1 s.
Label the points that represent the performances of Ruth and Bob.

2 A trader at a car auction notes the prices for a number of examples of a popular model of a car. He also notes the approximate mileage of each car.

Mileage (miles)	25 000	95 000	46 000	75 000	22 000	38 000
Price (£)	8500	3800	5300	5100	8900	6600

Use the horizontal axis for the mileage: 0–100 000 miles; 1 cm to represent 10 000 miles.
Use the vertical axis for the price: £3000–£9000; 1 cm to represent £1000.
Label the points that represent the car with a price of £8500 and the car that has travelled 46 000 miles.

3 Ahsan lists the results of his trial examinations and the results of the previous examinations:

Subject	Eng. Lang.	Eng. Lit.	Maths	Science	French	Geog.	Tech.	P.E.
Trial (%)	56	63	52	60	36	75	72	28
Exam (%)	48	68	54	65	25	68	72	30

Use the horizontal axis for the marks in the trial exams: 20–80%; 1 cm to represent 10%.
Use the vertical axis for the marks in the previous exams: 20–80%; 1 cm to represent 10%.
Label the points that represent Ahsan's results in French and Geography.

4 Members of a group of weight-watchers note their weights and heights.

Name	Omar	Brian	Wes	Sita	Dara	Eric	Gill
Height (cm)	177	183	174	165	160	171	158
Weight (kg)	78	89	85	71	75	76	70

Use the horizontal axis for height: 150–190 cm; 2 cm to represent 10 cm.
Use the vertical axis for weight: 60–90 kg; 2 cm to represent 10 kg.
Label the points that represent Wes and Dara.

5 Floyd is researching the connection between temperature at night and the amount of cloud cover. He measures the temperature at dawn for ten days in December. He also notes the number of hours that the sky was mainly clear of clouds.

Date	5th	6th	7th	8th	9th	10th	11th	12th	13th	14th
Hours of clear sky	9	7	3	0	8	12	10	8	3	2
Temperature (°C)	−5	−1	4	6	0	−7	−3	−2	3	5

Use the horizontal axis for the hours of clear sky: 0–12 hours; 1 cm to represent 1 hour.
Use the vertical axis for the temperature: −7 to +6°C; 1 cm to represent 1°C.
Label the points that represent 5th and 13th December.

6 Students are given a test at the end of a unit of study. The test is of twenty questions where it is necessary to pick the correct answer from a list of five suggestions. Students who have learned the work can complete the test very quickly. They are asked to say how many minutes the test took.

Candidate No.	1003	1015	1036	1060	1074	1101	1112	1125
Time (min)	25	20	18	22	15	17	28	14
Mark out of 20	3	7	14	6	20	16	2	19

Use the horizontal axis for the time: 0–30 min; 2 cm to represent 10 min.
Use the vertical axis for the mark: 0–20; 1 cm to represent 5 marks.
Label the points that represent the candidates with numbers 1003 and 1074.

Exercise 74B

Draw a scatter graph for each of the questions and label the required points.
Note: Keep your scatter diagrams – they will be useful for Exercises 75B and 76D.

1 Floyd is researching the number of hours of sunshine and the temperature at 1700 during a ten-day period in July.

Day	1st	2nd	3rd	4th	5th	6th	7th	8th	9th	10th
Hours of sunshine	8	6	3	9	9	4	7	10	8	5
Temperature (°C)	19	18	16	19	23	19	21	24	21	17

Use the horizontal axis for the hours of sunshine: 0–10; 1 cm to represent 1 hour.
Use the vertical axis for the temperature: 16–25°C; 1 cm to represent 1°C.
Label the points that represent 3 July and 10 July.

2 A small group of students are examined in Mathematics and History.

Name	Will	Huw	Rob	Awaz	Keith	Zaki	Sue	Nesta	Jon	Mary
Maths (%)	23	32	41	49	53	59	65	72	78	87
History (%)	78	69	68	60	64	60	54	46	30	48

Use the horizontal axis for the mark in Mathematics: 20–90%; 1 cm to represent 10%.
Use the vertical axis for the mark in History: 20–80%; 1 cm to represent 10%.
Label the points that represent Awaz and Huw.

3 The owner of a snack bar notes the number of cups of hot soup sold per day and the temperature forecast for the day on TV.

Day	1	2	3	4	5	6	7	8	9
Temperature (°C)	12	10	8	5	8	4	1	0	−2
Cups of soup	14	18	23	38	25	56	69	85	98

Use the horizontal axis for the temperature: −5– +15°C; 2 cm to represent 5°C.
Use the vertical axis for the number of cups of soup: 0–100 cups; 1 cm to represent 10 cups.
Label the points that represent Day 5 and Day 9.

4 The age and blood pressure for each of ten patients is noted.

Patient	A	B	C	D	E	F	G	H	I	J
Age (years)	20	24	27	32	38	45	49	54	58	65
Blood pressure	128	132	134	139	140	142	143	153	142	147

Use the horizontal axis for age: 0–70 years; 1 cm to represent 10 years.
Use the vertical axis for blood pressure: 120–160 mm; 2 cm to represent 10 mm.
Label the points that represent patients C and I.

5 Talat notes the cost of electricity used per month and the average daytime temperature for that month.

Month	J	F	M	A	M	J	J	A	S	O	N	D
Temp (°C)	2	4	8	12	14	18	20	19	15	11	7	5
Cost (£)	70	65	61	55	51	48	48	42	49	63	66	68

Use the horizontal axis for the temperature: 0–25°C; 2 cm to represent 5°C.
Use the vertical axis for the cost: £40–£70; 1 cm to represent £5.
Label the points that represent May and November.

6 A popular model of car is tested for fuel economy (miles per litre of petrol) at various speeds.

Speed (m.p.h.)	30	35	40	45	50	60	70	80
Economy (miles per litre)	11.8	11.6	11.3	10.9	10.4	9.3	8.1	7.0

Use the horizontal axis for the speed: 20–90 m.p.h.; 1 cm to represent 10 m.p.h.
Use the vertical axis for the fuel economy: 6.0–12.0 miles per litre; 1 cm to represent 1 mile per litre.
Label the points that represent speeds of 40 m.p.h. and 70 m.p.h.

75/ SCATTER DIAGRAMS: LINE OF 'BEST FIT'

The points of a scatter diagram often appear to tend towards being on a line. It is possible to draw a **line of best fit.** This is not a line passing through each point but a line which best describes the positions of all the points. The line does not need to pass through any of the points but *must* pass through a point that represents the mean of each of the variables.

EXAMPLE

▶ Brian lists the results of his trial examinations and the results of earlier examinations:

Subject	Eng. Lang.	Eng. Lit.	Maths	Science	Spanish	History	P.E.	R.E.
Trial (%)	65	74	78	82	56	45	48	60
Exam (%)	62	70	75	80	58	46	43	54

(a) Draw a scatter diagram of these results.
(b) Draw the line of best fit for the points of the scatter diagram.
(c) Use your line of best fit to predict the examination mark for a trial mark of 80%.
(d) Use your line of best fit to predict the trial mark for an examination mark of 50%.

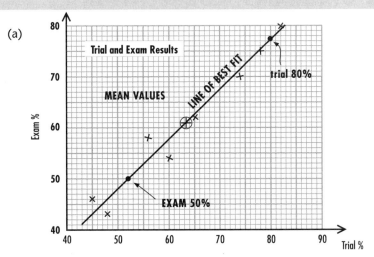

(a)

(b) The mean of the trial marks is 508 ÷ 8 = 63.5%.

The mean of exam marks is 488 ÷ 8 = 61.0%.

The point (63.5, 61.0) *must* be plotted and should be marked so as to stand out from other points. The line is now a matter of judgement but it *must* pass through the mean values point.

Note: The line does not need to pass through the point (0, 0).

Reading the values from the line of best fit:

(c) 80% → 77.5% (d) 50% → 52%

Exercise 75A

Refer to the examples in Exercise 74A. If you have drawn the scatter diagrams for these questions, you can use them to cut down the work in this exercise. If you do not have the scatter diagrams, you will need to plot them before starting.

(a) For each question calculate the mean value for each of the variables.

(b) Plot the point for these mean values.

(c) Draw a line of best fit.

(d) Use your line to predict the value of the other variable.

1 (d) (i) 15 s (100 m) (ii) 23 s (200 m)   **2** (d) (i) 80 000 miles (ii) £9000
3 (d) (i) 80% trial (ii) 20% exam   **4** (d) (i) 180 cm (ii) 71 kg
5 (d) (i) –4°C (ii) 3 hours   **6** (d) (i) 15 min (ii) 0 marks

Exercise 75B

Refer to the examples in Exercise 74B. If you have drawn the scatter diagrams for these questions, you can use them to cut down the work in this exercise. If you do not have the scatter diagrams, you will need to plot them before starting.

(a) For each question calculate the mean value for each of the variables.

(b) Plot the point for these mean values.

(c) Draw a line of best fit.

(d) Use your line to predict the value of the other variable.

1 (d) (i) 4 hours (ii) 22°C   **2** (d) (i) History 50% (ii) Maths 80%
3 (d) (i) 0°C (ii) 10 cups   **4** (d) (i) 60 years (ii) 130 mm
5 (d) (i) £52 per month (ii) 6°C   **6** (d) (i) 12 miles per litre (ii) 90 m.p.h.

76/ SCATTER DIAGRAMS: CORRELATION

If the points on a scatter diagram show no clear pattern, then there is no obvious connection between the two variables. There is **no correlation** between the variables.

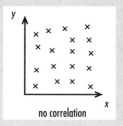

no correlation

If the points on a scatter diagram tend towards a line of best fit that has a positive gradient, then as one variable changes the other variable tends to change in the same way (**positive correlation**).
That is:
    Increase in variable 1 → increase in variable 2
    Decrease in variable 1 → decrease in variable 2

If the points on a scatter diagram tend towards a line of best fit that has a negative gradient, then as one variable changes the other variable tends to change in the opposite way (**negative correlation**).
That is:
    Increase in variable 1 → *decrease* in variable 2
    Decrease in variable 1 → *increase* in variable 2

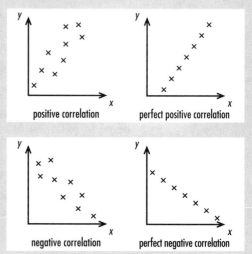

positive correlation   perfect positive correlation

negative correlation   perfect negative correlation

Exercise 76A

Examine the scatter diagrams sketched below and state the type of correlation for each. Choose from the following correlations: *perfect positive, positive, no correlation, negative, perfect negative.*

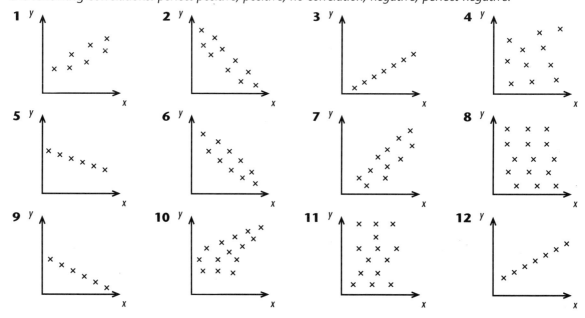

Exercise 76B

Examine the scatter diagrams sketched below and state the type of correlation for each. Choose from the following correlations: *perfect positive, positive, no correlation, negative, perfect negative.*

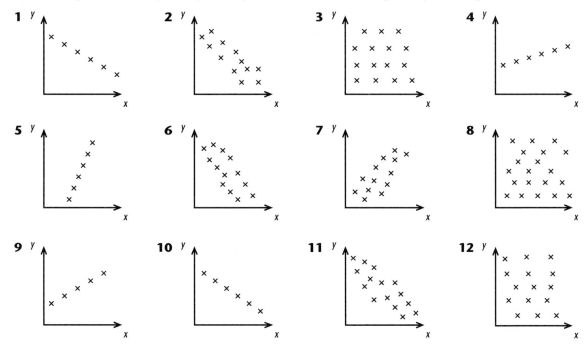

EXAMPLE

► State the type of correlation (if any) between NVR and Maths results.

Student	Colin	Dean	Julie	Harry	Bill	Alec	Norah	Anne	Neil	Ahmed
NVR	125	113	98	82	118	138	120	131	92	100
Maths (%)	83	75	43	34	67	98	77	89	39	56

Look at the lowest value for NVR – Harry 82. Unfortunately Harry is also bottom in the Mathematics examination.

Look at the highest value for NVR – Alec 138. Alec is also top in the Mathematics examination.

If you check out the others, you will see that the performance in the NVR gives you a very good idea of the performance in the Mathematics Examination.

There is positive correlation.

In fact the scatter diagram for this example confirms this (see section 74).

Exercise 76C

Examine the data for each of the questions in Exercise 74A and state whether there is any correlation. If there is correlation state whether this is *positive* or *negative* and try to comment on whether it is *moderate* or *good.* If you have drawn the scatter graphs for Exercise 74A, use these to confirm your answers.

Examine the data for each of the questions in Exercise 74B and state whether there is any correlation. If there is correlation state whether this is *positive* or *negative* and try to comment on whether it is *moderate* or *good.* If you have drawn the scatter graphs for Exercise 74B, use these to confirm your answers.

77/ PROBABILITY: RELATIVE FREQUENCY USED TO MAKE ESTIMATES

The results of experiments and surveys can be used to make **predictions** about the probability of future events.

If an event occurs 25 times out of 100 attempts then the **relative frequency** is $\frac{25}{100}$ or $\frac{1}{4}$. This can be used, with care, as the probability that the event will occur if another attempt is made.

EXAMPLE

▶ Tom makes a spinner like the one in the diagram; it is not made particularly well. He spins the spinner 100 times and notes the outcomes in a frequency table.

Score on spinner	1	2	3	4	5	6
Frequency	14	11	15	19	25	16

(a) Tom spins the spinner one more time; use the information in the table to answer the following:
  (i) State the score that has the greatest probability of occurring.
  (ii) What is the probability that the score is 5?
  (iii) What is the probability that the score is not 5?
  (iv) What is the probability that the score will be even?
(b) If Tom spins the spinner 1000 times more, about how many times will the score be 2?

(a) (i) 5

  (ii) $\frac{25}{100} = \frac{1}{4}$ or 0.25

  (iii) $\frac{1}{4}$ or 0.75

  (iv) $\frac{(11 + 19 + 16)}{100} = \frac{46}{100} = \frac{23}{50}$ or 0.46

(b) 1000 spins is 10 times the original 100 so the number of scores of 2 will be $11 \times 10 = 110$.

Remember: **This is a prediction based upon previous results.** You should not expect that this is exactly what will happen. It is likely that a score of 2 will occur less than $\frac{1}{6}$ of the total number of spins ($\frac{1000}{6} = 167$ spins).

Exercise 77A

In each of the following questions you are expected to *use relative frequency* as a method of predicting probability.

1 Pam runs a game at a fete that pays £5 for every double 6 achieved with two dice. Pam has 30 attempts before the fete starts. She scores double 6 only once. Using this information, estimate Pam's profit or loss on 180 goes at 25p a go.

2 Trevor Young is a candidate in a local election. A survey of 100 voters taken at random gives him 32 votes more than the other candidate. Estimate how many votes more than the other candidate he will receive if 2500 people vote.

3 Paul spins four coins and notes the number of tails. He does this 200 times and he obtains the following results:

Number of tails	0	1	2	3	4
Frequency	14	45	80	49	12

(a) What is the probability of getting two heads with four coins?
(b) State the relative frequency of four tails.
(c) State the probability of four heads.
(d) If Paul repeated the experiment with another 200 spins, would he get the same results? Comment on this.

4 There is a game at a fair that has three outcomes: 'WIN £1', 'WIN £5' and 'LOSE'. The results of 60 attempts are noted and are listed:

Result	WIN £1	WIN £5	LOSE
Frequency	7	1	52

(a) What is the probability of a win?
(b) If someone has a winner, what is the probability that it is a £1 win?
(c) What is the probability that one play will lead to a £5 win?
(d) Richard buys £10 worth of 20p tickets. What sort of profit or loss is he likely to make?

5 100 light bulbs are taken at random from boxes at a factory. They are tested and the time that each lasts is noted:

Time (hours)	0 (broken)	up to 600	600–999	1000–1999	2000 and over
Frequency	3	5	12	76	4

(a) What is the probability that a light bulb taken at random is broken?
(b) What is the probability that a light bulb taken at random will last for 1000 hours or more?
(c) In a batch of 1000 bulbs, how many are likely to be unacceptable if acceptable bulbs last 600 hours or more?
(d) Boxes contain 50 bulbs. How many light bulbs per box are likely to last 2000 hours or more?

6 A survey of sunglasses is made at a seaside resort. 1000 people who walk past are questioned and the results noted:

Category	Wearing sunglasses	Carrying sunglasses	No sunglasses
Frequency	203	97	700

(a) What is the probability that the next person taken at random is wearing sunglasses?
(b) What is the probability that a person who has sunglasses is wearing them?
(c) Out of 10 people taken at random, how many are likely to have no sunglasses?
(d) In the time when 100 people with no sunglasses walk past, how many people wearing sunglasses will be likely to walk past?

7 There are three candidates in an election, Ann Brown, Lloyd Peters and Wes Green. 53 000 people vote in the election. 100 of those who voted are selected at random and asked for whom they voted:

Vote	Ann Brown	Lloyd Peters	Wes Green	Will not say
Number of votes	64	42	72	22

(a) What percentage of those selected will not say how they voted?

(b) How many of the total number of 53 000 are likely to have definitely voted for Wes Green to the nearest thousand?

(c) How many of the total number of 53 000 are likely to have definitely voted for Ann Brown to the nearest thousand?

(d) If a quarter of those who were in the category 'will not say' voted for Ann Brown, is Wes Green likely to win?

8 As part of an experiment in probability Fiona spins two pentagonal spinners and notes the total of their scores:

Total score	2	3	4	5	6	7	8	9	10
Frequency	4	9	11	16	21	15	12	7	5

(a) Do the spinners appear to be biased? If so, towards what number?

(b) What is the probability of a score of 10?

(c) Which is more likely, an odd total or an even total? Give your reason for your answer.

(d) If Fiona invented a game that costs 10p a try with a prize of 50p for a score of 6, how much profit/loss should she make on 100 tries?

Exercise 77B

In each of the following questions you are expected to *use relative frequency* as a method of predicting probability.

1 In an experiment 135 out of 500 seeds failed to germinate. Estimate the weight of seeds that would fail to germinate in 2 kg of the seeds.

2 Alice takes 20 coins at random from a large bag of change. She finds that she has £1.80. Estimate the value of the bag of change if it holds 1500 coins.

3 Nathan rolls a dice 60 times and notes the scores:

Score on dice	1	2	3	4	5	6
Frequency	7	9	8	11	9	16

(a) Do you think that the dice is biased? If so, towards which number?

(b) What is the probability of scoring a six with one throw?

(c) What is the probability of an even score with one throw?

(d) Complete the following ratio – probability of odd number : probability of even number = 2 : ?

4 A garage notes the type of fuel used by 1000 customers:

Fuel type	Diesel	Leaded	Unleaded
No. of customers	210	240	550

    (a) Out of the next ten customers, how many are likely to use unleaded fuel?

    (b) What fraction of the customers, to the nearest simple fraction, use leaded fuel?

    (c) What percentage of customers are likely to use diesel?

    (d) If every 5th customer using unleaded petrol gets a raffle ticket, how many tickets are likely to be needed for 100 customers?

5 The owner of an ice cream van notes the number of 'good days' (sales over £300) and 'bad days' (sales under £100) for various temperature ranges over a period of 120 days:

Temperature range (°C)	0–5	6–10	11–15	16–20	21–25
No. of 'good days'	1	3	6	15	25
No. of 'bad days'	18	12	3	1	0
No. of other days	7	5	2	1	1

    (a) What is the probability that a day is neither 'good' nor 'bad'?

    (b) What is the probability that it will be a good day if the temperature is more than 15°C?

    (c) What is the probability of a good day if the temperature is below 6°C?

    (d) Is the probability of a good day likely to be more or less than $\frac{6}{11}$ if the temperature is 11°C? Explain your answer.

6 The ages of the passengers on a charter flight to Paris are noted and grouped to form the table:

Age group	under 12	12–19	20–29	30–49	50 and over
No. of passengers	15	35	70	15	21

    (a) What is the probability that a passenger taken at random is under 20 years old?

    (b) If a passenger is over 29, what is the probability that the passenger is also 50 or over?

    (c) What is the probability that a passenger taken at random is under 30 but not under 12?

    (d) Assuming that distribution of ages is the same, how many children's meals (under 12) will be required on a plane that has 300 passengers?

7 A sample of 100 out of the 60 000 voters in an election are asked for whom they would vote:

Candidate	Ned Bell	Jill Green	Tony Smith	Kate Long	Do not know
No. of votes	7	22	34	19	18

    (a) How many of the voters are likely to be in the group who 'do not know'?

    (b) What is likely to be the majority for Tony Smith (the number of votes that he gets compared with the number of votes of his nearest rival)?

    (c) Who will get more votes, the men or the women candidates (excluding those who do not know)?

    (d) If half those who 'do not know' vote for one candidate, which of the candidates can win?

8 Six coins are tossed in an experiment in probability. The number of 'heads' are noted:

No. of heads	0	1	2	3	4	5	6
Frequency	1	9	24	32	22	10	2

    (a) One outcome comes up approximately $\frac{1}{3}$ of the times. Which outcome is this?

    (b) What do you notice about the distribution?

    (c) What is the probability of getting all the coins the same?

    (d) Is six heads twice as likely as no heads? Explain your answer.

The **complement** of an event happening is that it will not happen. Since an event can either **happen** or **not happen**, the total probability = 1 (certain).

P(event) + P(complementary event) = 1

If P(E) is the probability that an event will happen and P(E') is the probability that the event will not happen then

P(E') = 1 – P(E)

EXAMPLE

▶ In each question state (i) the probability of the event happening
(ii) the complementary event (avoiding the word *not* if possible) and
(iii) the probability of the complementary event.
(a) Picking a black pencil from a bag containing five black and three red pencils.
(b) A score of 5 or more on a dice.
(c) Picking a vowel from SAUSAGES.
(d) Winning a raffle after buying 1 of the 200 tickets.

(a) (i) $\frac{5}{8}$ (ii) Picking a red pencil (iii) $1 - \frac{5}{8} = \frac{3}{8}$

(b) (i) $\frac{1}{3}$ (ii) Scoring less than 5 (iii) $1 - \frac{1}{3} = \frac{2}{3}$

(c) (i) $\frac{4}{8} = \frac{1}{2}$ (ii) Picking a consonant (iii) $1 - \frac{1}{2} = \frac{1}{2}$

(d) (i) $\frac{1}{200}$ (ii) Losing (iii) $1 - \frac{1}{200} = \frac{199}{200}$.

Exercise 78A

In each question all selections are at random and all outcomes can be assumed to be equally likely.
(a) State the probability of the event.
(b) State the complementary event.
(c) State the probability of the complementary event.
Probability answers should be fractions except in the questions marked * where they should be given in decimal form.

1 Picking a vowel from the word ESSENTIAL.

2* Choosing a day with six letters from the days of the week.

3 Selecting a 5p coin from £1 in 5p coins and £1 in 10p coins.

4* Getting a 5 with a pentagonal spinner (numbered 1, 2, 3, 4, 5).

5 Choosing a nought from two million in number form.

6 Getting a score of less than 3 on a dice.

7* Picking a yellow disc from a box containing 5 green, 2 blue and 3 yellow discs.

8 Selecting a 2p coin from £2 in 2p coins and £1 in 5p coins.

9* Winning a raffle having bought 10 tickets from a total of 2000 sold.

10 Choosing an even digit from the number 132 215.

11 Picking a day that does not have a letter *y* from the days of the week.

12* Choosing an odd digit from the number 23 759 225.

13 Picking a consonant from the word READY.

14 Choosing a month of the year that ends in the letter R.

15* Choosing a black pencil from a bag containing 5 black and 3 red pencils.

16 Selecting a 50p coin from £10 in 50p coins and £5 in 20p coins.

17* Winning a raffle having bought 5 tickets from a total of 400 sold.

18 Picking a shape that *must* have a right-angle from the list: rhombus, rectangle, trapezium, parallelogram, square, quadrilateral and triangle.

19 Picking a consonant from the word TELEPHONE.

20* Getting a score of 3 or more with an unbiased octagonal spinner (numbered 1, 2, 3, 4, 5, 6, 7, 8).

Exercise 78B

In each question all selections are at random and all outcomes can be assumed to be equally likely.
(a) State the probability of the event.
(b) State the complementary event.
(c) State the probability of the complementary event.

Probability answers should be fractions except in the questions marked * where they should be given in decimal form.

1 Getting a score of 2 or more on a dice.

2 Picking a vowel from the word UNLIKELY.

3* Not choosing a nought from fifty million in number form.

4 Choosing a day with eight letters from the days of the week.

5 Selecting a 2p coin from £1 in 2p coins and £1 in 5p coins.

6* Winning a raffle having bought 6 tickets from a total of 200 sold.

7 Picking a green disc from a box containing 7 green, 2 blue and 3 yellow discs.

8* Selecting a 10p coin from £1 in 10p coins and £3 in 20p coins.

9 Picking a vowel from the word CALCULATOR.

10 Choosing an odd digit from the number 1 254 344.

11* Choosing a red pencil from a bag containing 2 red and 3 blue pencils.

12 Getting 2 or less with an unbiased pentagonal spinner (numbered 0, 1, 2, 3, 4).

13* Choosing an even digit from the number 75 467.

14 Picking a 20p coin from twenty 5p coins.

15 Choosing a month of the year that ends in the letter Y.

16* Picking a card that is a diamond from a standard pack of cards.†

17 Picking a consonant from the word QUESTION.

18 Selecting a 20p coin from £10 in 50p coins and £2 in 20p coins.

19* Winning a raffle having bought 1 ticket from a total of 500 sold.

20 Getting a number less than 7 on an unbiased octagonal spinner (numbered 0, 1, 2, 3, 4, 5, 6, 7).

† See note on p.170

When two events are **independent** the outcome in one event does not affect the outcome in the other event in any way. For example, the outcome of spinning a coin does not affect the outcome of rolling a dice.

One way of solving this type of question is to create a **possibility space.** This means that you write all the possible outcomes in a neat and methodical manner. You are then in a position to answer questions about the outcomes.

EXAMPLE

▶ Brian spins a coin and rolls a dice. Create a possibility space and use it to calculate the probability of each of the following:
(a) A head and a six
(b) A tail and a score less than 5
(c) Either a six or a head.

Possibility space

		Dice					
		1	**2**	**3**	**4**	**5**	**6**
Coin	**T**	T1	T2	T3	T4	T5	T6
	H	H1	H2	H3	H4	H5	H6

(a) H6 appears once, so P = $\frac{1}{12}$

(b) T1, T2, T3 and T4 are all suitable, so P = $\frac{4}{12}$ = $\frac{1}{3}$

(c) T6, H1, H2, H3, H4, H5 and H6 are all suitable so P = $\frac{7}{12}$

Exercise 79A

For each of the following create a suitable possibility space to show all the possible outcomes and then use this to calculate the outcomes stated.

Give answers as fractions except for questions marked * where answers should be given in decimal form.

1 The score on a dice and picking a letter at random from ROLLING.
(a) A score of 3 and the letter I. (b) A score of 3 or more and the letter G.
(c) An even score and the letter L. (d) An odd score and the letter X.

2* Selecting a digit at random from 11 313 and the colour of a playing card picked at random from a pack.
(a) The digit 3 and a black card. (b) An odd digit and a red card.
(c) An even digit and a red card. (d) A black card and the digit 1.

3 The suit of a card picked from a pack of cards and the colour of a disc from a bag containing 4 green and 3 yellow discs.
(a) A diamond and a yellow disc. (b) A red card and a green disc.
(c) Either a green disc or a heart. (d) Either a yellow disc or a black card.

4* The colour of a disc from a bag containing 2 white and 4 black discs and picking a letter at random from COMMITTEE.
  (a) A white disc and the letter E.
  (b) A black disc and the letter O.
  (c) A black disc and the letter T.
  (d) A white disc and either a letter E or a letter M.

5* The suit of a card picked from a pack of playing cards and the score on a pentagonal spinner (numbered 1, 2, 3, 4, 5).
  (a) A spade and a score of 4.
  (b) A black card and an even score.
  (c) Either a club or a score of 4 or more.
  (d) An odd score and a spade.

6 The score on a dice and picking a coin from £1 in 20p coins and £1 in 50p coins.
  (a) A 20p coin and a score of 3.
  (b) An even score and a 50p coin.
  (c) Either a 50p coin or a score of 5.
  (d) A 20p coin and an even score.

7* The colour of a card picked from a pack of playing cards and picking a letter at random from TEETH.
  (a) A red card and a letter T.
  (b) A black card and a letter H
  (c) Either a red card or a letter T.
  (d) A red card and the letter Y.

8 The colour of a disc (which is then replaced) from a bag containing 2 red and 5 blue discs and the colour of a second disc taken from the bag.
  (a) Two red discs.
  (b) Two black discs.
  (c) Either two discs the same colour or two discs of different colours.
  (d) Two discs of different colours.

9* Selecting a digit at random from 25 050 and the score on a square spinner (numbered 6, 7, 8 9).
  (a) An odd digit and an odd score.
  (b) A nought and a score of 9.
  (c) 5 and a score of 7 or more.
  (d) 0 or 5 and a score of 7 or less.

10 The colour of a card picked from a pack of playing cards and selecting a digit at random from 12 432.
  (a) A red card and a 1.
  (b) A black card and an even digit.
  (c) A red card and either a 2 or a 4.
  (d) A red card and a 5.

Exercise 79B

For each of the following create a suitable possibility space to show all the possible outcomes and then use this to calculate the outcomes stated.

Give answers as fractions except for questions marked * where answers should be given in decimal form.

1* The score on a square spinner (numbered 0, 1, 2, 3) and the colour of a disc from a bag containing 3 red and 2 blue discs.
  (a) A score of 2 and a blue disc.
  (b) A score of 0 and a red disc.
  (c) A score of 2 or more and a blue disc.
  (d) A score of less than 4 and a red disc.

2 Picking a letter at random from CHOOSE and the score on a dice.
  (a) The letter E and a score of 4.
  (b) A letter O and a score of 5.
  (c) The letter S and a score of more than 2.
  (d) Either a letter O or a letter E and a score of 6.

3 The colour of a card picked from a pack of playing cards and selecting a digit at random from 441 554.
  (a) A red card and a 1.
  (b) A red card and a 4.
  (c) Either a black card or a 5.
  (d) A red card and a digit that is not a 5.

4 The colour of a disc from a bag containing 5 red and 3 black discs and the score on a dice.
  (a) A red disc and a score of 5.
  (b) Either a red disc or a score of 5.
  (c) A black disc and a score of 3 or more.
  (d) Either a black disc or an even score.

5* The suit of a card (which is replaced) picked at random from a pack of playing cards and the suit of a second card picked at random.
  (a) Two cards of the same suit.
  (b) Two cards of different suits.
  (c) One of the cards is a diamond.
  (d) One card is a diamond and the other is a spade.

6* The score on a pentagonal spinner (numbered 7, 8, 9, 9, 9) and the score on a dice.
   (a) Both scores are even.   (b) Both scores are odd.
   (c) Either the score on the spinner is 9 or the score on the dice is odd.
   (d) The scores are the same.

7 Selecting a digit at random from 200 001 and the score on a pentagonal spinner (numbered 1, 2, 3, 4, 5).
   (a) The digit is 1 and the score is odd.   (b) Both the digit and the score are 1.
   (c) The digit is a 0 and the score is even   (d) Either the digit is 0 or the score is 1.

8* The suit of a card picked from a pack of playing cards and selecting a letter at random from DAGGER.

   (a) A heart and the letter R.   (b) A club or a diamond and the letter A.
   (c) Either a club or the letter G.   (d) A spade and a vowel.

9 Picking a coin from £1 in 20p coins and £1 in 50p coins, replacing this coin, and then picking another coin.
   (a) Picking one of each type of coin.   (b) Picking two 50p coins.
   (c) Picking two 20p coins.   (d) Picking two coins that are the same.

10* The suit of a card (which is replaced) picked at random from a pack of playing cards and the suit of a second card picked at random.
   (a) Picking two clubs.   (b) Picking a club and a heart.
   (c) Picking two cards of the same suit.   (d) Picking two cards of different suits.

REVISION

Exercise H

1 The scatter diagram shows the marks of ten students in a Science examination and an English examination. The line of best fit has been drawn.

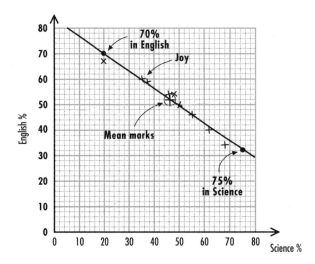

   (a) State the mean marks in Science and English.
   (b) State Joy's marks in Science and English.
   (c) Use the line of best fit to predict the mark in English for a student who gained 75% in Science.
   (d) Use the line of best fit to predict the mark in Science for a student who gained 70% in English.
   (e) What type of correlation is there between the marks in Science and English?

2 Describe the type of correlation between the two variables in each of the scatter diagrams. Choose from *perfect positive, positive, no correlation, negative* and *perfect negative*.

(a) 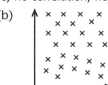   (b) 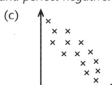   (c)   (d)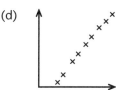

3 Anna makes a heptagonal spinner (7-sided) as shown in the diagram. She spins it 100 times and writes her results as a frequency diagram:

Result	A	B	C	D	E	F	G
Frequency	10	15	21	18	15	11	10

Use the relative frequencies of the results to answer the following.
(a) Do you think the spinner is biased? If so, say why.
(b) How many times do you think each of the outcomes should have occurred?
(c) State the probability that the outcome is either C or D.
(d) If the spinner had been spun 50 more times, predict the number of times C is likely to occur.

4 In each question all selections are at random and all outcomes can be assumed to be equally likely.
(i) State the probability of each event.
(ii) State the complementary event.
(iii) State the probability of the complementary event.
(a) Picking a vowel from the word MULTIPLICATION.
(b) Winning a raffle having bought 5 tickets out of a total of 2000.
(c) Getting less than 4 with an unbiased pentagonal spinner numbered 1, 2, 3, 4, 5.

5 Two dice are rolled and the resulting scores are noted.
(a) Create a possibility space to show all the possible results for the two dice.
   (for example, 1 and 1, 1 and 2)
(b) Create a frequency table to show how many times each total score for the two dice will occur.
(c) Draw a frequency diagram to show this information.

Exercise ⌗

1 Vijay notes the number of hours of sunshine in each day and also the temperature at 1800 h on that day.

Day (June)	6th	7th	8th	9th	10th	11th	12th	13th	14th	15th
Hours of sunshine	7	5	9	8	6	3	4	10	8	7
Temperature (°C)	21	18	24	22	20	15	17	25	24	20

(a) Calculate the mean of the temperature and the mean of the hours of sunshine.
(b) Draw a scatter diagram using 1 cm to represent 1 unit on each axis.
(c) Plot the mean values and draw a line of best fit.
(d) Use the line of best fit to predict:
   (i) The temperature on a day with 8 hours sunshine
   (ii) The number of hours sunshine when the temperature is 19°C.
(e) State the type of correlation between the two variables.

2 100 voters at random are asked for whom they will vote in the election.

Candidate	Bill Wicks	Kay Stark	Mo Foster	Do not know
Votes	24	27	21	28

45 000 people actually vote in the election. Use the relative frequencies of the votes of the 100 voters to predict the answers to the following.
(a) How many votes is Kay Stark likely to receive?
(b) Without the 'do not know' voters, what is likely to be Kay Stark's majority over Bill Wicks?
(c) How many voters 'do not know'?
(d) If half the 'do not know' voters vote for Mo Foster, who can win the election?

3 A box contains three red discs and five blue discs. One disc is picked at random and then returned to the box before a second disc is picked at random.
(a) Create a possibility space to show all the ways that the two discs can be selected.
(b) Use the possibility space to calculate the probability of each of the following:
  (i) Both discs are red.
  (ii) Both discs are blue.
  (iii) Both discs are the same.
  (iv) The discs are different.
  (v) Neither disc is blue.
  (vi) The discs are not different.
(c) If the first disc is a red and is not put back, create a possibility space for all the ways that the two discs can be selected.
(d) Use the possibility space to calculate the probability of each of the following:
  (i) Both discs are red.
  (ii) The discs are different.

Note on playing cards
A standard pack of playing cards has 52 cards. The cards are arranged into 4 'suits' called:

clubs (black)

hearts (red)

diamonds (red)

spades (black)

There are 13 cards in each suit.